Rostow, Kennedy, and the Rhetoric of Foreign Aid

Rhetoric and Public Affairs Series

Eisenhower's War of Words: Rhetoric and Leadership
Martin J. Medhurst, editor

The Nuclear Freeze Campaign:
Rhetoric and Foreign Policy in the Telepolitical Age
J. Michael Hogan

Mansfield and Vietnam: A Study in Rhetorical Adaptation
Gregory A. Olson

Truman and the Hiroshima Cult
Robert P. Newman

Post-Realism: The Rhetorical Turn in International Relations
F. A. Beer and R. Hariman, editors

Rhetoric and Political Culture in 19th-Century America
Thomas W. Benson, editor

Frederick Douglass: Freedom's Voice, 1818–1845
Gregory P. Lampe

Angelina Grimké: Rhetoric, Identity, and the Radical Imagination
Stephen Howard Browne

Strategic Deception: Rhetoric, Science, and Politics
in Missile Defense Advocacy
Gordon R. Mitchell

Rostow, Kennedy, and the Rhetoric of Foreign Aid

Kimber Charles Pearce

Michigan State University Press
East Lansing

(∞) The paper used in this publication meets the minimum requirements of ANSI/NISO Z39.48–1992 (R 1997) (Permanence of Paper).

Michigan State University Press
East Lansing, Michigan 48823–5202

Printed and bound in the United States of America.

07 06 05 04 03 02 01   1 2 3 4 5 6 7 8 9 10

LIBRARY OF CONGRESS CATALOGING-IN-PUBLICATION DATA

Rostow, Kennedy, and the rhetoric of foreign aid / Kimber Charles Pearce.
p. cm. — (Rhetoric and public affairs series)
Includes bibliographical references and index
ISBN 0-87013-578-3 (cloth : alk. paper)
1. Econonic assistance, American. 2. Economic development. 3. United States—Foreign relations—1953–1961. 4. Kennedy, John F. (John Fitzgerald), 1917–1963. 5. Rostow, W. W. (Walt Whitman), 1916– I. Title. I. Series.
HC60 .P3537 2001
327.1′11—dc21

2001002838

A Rhetoric and Public Affairs Series Publication
Series Editor: Martin J. Medhurst, *Texas A & M University*

Cover design by Heidi Dailey
Book design by Sans Serif, Inc.

Visit Michigan State University Press on the World Wide Web at:
www.msupress.msu.edu

For Dr. Richard B. Gregg,
a rhetorician of character and distinction.

Contents

Acknowledgments

I am indebted to Dr. Richard B. Gregg, Dr. Thomas W. Benson, and Dr. Stephen H. Browne, of the Department of Speech Communication at The Pennsylvania State University, for guiding the original version of the work through the dissertation process. Dr. Robert J. Maddox, professor of American history at Penn State, contributed to the manuscript during the dissertation stage as well.

Dr. Martin J. Medhurst, senior editor of the Michigan State University Press Series on Rhetoric and Public Affairs, made superb contributions to the book through his meticulous editing, recommendations concerning content, and steadfast dedication to the project. He was instrumental in helping me to acquire grant funding to complete the necessary research. I am grateful for the excellent advice of the three anonymous reviewers affiliated with the MSU Press Series on Rhetoric and Public Affairs.

Dr. Nan E. Woodruff, of the Department of History at Penn State, was the first who suggested to me that a study of Walt W. Rostow's influence on United States foreign aid policy would contribute to the literature on the rhetoric of inquiry and United States economic diplomacy during the cold war. Dr. Walt W. Rostow, of the Department of Economics at the University of Texas, Austin, was gracious in granting me a personal interview in 1995.

Dr. Dennis S. Gouran, of the Department of Speech Communication at Penn State, encouraged the project and arranged for travel funds which allowed me to conduct archival research at the Benson Latin American Collection at the University of Texas, Austin, and at the Lyndon Baines Johnson Presidential Library. The academic dean of Saint Anselm College, Rev. Peter J. Guerin, Order of Saint Benedict, contributed to the completion of the book by awarding me a research grant in 1998.

Early on, Dr. Leah Ceccarelli, of the Department of Communication at the University of Washington, offered meaningful insights concerning portions of the manuscript, particularly in the area of the rhetoric of inquiry. My wife, Dr. Vera E. Mouradian, of the Stone Center, Wellesley Centers for Women at Wellesley College, made significant contributions at every stage of the project by proofreading the text, making suggestions on content, and providing me with support during the research process. The archivists with whom I worked at the presidential libraries where I conducted research were knowledgeable and helpful. I especially wish to thank David Haight at the Dwight D. Eisenhower Presidential Library.

Introduction

> In the end, . . . a rude pragmatism shapes the content of intellectual life, and, in turn, the behavior of practical men is governed by the abstractions which men of ideas have created in an effort to give a degree of order to the world of human beings and things about them.
>
> Walt Whitman Rostow[1]

Questions concerning relations of social scientific discourse and public policy have been myriad and complex. How do social scientists contribute to the creation of policy? What political means and ends are served by the knowledge they generate? What conditions facilitate or impede the participation of social scientists in the polity? Should social scientists be interested in policy advocacy? And, if they should, what can they achieve as advocates?

Studies of the role of social scientific research in policy making have focused on relationships between knowledge and power,[2] the ways in which social scientists have gained access to policy communities,[3] and histories of national conditions that have created demands for social scientific research in the policy process.[4] Within the interdisciplinary rhetoric of inquiry movement that has arisen from the "linguistic turn" in social, scientific, and humanistic research, social scientists have been studied as advocates in the political process, along with politicians, bureaucrats, media figures, interest groups, and other participants in public policy debates.[5]

Economists have contributed to public policy for longer and in greater numbers than many of their colleagues in other disciplines. D. N. McCloskey's studies of the rhetoric of economics have demonstrated how economic theorists fuse fact and logic with the humanistic tropes of metaphor and narrative to make economic models persuasive to both general and expert audiences.[6] Among eminent twentieth-century economists, American economic historian and presidential adviser Walt Whitman Rostow is one theorist who has exhibited convincingly the rhetorical skills of storytelling, metaphor making, and model building, yet his discourse has received scant notice in the literature of the rhetoric of economics.

During the 1950s and 1960s, Rostow narrated and applied to the advocacy of cold war foreign policy his theory of the five "stages of economic growth" as "an alternative to Karl Marx's theory of modern history."[7] His model of economic development inspired a conceptual revolt in macroeconomics during the early 1950s against the dominant neoclassical paradigm, which held that short-period factors were the appropriate units for the statistical analysis of economic growth trends. In contrast to the mathematical imperative of the neoclassicists, such as Simon Kuznets,[8] Rostow used narrative to reconstruct historical patterns and predict future trends in long-term economic growth.[9]

Beyond the academy, Rostow's promotion of his "stages of economic growth" narrative as a countertheory to Marxism won the attention of policy makers in the Eisenhower, Kennedy, and Johnson administrations, who used it as a blueprint for deploying foreign aid programs to contain Soviet expansionism in Asia, Africa, Latin America, and the Middle East. In his role as a cofounder of the Massachusetts Institute of Technology (MIT) Center for International Studies (CENIS)—a forum he established with economist Max F. Millikan in 1951 to advance developmental economic theory and U.S. foreign aid policy[10]—he was called upon to assist in the efforts of foreign aid advocates in the Eisenhower administration.[11] After a decade of lobbying in Congress and elsewhere on behalf of U.S. development aid programs, he was appointed deputy special assistant for national security affairs under President John F. Kennedy in 1961.[12] In 1968 Rostow ended his career in government service as President Lyndon B. Johnson's national security adviser during the Vietnam conflict. Rostow's dual role as a leading architect of both U.S. economic development programs and U.S. military escalation in South Vietnam made him a key figure in the history of both developmental economic theory and U.S. diplomacy during the cold war. For this reason, and because of his enduring influence on post–cold war policy discussions concerning regionalism and globalism, his economic discourse is singularly significant as a subject of analysis in the rhetoric of inquiry.[13]

Rostow, the Policy Sciences, and Modernization Theory

In the United States, following World War Two, Rostow and other scholars devoted great effort to answering questions about the role of the social sciences in political decision making and policy planning. Massive societal transformations in America, newly acquired responsibilities in world affairs, and the rise of a cold war competition with the Soviet Union afforded new opportunities for social scientists to contribute to solving global problems. With the emergence of the

United States from World War Two as an atomic and economic superpower, an institutional infrastructure supporting the social sciences was expanded with the growth of government granting agencies, private foundations, and modern research multiversities. Relations among the social sciences, policymaking, and governance became of paramount importance as the academic disciplines were professionalized and greater numbers of social scientists joined policy circles.

As more social scientists were invited to assume positions as policy advisers in the U.S. government, some of the more action-oriented scholars began to envision a basic and programmatic social science that political leaders could apply to formulate policy. In the early 1950s, two political scientists, Daniel Lerner and Harold D. Lasswell, were recognized as pioneers of a new "policy sciences" approach, which was intended to address ultimate issues of world peace and economic stability, rather than situational and transient problems in world affairs. As Lasswell explained the mission: "The basic emphasis of the policy approach . . . is upon the fundamental problems of man in society, rather than upon the topical issues of the moment."[14]

As an interdisciplinary perspective, the policy sciences movement attracted scholars from across the academy during the 1950s. Political scientists, sociologists, and economists began to define their research mission as one of providing direction for political action in order to alleviate the problems of twentieth-century civilization. One policy area that engaged social science on a large scale was the U.S. foreign aid program, which had become a staple of American foreign policy after President Harry S. Truman announced the Marshall Plan to reconstruct Europe in June 1947.

During the 1950s and 1960s, social scientists assisted in crafting such foreign aid initiatives as the Point Four Program, the Mutual Security Program, the Development Loan Fund, the Foreign Assistance Act of 1961, President John F. Kennedy's Alliance for Progress to develop Latin America, and a range of efforts in Korea and Vietnam. All of the aid programs aimed to encourage newly decolonized nations in Asia, Africa, Latin America, and the Middle East to adopt the tenets of liberal democratic capitalism as an alternative to socialism and communism.

In response to the new policy emphasis on the instrument of foreign aid, American social scientists generated a variety of approaches to the study of development and modernization. Collectively, the research that emerged during the 1950s and 1960s was subsumed under the heading of "modernization theory." As a paradigm that encompassed, among other areas of study, economics, sociology, anthropology, and political science, modernization theory embodied the interdisciplinarity Lerner and Lasswell had envisioned for the policy sciences in 1951. Manning Nash has written of the leading modernization theorists of the cold war era in the United States:

> The reigning ideas of this period, as well as some of its factual and theoretical contributions, are associated with T. Parsons (1966), M. Levy, Jr. (1966), S. N. Eisenstadt (1966), E. A. Shils (1970), G. A. Almond and J. S. Coleman (1960), W. W. Rostow (1960), E. E. Hagen (1962), W. A. Lewis (1966), D. McClelland (1961), and A. Inkles and D. H. Smith (1974), to single out a few of the most typical and widely read of this new wave of theorists.[15]

C. E. Black has captured the general emphasis of the modernization theorists in his definition of modernization as "the process by which historically evolved institutions are adapted to the rapidly changing functions that reflect the unprecedented increase in man's knowledge, permitting control over his environment, that accompanied the scientific revolution."[16] Theorizing from the premise identified by Black, modernization researchers constructed assorted models of the "universal" stages of societal development in an attempt to ascertain the evolutionary dynamics of traditional, transitional, and modernized societies. Their generalized perspective on societal growth offered policy makers guidelines for designing foreign aid packages to induce economic, political, and social reforms in the nearly one hundred nations that had gained independence from European- and Asian-based empires after World War Two.

Among the many scholars who worked within the paradigm of modernization theory, few were as successful at advocating their research for policy purposes as was Walt W. Rostow, who performed his studies of economic growth during the 1950s at the Center for International Studies at MIT. As an economic historian, Rostow shared with other modernization theorists a general style of theory building that can be characterized as deductivist and taxonomical.[17] A committed policy scientist in the Lasswellian mold, he argued in his first book on development, *The Process of Economic Growth,* that the social scientist, who most importantly serves society in the function of perception, "cannot afford to lag in his scientific formulations too far behind the events and problems of the active world."[18]

The geopolitical edifice of the cold war created a climate during the 1950s in which Rostow's themes of economic growth, its taxonomy, and its sociopolitical implications acquired a powerful appeal in academia and government. His theory of the "stages of economic growth," a model he framed over the course of a decade to summarize "a way of generalizing the sweep of modern economic history,"[19] found its relevance to three major problems on the world scene:

"development assistance policy; managing the competition between older and newer industrial societies; and phasing out the cold war."[20]

During the 1950s, the expansion of Soviet aid programs in Africa, Indochina, and the Caribbean kindled a policy debate in Congress and elsewhere about the strategic potential of development aid to offset communist infiltration of impoverished areas. Rostow has recalled that the arguments centered on several complex matters, including "the nature of the process of modernization in developing countries; the relation of external assistance to it; and the U.S. (and Western) interest, if any, in the success or failure of the developing nations in achieving sustained economic and social progress."[21]

Acting in the spirit of the "policy sciences" directive, which pointed social scientific inquiry toward the discovery of solutions for world problems, Rostow developed his theory of the stages of economic growth and participated in a protracted political debate during the Eisenhower years by crusading for a comprehensive development aid program to counter Soviet foreign aid initiatives in the third world. In 1961, the decade-long controversy culminated in the implementation of President Kennedy's Alliance for Progress program to develop Latin America, which was an initiative that marked the height of Rostow's influence on foreign aid policy as an economist and policy planner.

By the time the Kennedy administration activated the massive Alliance for Progress in 1961, Rostow's approach to the study of economic growth had become archetypal within the modernization paradigm. His five stages of economic growth—the traditional society, preconditions stage, "take-off" stage, drive to maturity, and age of high mass consumption—provided an analytic bone structure that was widely cited and applied by both scholars and government officials in the United States and Latin America.

Many of the assumptions that guided the Alliance for Progress and other aid programs were set forth by Rostow in three of his books: *The Process of Economic Growth,* published in 1952, *A Proposal: Key to an Effective Foreign Policy,* coauthored with Max F. Millikan in 1957, and *The Stages of Economic Growth: A Non-communist Manifesto,* published in 1960. Rostow argued in these volumes that foreign aid, if properly distributed, could create and reinforce liberal democratic capitalism in third-world nations. The texts elaborated Rostovian theory as a general model of economic growth and advocated an expansive U.S. development aid program as a solution to the cold war predicaments of impoverished regions. For this reason, a concentrated study of the texts can reveal much about the process of social scientific advocacy and the role of social scientists as managers of argumentation and rhetorical appeals in the political arena.[22]

In this book, the analysis of the production and utilization of Rostow's modernization theory in U.S. foreign aid policy illuminates the means through which his social scientific concepts were created, circulated, and applied by policy makers in cold war economic diplomacy. The purpose of the analysis, performed from the vantage point of a rhetorician, is to frame a partial reply to the questions, "How did Rostow use argumentation and rhetorical appeals to promote his theory in the field of macroeconomics and in U.S. foreign aid policy?"; "How was his theory of the stages of economic growth translated into political language by members of the Eisenhower, Kennedy, and Johnson administrations to further development aid as an instrument of foreign policy?"; "How were Rostovian economic principles incorporated into the advocacy and implementation of Kennedy's Alliance for Progress?"; and finally, "What were the outcomes of this assimilation of Rostow's model of the stages of economic growth into U.S. foreign aid policy?"

The Rhetoric of Inquiry and Critical Methodology

The analysis in this book approaches the study of the production and dissemination of Rostovian theory in academia and government from the standpoint of rhetorical studies, which employs research methods that focus on argumentation and persuasive appeals as objects of critical inquiry. As John S. Nelson, Allan Megill, and D. N. McCloskey have observed, "Scholarship uses argument, and argument uses rhetoric."[23] Thus, it is assumed that the explication of modalities of social scientific argumentation in texts can reveal ways in which social scientists position their ideas in relation to the academic and political contexts in which they frame theory. Following the suggestions of Bjorn Wittrock and Peter Wagner, the present study focuses on Rostovian discourse in order to discern means through which social scientists are able

> [to] find an epistemic grounding in important intellectual traditions; to find ways to institutionalize and reproduce their particular forms of discourse in *knowledge-producing* institutions; to establish some kind of linkage to *political-administrative* institutions; and to be able to draw on some kind of discursive affinity with societally significant broad policy traditions—i.e., to achieve a minimum of intellectual, institutional, political-administrative, and social legitimacy.[24]

The rhetorical activities of Rostow, as an economic historian, provide a starting point for inquiry from which one can discern the dynamics of social scientific advocacy in the area of U.S. foreign aid policy at the height of the cold war. This analysis of the production and articulation of Rostow's modernization theory and the promulgation of it in the foreign policies of Presidents Eisenhower,

Kennedy, and Johnson demonstrates ways in which social scientists use rhetoric to gain access to policy communities within the constraints of particular institutional settings. Rhetorical history, as conveyed through the criticism of texts, provides insights into various facets of relations of knowledge to power, ideas to action, and theory to practice, including decision making, diffusion of information, and the influence of discourse communities on research and policy design.

Materials for this book were drawn from a variety of archival sources, including the records of the Dwight D. Eisenhower Presidential Library, the John F. Kennedy Presidential Library, the Lyndon Baines Johnson Presidential Library, the Benson Latin American Collection at the University of Texas, Austin, and a personal interview Professor Rostow granted the author in 1995 at the University of Texas, Austin.

Chapter one offers a biographical sketch of Rostow's early life, education, military service, diplomatic and academic careers, and government service in the Eisenhower, Kennedy, and Johnson administrations. The survey of Rostow's background covers the years from 1916 through the late 1960s. Special attention is devoted to Rostow's association with John F. Kennedy, during Kennedy's years in the Senate, his 1960 presidential campaign, and his time in the White House. Rostow's relationship with Kennedy laid the foundation for his long-term involvement in the planning, advocacy, and implementation of the Alliance for Progress to develop Latin America, which is taken up in chapters five and six.

Chapter two examines the production and rhetorical character of Rostow's 1952 publication, *The Process of Economic Growth,* which represented his first attempt to produce a general model of economic development to counter Marxist theory. The book is analyzed as a countertheory to Marxism in which Rostow criticized the research of neoclassical economists, the mutual security approach to U.S. foreign aid policy developed by the Truman administration, and communist methods of modernization. Rostow's rhetorical goal was to achieve academic novelty for his new method of long-term economic analysis as presented in *The Process of Economic Growth.*

Chapter three focuses on Rostow's involvement in the production of a proposal for a "World Economic Plan," which was commissioned by the Eisenhower administration in 1954, and drafted in a meeting of figures from economics, banking, industry, labor, and government at the Princeton Inn, in Princeton, New Jersey, on 15 and 16 May of that same year. The Princeton Inn proposal ultimately was rejected by President Eisenhower, at the behest of fiscal conservatives in his administration, but Millikan and Rostow continued to develop the arguments in the report and published a book based on it in 1957, *A Proposal: Key to an Effective Foreign Policy.* The publication of the book version of the Princeton Inn proposal was timed to influence debates concerning foreign aid policy in the U.S. Congress. The history of Millikan and Rostow's social scientific advocacy of the "World Economic Plan" is covered in chapter three, and the text of their 1957 book is analyzed as a discourse that sought to advance a view of the cold war as a global diffusion of power, in which the United States was perceived as having an opportunity to use foreign aid to influence the configuration of what the economists believed would become a multi-hegemonic world after the demise of the cold war.

Chapter four studies Rostow's use of narrative and metaphor in constructing his five-stage model of economic growth in his magnum opus and landmark analysis of modernization, *The Stages of Economic Growth: A Non-communist Manifesto,* published in 1960. Rostow's method of combining historical narration and developmental economic theory is examined to demonstrate how he applied the conventional framework of economic analysis, which had guided scholars of economic development since the time of Adam Smith and John Stuart Mill, to the study of the global economy of the cold war. The chapter reveals the discursive strategies Rostow used to reestablish historical narration in the methodological tradition of economic history, to refute Marxist theory in order to achieve academic and political legitimacy for his ideas during the cold war, and to link his theory to foreign aid policies that responded to the global decolonization that had occurred in the wake of World War Two.

Together, chapters five and six comprise an extended case study of how Rostovian theory was applied to the advocacy and implementation of President Kennedy's Alliance for Progress to develop Latin America. Chapter five offers a rhetorical history of Rostow's influence on Kennedy's early advocacy of the Alliance program in 1961. Chapter five demonstrates how Kennedy's references to the motifs of "counter" and "peaceful" revolution in his advocacy of the Alliance registered Rostow's contributions to his Latin American policy rhetoric. Kennedy's use of the "Rostow Doctrine" of foreign aid policy in his promotion of the Alliance for Progress was intended to make the program appear applicable to all Latin American countries, regardless of differences in culture, attitudes, aims, and interests among the nations. The "counterinsurgency" side of the Rostow Doctrine made for powerful appeals to members of the U.S. Congress, who were interested in immunizing the Western Hemisphere against communism and Castroism.

Chapter six examines Rostow's influence on the activation and maintenance of the Alliance for Progress during his years in the Kennedy and Johnson administrations, from 1961 to 1968. The chapter focuses most directly on Rostow's contributions to the development of the foundational documents of the Alliance program, which were approved at a meeting of the Council of the Organization of American States (OAS), at Punta del Este, Uruguay, from 5–17 August 1961.

Rostow's involvement in the Alliance during the Johnson years also is scrutinized, and especially the planning of the OAS Summit of 1967, which was promoted as a return to the birthplace of the Alliance at Punta del Este. The ostensible purpose of the summit was to revitalize the Alliance program, but it also was designed to generate positive publicity for President Johnson as a way of counterbalancing negative media coverage of the American involvement in Vietnam.

As a whole, this study traces the formulation of Walt Whitman Rostow's theory of "the stages of economic growth" within the field of macroeconomics, and it chronicles the dissemination of his model of modernization throughout U.S. foreign aid policy communities in the 1950s and 1960s. It is my intention for the study to contribute a rhetorician's view of the history of the influence of Rostovian theory on U.S. foreign aid policy during the second half of the twentieth century. It is my hope that communication researchers, diplomatic historians, political scientists, and other scholars will find this demonstration of rhetorical analysis useful in understanding relations between social scientific research, public policy advocacy, and political power in the context of American economic diplomacy during the cold war.

CHAPTER 1

From the Academy to the White House: Rostow, Foreign Aid, and Social Scientific Advocacy

1916–50: The Early Years

Walt Whitman Rostow was born in New York City, on 7 October 1916. His parents were Victor Aaron Rostow, a Russian immigrant, and American-born Lillian Helman Rostow. Victor Rostow came to the United States when he was eighteen years old and worked his way through the Pratt Institute in New York to become a metallurgical engineer. An idealist and ardent socialist, he named his three sons after visionaries. Walt Whitman Rostow was the namesake of the nineteenth-century American poet. Eugene V. Rostow's name honored the socialist leader Eugene V. Debs. Ralph Emerson Rostow's name was inspired by the American transcendentalist philosopher and poet Ralph Waldo Emerson.

The Rostow brothers grew up in New Haven, Connecticut, and attended New Haven High School. Victor and Lillian Rostow were zealous in promoting their sons' success. Ralph went on to run a clothing store in Plymouth, Michigan, while Walt and his older brother Eugene both received B.A. degrees in economics from Yale University.[1] Eugene graduated Phi Beta Kappa from Yale in 1933 and studied economics on a Henry Fellowship at King's College in Cambridge, England, in 1933 and 1934. Afterward, he attended Yale Law School and graduated *magna cum laude* with an LL.B. degree in 1937. His law career began with the firm of Cravath, deGersdorff, Swaine & Wood in New York City the same year. He joined the law faculty at Yale one year later, and by 1955 he had been appointed dean of the Yale Law School. During the late 1960s, Eugene Rostow served as undersecretary of political affairs in President Lyndon B. Johnson's administration with his brother Walt.

Walt Rostow's early life was remarkably similar to that of Eugene's. In 1936, when he was nineteen years old, he received the B.A. degree in economics from Yale. It was at Yale, he said, that he made a decision that influenced the course of his entire life. He explained: "I decided as an undergraduate I would work on two problems. One was economic history and the other was Karl Marx. Marx raised some interesting questions but gave some bloody bad answers. I would do an answer one day to Marx's theory of history."[2] Rostow recalled that it was during his sophomore year at Yale that Richard M. Bissell, who would serve as the deputy director of the Central Intelligence Agency (CIA) from 1959 to 1962, taught him his first "serious" economics, which he applied in his efforts to answer what he saw as the basic errors of Marxism: "[Bissell] laid out both micro- and macrotheory in mathematical terms to four of us in a kind of black market seminar on Thursday evenings. It was an extraordinarily exciting experience. I decided then, at the age of seventeen, that I would try to combine economic theory and economic history. . . ."[3]

Rostow distinguished himself in his studies of economic history at Yale, and upon graduation he received a Rhodes scholarship to attend Balliol College at Oxford University from 1936 to 1938. While he was in England, his friend Max F. Millikan, with whom he would later cofound the Center for International Studies (CENIS) at the Massachusetts Institute of Technology (MIT), wrote him a letter and included a newspaper clipping from the *New York Times* about a Barnard woman, Elspeth Vaughan Davies, who had won a scholarship to a summer school at Geneva in 1937. En route to the same summer program, Rostow met Elspeth Davies in Paris. Ten years later, the two married on 26 June 1947. Like her husband, Elspeth Davies Rostow became a distinguished economic historian, and she went on to teach at Barnard, Sarah Lawrence, MIT, and the Lyndon Baines Johnson School of Government at the University of Texas, Austin. The Rostows had two children, Peter Vaughan and Ann Larner Rostow.

After completing his studies at Oxford in 1938, Rostow returned to Yale for his Ph.D. He wrote his dissertation on the British industrial revolution and earned his degree in 1940. Oxford granted him a M.A. degree in 1946, and Cambridge University granted him another M.A. in 1949. His career as an educator began at Columbia University as an instructor in economics during the 1940–41 academic year, but he quickly enlisted for military service during World War Two.

Rostow's time in the military was formative in directing him toward a career in government service, economic diplomacy, and policy planning. He entered wartime service with the Department of State and the Office of Strategic Services (OSS), which was the predecessor to the CIA. As an OSS staff officer who was assigned to work with the British Air Ministry, he achieved the rank of an army major in England. His job was to help select bombing targets in Europe. Rostow was aboard the British tanker *Empire Mersey* on 13 October 1942, when it was sunk by a German submarine. Five years after the sinking, he was able to convince

Representative Ellsworth Bishop Foote of Connecticut to introduce a bill for his private relief, which was adopted on 19 May 1947. The bill reimbursed him the amount of $585.50 for the loss of his belongings. For his work with the British Air Ministry in dealing with the German Air Force, he was awarded the Legion of Merit and made an honorary member of the Order of the British Empire.

After the war, in 1945, Rostow continued in government service by assuming a one-year post in the State Department as assistant chief of the German-Austrian Economic Division, in which he played an important middle-echelon role in the development of German economic reconstruction. In 1946, he returned to academic life at Oxford as the Harmsworth Professor of American History. There he completed two works, *The American Diplomatic Revolution* and *British Economy of the Nineteenth Century.*[4] When the academic year ended in England, he was offered a faculty position at Harvard, but, at the age of thirty, he declined, instead accepting an offer to become the assistant to the executive secretary of the Economic Commission for Europe, which was an organization established by the United Nations. At the beginning of the era of the Marshall Plan, Rostow worked on European recovery for two years with the Swedish economist Gunnar Myrdal, who headed the commission. In 1949, when his stint with the Economic Commission for Europe came to an end, Rostow returned to England, where he taught at Cambridge for a year as the Pitt Professor of American History. He returned to the United States in 1950 to assume a faculty position at MIT as a professor of economic history.

In 1951, Rostow's friend Max F. Millikan left a position at the CIA to found and direct CENIS at MIT. Upon his arrival on campus, Millikan invited Rostow to become a staff member and to assist in cofounding the Center, which was funded by the Ford and Rockefeller Foundations, and less publicly by the CIA. With his acceptance of Millikan's offer Rostow began a phase of his academic and political life in which his theory of the stages of economic growth would be disseminated throughout the foreign aid policy community. It was Rostow's work at CENIS that brought him to prominence as an economic historian and as a foreign policy adviser in the administrations of Presidents Eisenhower, Kennedy, and Johnson.

1951–59: The CENIS Years

At CENIS, Rostow, Millikan, and their colleagues orchestrated a strategy of academic advocacy on behalf of the establishment of a world economic plan in U.S. foreign policy. The research team was only one of many that argued for an unprecedented U.S. development aid program, but the breadth and duration of the center's efforts distinguished it from other academic enterprises of the 1950s.

The group seized numerous opportunities to promote ideas about how development aid initiatives could be used to wage cold war against the Soviet Union. Rostow described CENIS's attempts to expand the U.S. foreign aid program as "a considerable propaganda activity conducted by political and academic figures: books, articles, and letters to assorted editors; speeches and symposia; appearances before congressional committees, etc."[5]

CENIS's institutional mission to study the dynamics of the communist system and theorize about the economic and sociopolitical evolution of developing countries placed the group in an advantageous position to contend with the circuitous routes through which social scientific theory enlightens policy communities in government.[6] Rostow wrote of the mission:

> CENIS . . . felt that part of its duty was to understand the political context of action well enough to present its notions in ways which working politicians could recognize as potentially realistic. There was thus an interacting osmotic process between those conducting research and generating ideas and those charged to act.[7]

Among the CENIS staff members, Rostow was one of the most active in attempting to bridge academic and governmental interests in foreign aid. He published and collaborated in the production of eight books and a number of scholarly articles on economic growth and foreign aid policy during his decade of research and political lobbying at the Center, including works that laid the groundwork for his best-known contribution to developmental economics—his five-part model of the stages of economic growth.[8]

Early on, in 1953 and 1954, he was commissioned by the Eisenhower administration to study the Russian and Chinese economies.[9] He served as a foreign policy consultant to Eisenhower and chaired the Quantico Panel that evolved the "open skies" proposal the president presented at the Geneva Conference in 1955, in which Eisenhower attempted to negotiate an agreement on a program of mutual aerial inspection of Soviet and U.S. missile sites.[10] Rostow penned Eisenhower's address to the United Nations Assembly during the Middle East debate of 13 August 1958, and he worked with Eisenhower confidant C. D. Jackson to draft a world development plan.[11]

Concerning the political situation during the Eisenhower years that prompted the ruminations of both opponents and supporters of a world development plan, Rostow wrote:

> The protracted debate on foreign aid was, in a quiet way, one of the most dramatic and illuminating strands in the Eisenhower Administration. The major

> actors can be characterized as: a President who wanted to expand foreign aid in this direction but who was deeply concerned with its budgetary consequences; a secretary of state who felt an expansion was needed but who would not throw his weight fully into the scales unless the President made an unambiguous policy decision; a conservative phalanx (George Humphrey, Herbert Hoover, Jr., etc.) that did not believe in development aid; and a liberal cohort (Harold Stassen, C. D. Jackson, Nelson Rockefeller, Allen Dulles, Clarence Randall, etc.) that believed this new dimension of policy was urgently required.[12]

In the contentious political environment that arose from deliberations on foreign aid policy during the early years of the Eisenhower administration after the Korean War, the CENIS mission to study the processes of societal modernization proved especially relevant to U.S. policy as a different kind of cold war emerged. Rostow attributed U.S. policy makers' rising interest in modernization theory to the fact that Moscow had devised a new approach to the developing world that "was part of a general strategy broadly enunciated in October 1952 at the Nineteenth Party Congress, but it emerged operationally only in the wake of Stalin's death."[13] It represented a new phase in a "protracted test between communist and non-communist methods of modernization in the developing regions, launched with President Truman's Point Four."[14] The objective of the Soviet Union's program was to expand communist influence in the third world through trade, loans, technical assistance, and other means of political persuasion. The timing of the offensive coincided with intensified development efforts in communist China, which, in 1953, adopted a Five-Year-Plan based on the Russian model of 1928. These developments required a coherent counteroffensive by the United States.

In response to the Sino-Soviet turn toward modernization as a cold war strategy, Rostow and the CENIS group analyzed the Soviet and Chinese economies and those of developing nations caught in the East-West struggle. Meanwhile, the foreign aid policies of the Eisenhower administration extended the policies of the Truman administration and moved in directions oriented more toward security than toward development interests. Foreign aid efforts to counter communist infiltration of developing areas were centered in the activities of the Economic Cooperation Administration (the Point Four Agency) and the Mutual Defense assistance program. These operations had been gathered by the Mutual Security Act (MSA) of 1951 under a single legislative authorization. Codified between 1947 and 1951, the joint initiatives were designed to build free world alliances, develop defense and economic resources, and raise living standards in developing areas.

The cold war motive of the MSA was to lessen the appeal of communism and provide the United States with a defense that would not endanger the economies of allies. To further these goals, military and economic aid were distributed primarily for short-term purposes rather than for long-term development projects. Robert A. Packenham has written of the shortcomings of the strategy behind the mutual security initiatives the Eisenhower administration carried over from the Truman years: "As in the case of Point Four Aid, the linkages between mutual security aid and its goals were often unclear and open to question."[15]

Rostow and his colleagues at CENIS criticized Eisenhower's continuation of the Truman administration's mutual security approach to the developing world for not capitalizing on opportunities to link foreign aid with democratic development. The practice of responding only to immediate exigencies in developing countries represented a dangerously shortsighted foreign aid strategy, in the opinion of the CENIS group. Rostow, Millikan, and others at MIT aimed to provide a persuasive, alternate policy design that could produce long-term solutions to the socioeconomic problems of developing regions, in order to shield them from communist influence.

At CENIS, Rostow oriented his research program toward supporting the arguments of development aid proponents in the Eisenhower administration, and during the 1950s he conducted a series of influential studies of economic evolution that culminated in the production of his five-stage model of economic growth. He set forth his model in a 1959 article in the *Economic History Review*, "The Stages of Economic Growth," and then expanded it in his best-known book, *The Stages of Economic Growth: A Non-communist Manifesto*, published in 1960.[16] The stages of growth model became the basis for his arguments on behalf of an extensive plan to institute development aid as a mainstay of U.S. foreign policy.

On three occasions between 1956 and 1959, Rostow testified before congressional committees on foreign relations and economic policy about "the place of the Soviet economic offensive in the total Communist strategy in the underdeveloped areas; and on the implications of that strategy for American policy."[17] In 1956, he made a statement about the communist policy of providing aid to developing nations at hearings before the Subcommittee on Foreign Economic Policy of the Joint Economic Committee. He appeared before the Senate Committee on Foreign Relations in 1958 and was questioned about development in India. Late in 1959, at hearings before the Joint Economic Committee, Rostow offered a comparison of the United States and Russian economics.

The primary sources of concern that gave rise to the congressional hearings at which Rostow testified after 1957 were the launching of the first Sputnik satellite by the Soviet Union on 4 October 1957 and a gathering conviction during

Eisenhower's second term that, in a broad sense, the nation was not dealing with its military, diplomatic, and domestic problems.[18] Stephen G. Rabe has written of the causes of the widespread debate that arose in 1958 about Eisenhower's policies:

> The Soviets' scientific and technological triumph [with the launching of Sputnik] shattered the confidence of the U.S. public; it also suggested that the Soviets would soon threaten the United States with new nuclear weapon delivery systems. The Administration was further beset by cold-war crises in Lebanon, Berlin, Quemoy and Matsu. At home, the Administration had deep political problems as the U.S. economy went into severe recession: unemployment rates rose to 7 percent, and the nation's industrial output fell by 14 percent. President Eisenhower, who had an approval rating from fellow citizens of 79 percent in early 1957, saw his approval ratings plunge below 50 percent in 1958.[19]

One Democrat who exploited Eisenhower's weaknesses in the area of foreign policy was John F. Kennedy. His assignment to the Senate Foreign Relations Committee in 1957 provided him a forum from which to articulate an oppositional foreign policy as a relatively undistinguished junior senator from Massachusetts with presidential aspirations. His interest in the issue of expanding foreign aid to promote third world development, as a cause with which to distance himself from conservatives in the Democratic Party, brought him into contact with Rostow.[20] Initially, the senator narrowed his focus to the economic plight of Nehru's India—an issue that Rostow and the CENIS staff had studied in depth.

In November 1957, Kennedy dispatched Senate staffer Fred Holborn to MIT to seek information from the CENIS group about India. From that time forward, Rostow and others at the Center collaborated with Kennedy on a regular basis.[21] According to Rostow, "From the autumn of 1957 CENIS was in regular contact with Kennedy, mainly through Holborn, and generating a quite steady flow of analytic material, responses to specific questions, and information on attitudes in India and Western Europe."[22]

In February 1958, Rostow traveled to Washington to testify in the Senate about the question of Indian development before the Foreign Relations Committee. Kennedy arranged a meeting with Rostow and recruited him to write speeches for his efforts in Congress during 1958 and 1959 to gain passage of a resolution he co-sponsored with Republican senator John Sherman Cooper of Kentucky to assist India in salvaging a faltering second Five-Year Plan. The working relationship the senator and the economist established on the basis of their mutual commitment to foreign aid was apparent when Kennedy questioned

Rostow at the Senate's 1958 review of foreign policy in the Foreign Relations Committee.[23] The Kennedy-Rostow exchange concerning Indian development reflected the basic theme of the danger of an "economic gap" between rich and poor countries, which the economist contributed to the senator's rhetorical efforts during 1958 and 1959 to gain passage of an aid package to India.

In a pair of speeches Rostow assisted in writing on the topic of foreign aid policy, Kennedy accused the Eisenhower administration, on the Senate floor, of abdicating responsibilities to demonstrate to the third world the fiscal power of liberal democratic capitalism.[24] He warned that the Soviet Union was devoting maximum resources to China to confirm the superiority of the communist model of development, and that developing nations, in the words of Professor Rostow, might

> emerge to maturity from a totalitarian setting, their outlook dominated by bitter memories of colonialism and by memories of transition made without help, while the rich West sat by, concerned only with the problems of defense.[25]

Barely a month after Kennedy delivered his first address on India in 1958, Vice President Richard M. Nixon embarked in May on an ill-fated tour of South America, where, as Rabe has recounted, he "was harassed by law students in Montevideo, stoned by university students in Lima, and assaulted by a mob in Caracas."[26] On 19 February 1959, Kennedy exploited the Nixon trip in his "Economic Gap" address in the Senate by pointing to the incident as evidence that a third world revolution was not only transpiring, but reaching a critical mass in Asia, the Middle East, and closer to home, in the Western Hemisphere. In late 1958 and early 1959, Kennedy and Rostow recognized that issues concerning developing areas, and especially Latin America, were gaining momentum in Congress, and that the political potential for enlarging the U.S. foreign aid program was better than it had been at any other time during the 1950s. Kennedy became emboldened enough to extend his proposals beyond aid to India to arguments for a significant increase in the resources of the Development Loan Fund, the major U.S. source of long-term, low-interest loans to developing nations.

From September 1958 to September 1959, Rostow took sabbatical leave from MIT to write and lecture at Cambridge University, where he produced what would become his best-known book, *The Stages of Economic Growth: A Non-communist Manifesto.* Acting as Kennedy's agent in Europe, he corresponded frequently with the senator and with staffer Fred Holborn, providing information about aid, speech drafts, and suggestions for the 1960 campaign. He also worked to stimulate European interest in the strengthening of the Development Loan

Fund by meeting with influential figures to make the case for international cooperation.[27]

When Rostow returned from England in late 1959, questions about Latin America were being thrust to the forefront of foreign aid debates. Asia, the Middle East, and Africa had been, to differing degrees, the main areas of scrutiny in Congress with regard to development and security issues prior to 1958. The Nixon trip to South America had served to direct attention toward troubles brewing in the Western Hemisphere. Notwithstanding the impact of the vice president's ill-fated junket, U.S. national interest in Latin America solidified in the early days of 1959, when Fidel Castro and his 26th of July Movement seized control of Cuba and its capital city, Havana. Policy makers and the national media became transfixed by the triumph of the rebels who had spent two years in the southeastern mountains of the Sierra Maestra plotting against the Cuban strongman Fulgencio Batista, who had dominated the political life of the island since 1934. Castro's actions during 1959 did more to influence U.S. foreign aid policy in Latin America than any other single factor.[28]

U.S. officials, the press, and members of the business community watched and waited to see which political path the enigmatic leader would choose in Cuba. Would he enact the pledges of his famous "History Will Absolve Me" speech of 1953,[29] in which he championed liberal and progressive policies, agrarian and industrial reform, and honesty in government? Or would he veer toward radicalism and socialism, as he had hinted in letters and declarations released from the mountains between 1957 and 1959? The State Department reluctantly recognized the Cuban government early in 1959, in the hope that diplomacy might persuade Castro to aim toward moderate reformist goals. Despite this effort, he meandered toward radicalism and the Soviet Union over the course of the year, and the United States found it impossible to direct his activities toward American interests. In April, the Eisenhower administration had expressed a willingness to offer Cuba economic aid in order to preserve U.S. hegemony in the Western Hemisphere. By December, Castro's neutralist foreign policies, appointment of Communists to key government posts, and nationalization of the Cuban economy spawned talk among U.S. officials of the need for an overthrow to preserve the political, social, and economic integrity of the Americas.

Even before the Cuban Revolution, the Eisenhower administration had begun to act to improve relations with Latin America, on the advice of the president's brother, Dr. Milton Eisenhower, who had toured Latin America in 1953 and submitted a report to the president.[30] In 1958, President Juscelino Kubitschek of Brazil had taken the initiative to contact Eisenhower in the aftermath of the disastrous Nixon junket. The presidents exchanged letters and Kubitschek proposed a development aid program for the Western Hemisphere—an "Operation

Pan-America."[31] Eisenhower agreed that regional cooperation should be broadened to stimulate more rapid development, but stopped short of supporting a comprehensive plan. L. Ronald Scheman has written of the initiatives instituted after Kubitschek's appeal:

> The Act of Bogota, which followed shortly thereafter in 1959, gave birth to the Inter-American Development Bank and led President Eisenhower to recommend to the U.S. Congress the establishment of a fund for social development, which later became the Social Progress Trust Fund.[32]

The Act of Bogota, the Development Bank, and the Social Progress Trust Fund, which was established in late 1960, were programs designed to immunize the poor of Latin America against revolutionary nationalism. Officials in the Eisenhower administration believed that they had achieved a diplomatic breakthrough with a dual-track policy of collective interventionism—an anticommunist strategy based on the Declaration of Caracas of 1954, which was drawn up to combat communist imperialism in the hemisphere, along with the Act of Bogota, which was designed to alleviate social and economic ills. They also assumed that they had generated a rejoinder to Democratic attacks on their Latin American record and handling of the Cuban situation, many of which had been voiced by Kennedy, who, at the behest of Rostow and other advisers, had expressed interest in an encompassing effort to improve economic conditions in the Americas.[33]

The Latin American initiatives Eisenhower and his advisers deployed in 1959 and 1960 failed to allay election year questions about "Who lost Cuba?"—a query that dampened the administration's claims that it had "risen to the challenge of the 1960s." In effect, the Development Bank and the Social Progress Trust Fund laid the foundations for what would become Kennedy's Alliance for Progress program to develop Latin America. During the 1960 campaign, Rostow's newly framed model of the stages of economic growth supplied Kennedy with concepts that allowed him to talk about development aid issues in clear and proactive terms, just as he had done in the Senate in the late 1950s in his efforts to secure aid to India. After 2 January 1960, when Kennedy officially announced his candidacy for president, the ideas Rostow provided—of an "economic gap" and its related themes—remained a prominent plank in his foreign policy platform.[34]

1960–68: Rostow and the Rise and Fall of the Alliance for Progress

In January 1960 Kennedy moved quickly to solidify his campaign base within the academic community.[35] He gathered some thirty Boston-area scholars together at the Harvard Club on a Sunday afternoon shortly after announcing his candidacy. He told them he did not expect their support in the primaries but he wished to speak to the issues seriously, and that he wanted each, in his or her own field, to give him the kind of advice they would give to a person who might bear the responsibility of the presidency. Rostow, Max Millikan, and Ithiel de Sola Pool of CENIS attended the meeting, along with others who later contributed to a presidential brain trust, the "Charles River School of action intellectuals," as Arthur Schlesinger Jr. labeled the group.[36]

During the primaries, Richard Goodwin, Archibald Cox, John Bartlow Martin, Mike Feldman, and others assisted in organizing the policy-formulation and speech-writing side of Kennedy's post-convention campaign. In June, Cox proposed that academic advisers be utilized after the convention as background experts, political researchers, and speechwriters to develop position papers, analyze Nixon's campaign, and assist directly in the presentation of major speeches.[37] Cox believed that materials provided by university groups should "flow in considerable volume" in the form of facts, analyses, themes, quotes, and original ideas.[38] The materials would be incorporated into three basic types of speeches in the campaign against Nixon: "off-the-cuff" speeches for local occasions, "minor speeches" for whistle stops and press releases, and major speeches for large audiences and television. Among a group of scholars that Cox, Goodwin, and others planned to consult, Rostow's name topped the list.[39]

Having served Kennedy as a senatorial consultant, Rostow worked in 1960 during the primaries and general election campaign to frame messages centered around "the need for the nation to transcend a strong historically rooted aspect of the national style: a tendency to innovate incrementally and to await acute crisis before radically changing course."[40] The messages and slogans Rostow devised revolved around the concept of establishing links between the growth of the domestic economy and foreign policy, with an emphasis on "the need for increased attention in U.S. policy to economic growth in the developing regions."[41] The sluggish economy of the late 1950s and Eisenhower's lackluster performance in Latin America made choice marks for Kennedy to assail with his campaign slogans, "Let's Get This Country Moving Again" and "The New Frontier," both of which Rostow claimed to have formulated.[42] Schlesinger has noted that "the candidate repeatedly cited Latin America as a signal Republican failure in foreign affairs."[43]

Kennedy utilized Rostow's "economic gap" themes during the primaries mostly for "off-the-cuff" speeches he delivered in states with large immigrant populations. In the early months of 1960, he had neither conceived of the Alliance for Progress program nor had the input of his academic advisers on Latin America been assimilated into a coherent policy platform. The lack of early deliberation was evidenced by a "whistle stop" address he delivered to an audience at Stanford University, Palo Alto, California, on 12 February. He told the assembly there that, as a member of the Senate Foreign Relations Committee who had served on the Special Subcommittee for Latin American Affairs, he believed "it would be a mistake to propose a new 'program for Latin America,'" and, on the contrary, "our task is to work out separate policies and proposals for each nation with the leaders of that nation."[44] Kennedy reversed this position within weeks, after Eisenhower embarked on a resoundingly successful goodwill trip to South America, which was staged to exhibit a "new diplomacy" and to deflect criticisms of his hemispheric policy. The South American tour and the president's efforts to pass the Social Progress Trust Fund in Congress motivated Kennedy to change his position toward Latin America as the primary campaign ensued.

In March and April, Kennedy reacted to Eisenhower's trip by charging that an act of deception lay behind the applause. "I know that all Americans were pleased and warmed by the acclaim," he suggested in March at Dartmouth College in Hanover, New Hampshire. In April at St. Mary's College in South Bend, Indiana, he continued his comments in a repeat performance of the speech:

> But let us not be misled by the display. For behind those cheers—behind the handshakes and smiles—lurk the same unsolved problems—the same bitter resentments—the same disappointed hopes—which resulted in the violent attacks on Vice President Nixon when he went to South America as a representative of the United States.[45]

After the Democratic Convention in July, Kennedy's Latin American plans became more focused as Eisenhower officials stepped up efforts to get the Social Progress Trust Fund through Congress in advance of a September meeting of the Organization of American States (OAS) in Bogota. As the nominee of the Democratic Party, Kennedy was given a post-convention briefing by CIA director Allen Dulles on the international situation, in which there was much discussion about Castro and Cuba. The information Dulles conveyed at the meeting magnified Kennedy's view of the gravity of hemispheric affairs, as well as his opinion of the importance of Latin American policy as an issue in the campaign against Nixon.

In May, Cuba had formally inaugurated diplomatic relations with the Soviet Union. In June, the Eisenhower administration cut off Cuba's sugar quota and later broke diplomatic relations. Castro retaliated by stepping up expropriations of American-owned properties and signed a barter agreement with China for the exchange of sugar for rice. In September, Cuba became the first Latin American nation to formally recognize the People's Republic of China. Reports about the rift between the Eisenhower administration and Castro's Cuba were in the U.S. news continually between May and November 1960.

On 24 July, the *New York Times* reported that after Kennedy's meeting with Dulles, which served to provide the nominee of the Democratic Party with "guidance for his campaign utterances dealing with foreign policy and defense," the "Kennedy high command began deploying the forces that . . . worked closely with the Senator during the primary campaigns and Democratic convention."[46] The list of scholars recruited from American universities was the longest ever compiled for a presidential campaign. Rostow, Max Millikan, and other CENIS staffers led the effort in the area of foreign policy and defense. The team provided a great deal of assistance in speech writing to Richard Goodwin, Kennedy's man on Latin America.

In August, the Eisenhower administration was ready to push for congressional action on the Social Progress Trust Fund. Undersecretary of State C. Douglas Dillon solicited Kennedy's support, knowing that the fate of the legislation depended on the Democratic nominee. By then, Kennedy's foreign policy and defense team had begun framing a comprehensive program to improve economic conditions in Latin America. In light of the imminent unveiling of what John Kenneth Galbraith phrased a "Partnership in Progress," which would "identify the young leadership of the United States with the young countries abroad,"[47] the senator felt that the Eisenhower proposal would dilute a promising campaign issue. Nevertheless, after Dillon emphasized the importance of the upcoming Bogota meeting, Kennedy struck a compromise. Dillon wrote:

> [H]e relented and most magnanimously made me a compromise proposal. He would support legislation authorizing the fund and would work to get it passed in time for the conference, but the actual appropriation of funds would have to come later, in early 1961. In this way, if elected, he could include it as part of his overall proposal for the Alliance. . . . The way had been paved for the arrival of the Alliance for Progress.[48]

Although Kennedy had won concessions for supporting the Social Progress Trust Fund, he sensed that the time was right for a brimming exposition of his Latin American views. Richard Goodwin, who had adopted Galbraith's "Partnership in Progress" phrase, "was charged with preparing a [speech] draft [to announce a new Latin American initiative], presumably for delivery at the Alamo [in September]."[49] Having versed himself in Rostow's ideas about the "demonstrative effects of democracy" on third world development, Goodwin incorporated two points from the economist's research into Kennedy's announcement of the new program for Latin America. In a confidential memorandum, he explained that the candidate should associate his Latin American policy with motives of benevolence and equality in the spirit of Franklin Delano Roosevelt's Good Neighborism, rather than with superpower rivalry or global missionary zeal:

> (1) Let us see our role not as Uncle Shylock purchasing security but as partners in life's adventure. (2) We must identify ourselves with the peoples of emerging nations by demonstrating that we share, and will work with them to realize, their aspirations.[50]

Goodwin's announcement draft embraced Rostow's assumption that American values and economic prosperity would be more likely to flourish at home if they were shared abroad. He drew from various sections of Rostow's 1958 Cambridge lectures to differentiate Kennedy's proposal from President Eisenhower's Latin American policy, a policy that Tony Smith has described as a "selective liberal democratic internationalism"[51] that harbored a questionable willingness to work with authoritarian regimes. The notion of a "partnership," in which the United States would help Latin American countries to help themselves, subscribed to Rostow's long-standing argument about freeing economic assistance from short-term U.S. political objectives. What Goodwin needed to get the message of mutual respect and economic assistance across was a phrase, as Schlesinger wrote, "which would express for Kennedy what the phrase Good Neighbor policy had expressed for Roosevelt":

> On a campaign bus rolling across Texas in September 1960 . . . [Goodwin's] eye happened to catch the title of a Spanish-language magazine which someone had left on the bus in Arizona. The magazine, published by the Alianza Hispanico-Americana in Tucson, was simply called *Alianza*.[52]

Kennedy favored using the term "alliance," so Goodwin sought suggestions from his friend Karl Meyer, who wrote editorials on Latin America for the *Washington Post.* Meyer telephoned Ernesto Betancourt, a Cuban expatriate who had broken from Castro to join the Pan American Union. Betancourt offered two possibilities: *Alianza para el Desarrollo* (Alliance for Development) or *Alianza para el Progreso* (Alliance for Progress). Schlesinger described the humorous circumstances that prompted the final choice: "When Meyer reported [the two alternatives], Goodwin laughed and said that Kennedy could not possibly pronounce *Alianza para el Desarrollo.* Moreover, 'progress' had the advantage of being essentially the same word in both languages."[53]

Kennedy's announcement of the Alliance for Progress, which was initially scheduled for September at the Alamo, was rescheduled for October, in front of the county courthouse in Tampa, Florida—a location closer to Cuba than had been the first choice of San Antonio, Texas. His description of the program involved a number of departures in U.S. policy: support for democracy and opposition to dictatorship, long-term development assistance, land reform, stimulus to private investment and technical assistance, exchange of information and students, arms control for the Hemisphere, collaboration with the OAS, and the appointment of uniquely qualified ambassadors to Latin American posts. The text of the Tampa speech was distributed widely in print, and it represented the most extensive summary of Kennedy's Latin American policy during the campaign. He aroused high expectations in the Hemisphere by suggesting that prospects for the Americas were approaching a "historical moment," in which the United States and its southern "partners" must work together, in the spirit of cooperation first achieved by Roosevelt, to find new solutions to conflicts in the area.

Having excited the Hispanic community in the United States and across the Western Hemisphere, Kennedy realized that he had opened himself to charges of exaggeration and distortion—that his campaign promises might be viewed as overselling the guarantee of an easy accomplishment of unattainable goals. To offset criticisms that might breed disillusionment and resentment among key figures in Latin America, Goodwin began setting up a Latin American Task Force shortly after the Tampa speech was published, to signal the candidate's seriousness about the Alliance initiative. The task force operated in close conjunction with the foreign policy and defense team, on which Rostow, Millikan, and other CENIS staffers were charged with addressing development aid issues.

During the post-election transition period, the policy planners stepped up efforts to articulate the clarity, scale, and continuity of Kennedy's legislative agenda for Latin America and foreign aid. Members of the task force on Latin America believed that the success of the Alliance and other programs would depend on the timing of rhetorical efforts and the delineation of effective appeals to both national and international audiences. Millikan suggested that Kennedy should "persuade the underdeveloped world that our main purpose and interest is in nation building rather than in the cold war, an alliance system, or the cultivation of friendship."[54] Rostow added:

> These soundings should permit the new President to project his [foreign aid] program with confidence, from the beginning, as a co operative Free World program, and, given the role of our partners, he should with some delicacy project the Kennedy Plan in somewhat less national terms than the Marshall Plan was launched. . . . [T]he relevant portions of the Inaugural . . . should be revealed before the event to our incipient partners.[55]

On the national front, the foreign aid planners were aware that, in order for budgetary and legislative authority for the new program to become fully operative by the beginning of Fiscal Year 1962 (1 July 1961), Kennedy would have to introduce an executive and legislative action blueprint to Congress by 1 March 1961. In speculating about the need for an early submission of the president's program, Fred Holborn noted: "The beginning of a new Administration presents a unique opportunity to make the basic changes required."[56] The consensus among the planners was that the first three months of the new administration would be vital to Kennedy's success at launching the Alliance for Progress and other aid programs. They agreed that the public and Congress, as Holborn put it, must have "a more concrete sense of association with the assistance programs," and that the new administration "should develop some new terms for present expressions which now cause misunderstanding abroad."[57]

The challenge for Kennedy, in mobilizing the Alliance as a newly elected president, was to motivate both Latin American leaders and members of Congress to support the plan without alienating either set of auditors. He was confronted with the task of selling the foreign aid package as an anti-Castro, anticommunist initiative at home, while at the same time working to excite Latin Americans with images of economic progress and "peaceful revolution" abroad. Rostovian developmental theory provided a rhetorical framework that addressed the two issues simultaneously by wedding an anti-Marxist philosophy and a comprehensive vision of the process of societal development. The theory informed Kennedy's rhetorical efforts to mobilize the Alliance in the motivational phase of advocacy that occurred between January and March 1961.

Rostow's long-standing association with Kennedy's foreign policy team and his intellectual appeal to Latin American "democratic-progressives," such as Presidents Romulo Betancourt of Venezuela and Alberto Lleras Camargo of Colombia, among others, precipitated the application of his theory of the stages of economic growth to the Alliance program. As self-proclaimed agents of social reform and democratic change, leaders of a freshly emergent democratic Left in the Western Hemisphere fell in naturally with Kennedy's "New Frontier" outlook. Many were familiar with Rostow's principles of developmental economics, which had come to pervade the curricula of economics departments in the United States and abroad by 1960.

Another important factor in Rostow's involvement in planning and promoting the Alliance program in the United States was his fervent anticommunism, which he expressed frequently in both his theorizing and his public pronouncements. Among the economists in the Kennedy administration, he was distinguished by his World War Two credentials as a member of the OSS, by the depth of his involvement in the Eisenhower administration, and by the fact that, in

1959, he had traveled to Moscow to inform a hostile gathering of Soviet economists that Marxism represented an aberration in the stages of economic growth. David Halberstam has written that some officials, and especially Secretary of State Dean Rusk, found Rostow "irritating—this verbose, theoretical man who intended to make all of his theories work."[58] Yet, regardless of Rostow's interpersonal relationships with some policy makers, his friendship with Richard Goodwin, to whom President Kennedy assigned high-level Latin American functions, was cordial by Rostow's own account, and, at times, somewhat paternal.[59] It was Rostow's rapport with Goodwin, in particular, that provided him with a firsthand channel of input into the president's Latin American policy and rhetoric.[60]

Rostow's influence on Goodwin and other members of the Kennedy administration was, by many accounts, formidable for an academic economist. His anti-Marxist philosophy of economic development and his commitment to an "anti-guerrilla" warfare strategy in U.S. foreign aid policy coincided with the sentiments of a number of U.S. officials who believed that the elimination of Castro and the protection of the Western Hemisphere were of the highest priority for the new administration. As Rostow assisted in instituting the Alliance program, he sat in on the planning and deployment of the disastrous Bay of Pigs invasion of Cuba during the early months of 1961. The two initiatives would come to reflect the evolution and pitfalls of Kennedy's Latin American policy, as the new president sought to activate a "flexible response" policy in the Western Hemisphere, which would attempt to synchronize the military means of "counterinsurgency" with the process of "peaceful revolution" through the disbursement of development aid.

Rostow's ill-fated involvement in the planning of the Bay of Pigs led to his reassignment by President Kennedy to the position of chair of the Policy Planning Council in the Department of State in 1961. From that post, Rostow worked to reorganize U.S. foreign aid policy and, at times, to support the faltering Alliance for Progress, which began to fail soon after its inception in 1961. In 1964, President Johnson made Rostow the U.S. representative on the Inter-American Committee for the Alliance for Progress (CIAP). After 1966, when Johnson appointed Rostow as his national security adviser, he became the president's primary contact with administration officials involved in the Alliance program. During the mid- to late 1960s, Rostow's and Johnson's attention turned more and more toward the escalating conflict in Vietnam, and the Alliance for Progress became a shadow of its original conception. In the end, the program did not lead to the optimistic, upward curve of Rostow's stages of economic growth in the republics of Latin America. Instead, the Alliance for Progress became a public relations vehicle for the Johnson administration's efforts to divert the eyes of the nation from the expanding crisis in Southeast Asia.

CHAPTER 2

Theory, Countertheory, and Rostow's Pursuit of Academic Novelty: *The Process of Economic Growth*

After languishing for a century following the publication of John Stuart Mill's *Principles of Political Economy* in 1848, the study of economic development was revitalized immediately after World War Two, when the colonies of European and Asian-based empires were transformed into a "third world." The advent of the cold war brought the political, social, and economic prospects of nearly one hundred new nations into sharp focus in government and academia. Poverty and instability in decolonized countries motivated W. W. Rostow and other economists to turn, in the tradition of Adam Smith and J. S. Mill, to the concentrated study of economic growth.

The resurgence of developmental economic theory provided Rostow, as an economic historian, with a conceptual platform from which to challenge the assumptions of neoclassical economists. Neoclassicists applied a physics-based framework of analysis to isolate and quantify fixed economic variables in order to formulate short-term equilibrium equations. The neoclassicists' mathematical focus on short-period economic trends generated the Keynesian revolution in America during the 1930s. In contrast, Rostow adopted a qualitative, longitudinal perspective, in which he applied biological metaphors to analyze relationships between patterns of "organic" growth operating in past and present economic frameworks. He and like-minded researchers, who were known as "modernization theorists," deemed the scrutiny of external social and political variables to be of equal importance to the analysis of internal (fixed) economic factors for the investigation of growth trends. The modernization theorists argued that their qualitative focus on long-term development issues was more relevant to policy applications in the protracted struggle of the cold war than was that of short-term analysts, who they charged with being unable to extend the focus of their statistical methods or operationalize their theories in defense of the Western world. This new wave of theorists assembled models of societal development intended to persuade developing nations to adopt the tenets of liberal democratic capitalism in lieu of socialism and communism.

In their efforts to make U.S. foreign aid programs more effective, Rostow and his fellow modernization researchers were influenced by the interdisciplinary "policy sciences" movement pioneered by political scientists Daniel Lerner and Harold D. Lasswell in 1951.[1] Following the philosophy of the policy sciences, modernization theorists attempted to make policy contributions to aid programs for needy nations caught in the cold war. Modernization theory became increasingly important to U.S. foreign policy after the Soviet Nineteenth Party Congress of 1952 enunciated a program to meet the needs of developing countries and bring them under communist influence.[2]

Rostow's book *The Process of Economic Growth,* published in 1952, was his first attempt to produce a general model of societal development to counter Karl Marx's framework for relating socioeconomic factors to societal evolution. As both a theory of economic growth and a countertheory to Marxism, the book offered a capitalistic approach to modernization in the context of the cold war struggle between democracy and communism in the impoverished third world. Similar to Marxist theory, Rostow's model of economic growth conceived of modernization as a historical process. In contrast, however, Rostow outlined the expansion, rather than the decline, of Western-style, capitalist democracies. In this regard, *The Process of Economic Growth* fit into a genre of cold war theorizing that Richard Bellamy has described as one "dedicated to contrasting the ideas and practices of Western liberal democracies with the supposedly totalitarian regimes of left and right."[3]

As an innovation in macroeconomic theory and U.S. foreign aid policy, Rostow presented his research as practical knowledge, by outlining procedures for economic action and political transformation in developing countries. His analysis in *The Process of Economic Growth* explored connections between the dynamics of free-market economies, long-term growth, and democracy. The purpose of his investigation was to produce a new taxonomic device that could account for the character of economic growth in developing nations and the kinds of interventions needed to sustain growth in a liberal democracy. Rostow's model of economic development catalogued the psychological propensities of national communities, which he claimed would shape the character of individuals and, by extension, the political economy of whole societies.

By considering strategies for altering national character and societal propensities for modernization in *The Process of Economic Growth,* Rostow offered policy makers a method for inducing capitalist transformations of the economic, social, and political traits of developing countries. By the end of the 1950s, the ideas he had generated about human motivation and the mechanisms of modernization had influenced the thinking of a generation of economists and foreign affairs specialists.

The Process of Economic Growth in the Intellectual and Political Contexts of Cold War Modernization

In *The Process of Economic Growth* Rostow detailed a set of economic and psychological means for advancing Western principles of capitalism in the global context of the cold war. The pensive tone of his book fit a rhetorical pattern that was discernible in all of his works on modernization and foreign aid. Rostow's writings, as Barry Supple has noted, were "provocatively characterized by a presumption that their themes were not merely graceful intellectual exercises, but were intimately and critically related to the stability of the world around us and to the future that awaits our descendants."[4]

As a starting point for his foundational 1952 exposition on economic growth, Rostow analyzed the British industrial revolution as an archetype of the general process of modernization. Drawing from the British experience, he prescribed means for inducing democratic development in the third world during the twentieth century. His recommendations pitted the liberal democratic emphasis on human liberty in economic affairs against what he saw as the autocracy of communist central planning inspired by the works of Marx.

As an economic theory, the anticommunist pretext of *The Process of Economic Growth* made it amenable to the ideology of development aid activists in the United States during the early-to-middle 1950s, even as it challenged deeply held academic and political ideas about modernization and U.S. foreign aid policy. At a time when a host of new nations had gained independence from imperial powers, Rostow approached the challenge of achieving academic novelty for his work in the field of macroeconomics by staking a claim against neoclassical economic theory and by legitimizing his economic growth theory as a capitalist answer to communist methods of modernization. The modalities of argument through which Rostow positioned *The Process of Economic Growth* in the field of developmental economic theory and U.S. foreign policy communities emerged from the academic and political management of his social scientific discourse during his early career as a member of CENIS at MIT.

In *The Process of Economic Growth,* Rostow set for himself the arduous task of positing a theoretical apparatus to account for patterns of growth and fluctuation in the world economy since the mid-eighteenth century. In doing so, he found himself in the midst of a theoretical debate that marked a schism between the mathematical imperatives of neoclassical analysts he referred to as "neo-Newtonians," such as his primary detractor, Simon Kuznets,[5] who considered the statistical analysis of short-period factors to be the appropriate units for economic calculation, and "biologist-economists," such as Rostow himself, who used a narrative methodology to reconstruct historical patterns and predict future trends in long-term growth.[6] Rostow cited the philosophical and methodological differences between neo-Newtonians and biologist-economists as providing the rationale for the construction of his economic growth model. He wrote:

> The most vital and fully articulated bodies of modern economic thought have been developed within Marshallian short-period assumptions; that is, the social and political framework of the economy, the state of the arts, and the levels of fixed capacity are assumed to be given, and usually, fixed. Except for an extremely limited range of problems, these are intolerable assumptions for the historian. The economic historians, from their formal nineteenth-century beginnings, have in fact mainly devoted themselves to telling the story of how the social and political framework of the economy, the state of the arts, and the levels of fixed capacity have changed in various regions of the world. It is this fundamental divergence of interest and outlook as between economists and economic historians which accounts, principally, for the limited nature of their useful professional exchanges in recent decades.[7]

In proposing new directions for the analysis of economic growth, Rostow rationalized his study as one that sought to fulfill a need for a more comprehensive perspective on macroeconomics than that of the neoclassicists, and one that could further the moral imperatives of the West in the development of the third world. He began his project by declaring that the "verbal landscape of macroeconomics is already sufficiently cluttered,"[8] but he went on to argue that the problem of opposing Marxism—the guiding doctrine of communist modernization—demanded that all political, social, and economic analysis be made to converge on the issue of contesting Marxist theory. The problem of countering Marxism, which he described as an "urgent item on the agenda of the social sciences,"[9] supported his claim of academic novelty for his theory within the field of macroeconomics.

Rostow set forth his claim of academic novelty to amplify the utility of his "biological" analysis of economic growth as a way of understanding the developmental problems of the third world. This argument not only justified his research focus on economic growth over the long period, as an effective method for contesting Marxism and guiding U.S. foreign aid policy, but it also allowed him to subsume the disciplinary practices of short-term analysts as he sought to direct the field of macroeconomic inquiry toward the analysis of long-term growth trends. Rostow's association and dissociation of short- and long-period approaches to macroeconomic inquiry were sophisticated rhetorical strategies, for as David S. Kaufer and Cheryl Geisler have argued, "[academic] newness turns on a delicate balance between the inertia of the past and the drive to change it."[10] In this respect, Kaufer and Geisler have made the case that innovative scholars must represent knowledge by persuading readers "in the very points of consensus they ultimately wish to break."[11] Thus, in discriminating and modulating the importance of a novel claim against a current stock of consensual thought, a potential innovator "must be able to perceive and manipulate structures of knowledge at varying levels of complexity."[12] This is what Rostow did when he offered his "biological" perspective on economic growth as an alternative to the dominant neoclassical paradigm of macroeconomics.

In fact, in *The Process of Economic Growth,* Rostow sought to reconfigure macroeconomic principles of inquiry at the highest level of complexity through what he termed his "effort to explore a method for permitting the introduction of long-period factors into economic analysis, including within them the changing social and political framework of the economy."[13] "Frameworks and complex schemas," as Kaufer and Geisler have written, "derive from analogies drawn from multiple historical sources, cross-fertilized ideas that have now 'stabilized' into specialized assumptions, methods, and modes of inference."[14]

In this regard, Rostow's quest to champion a new "biological" paradigm of economics to capture the shape, motion, and pattern of long-term growth in a general model of economic change represented nothing less than a bid to swell the boundaries of macroeconomics as a mode of inquiry. He wrote of the task he set for himself in a deliberate and self-conscious manner:

> It appears a general characteristic of scientific progress that certain models dominate the main lines of thought in particular periods. In the meanwhile, clusters of empirical evidence and partial analyses accumulate which are not strictly explicable in terms of current models. Then, at some stage, a new framework is created which contains the old and puts the new evidence and partial analyses into a more general frame of theory.[15]

As Rostow moved to expand the focus of macroeconomic modes of inference to the investigation of long-term economic growth trends, he also worked to provide legitimacy for his new approach in what Gene M. Lyons has termed the "seamless web" of policy formulation—"a complex process [with no fixed starting point] that involves empirical analysis, political bargaining, weighing historical precedents, and consulting the experience or intuition of executive officials and legislators."[16] Rostow's sensitivity to the discrepancies between invention and inquiry in formal social science and their counterparts in policy formulation was evidenced by his concern in *The Process of Economic Growth* with the ways that theory influences policy. He worked to register with readers his awareness of the different epistemological grammars of social science and policy planning. He wrote:

> The informal, partially unorganized knowledge and awareness of scientists is something different from the knowledge which is incorporated in formal, general logical structures. It is the latter which mainly serve as guides to the selection of relevant data, in confronting a problem; and, as noted earlier, the factors assumed formally to be fixed tend to disappear from among the objects of policy when issues for action are under consideration.[17]

Rostow's focus on the political economist's obligations to observe both formal rules of social science as well as the practical demands of the policy process served to strengthen the rationale for his general model of economic growth as a blueprint for U.S. foreign aid policy. By drawing attention to the inadequacies of short-period economic analysis for cold war policy applications, he faulted the neoclassicists, or neo-Newtonians, as he called them, for failing to answer Marx and contribute to the containment of communism in the contemporary world. Rostow's assessment of short-period, neo-Newtonian analysts' inability to fulfill the needs of the cold war policy process marked a locus of dissociation from biologist-economists, such as himself, not so much on purely theoretical grounds as in practical applications. Whereas Rostow argued that the elongated focus of biologist-economists found applications in the protracted struggle of the cold war, he depicted neo-Newtonian macroeconomists as being unable to lengthen their mathematical focus on behalf of the common good of the Free World.

Perhaps the most telling instance of Rostow's dissociation of biologist-economists and neo-Newtonians came at a point in *The Process of Economic Growth* at which he discussed John Maynard Keynes, who was the architect of the economy of the liberal consensus in America and an inspiration to the neoclassicists of the early 1950s. Rostow lauded Keynes for his commitment to the moral values of the Western world, but underscored the failure of the Keynesian revolution to provide long-term direction for Free World social and political structures. He wrote:

> If the short-period formulations generated in recent decades are an insufficient analytic framework for our times, they incorporate a spirit and an aspiration which should not be lost in the elaborations that must come. Keynes in particular was dominated by a desire to defeat the notion that the underlying individualistic moral and ethical values of the Western world must be lost if the economic problems of this century were to be conquered. . . . Serious, indeed, are the issues posed for democratic societies by the need to draw a line of

> policy between full employment and chronic inflation and by the need to consider consciously the appropriate pattern of investment, as well as its scale. Their solution will require changes in outlook and economic analysis of a major kind, among economists and other social scientists, among politicians and civil servants, and, ultimately, among the peoples of the democratic world. These are changes no less profound than those wrought by the Keynesian revolution, which has brought the majority of men to the view that the short-run level of income is a matter that lies within the compass of conscious policy. And unless these newer issues [of the long-run] are faced they will constitute a threat to relatively free social and political structures. They cannot be ignored with impunity any more than could the depression after 1929.[18]

Rostow contra Marx

Rostow's diminishment of the practical applications of short-period economic analysis and his amplification of the advantages of studying long-term growth placed his "biological" theoretical perspective in an effectual position to rival Marxist theory as an account of the modernization process. Having subsumed and rejected portions of neoclassical economic theory, he distinguished his own view of economic development from that of Marx, who also focused on long-period patterns of economic growth and the relations among the economic, social, and political forces in a society. Rostow worked in *The Process of Economic Growth* to break points of conceptual overlap with Marx by offering his own model as a countertheory to remedy what he charged were Marx's oversimplifications and ad hoc theorizing in his analysis of dynamic causation in economic trends.

In attempting to demonstrate a philosophical division from Marx, Rostow avoided a consideration of the relevance of Marx's system as a practical guide to policy formulation and instead concentrated on its inadequacies as abstract theory. This strategy of dissociation was the converse of the one he used to attack the usefulness of the theories of twentieth-century neo-Newtonian economists for guiding cold war foreign policy in the United States. Instead of attacking Marxist theory on the basis of its shortcomings in terms of practical applications, as he did in his arguments against neo-Newtonian macroeconomic research, Rostow labored to dissolve all pragmatic similarities between his and Marx's models of economic growth. He questioned the logical consistency and validity of Marx's ideas and emphasized repeatedly his belief in the need for an interdisciplinary imperative to purge Marxist concepts from the stock of Western thought.

One instance of Rostow's indictment of Marxism, penned at the peak of the McCarthy era in the United States, indirectly supported assumptions from Marxist theory in the context of a denunciation. The passage revealed the fact that Rostow's model of economic growth had certain methodological similarities to Marxist theory; in particular, the problem of dealing with the issue of dynamic causation in the process of economic evolution. Rostow wrote:

> It may . . . be proper . . . to call attention to an issue which arose in the context of this analysis and which historians and social scientists must face if they are to make progress in many important directions, including the analysis of economic growth; namely the inadequacies of the Marxist analysis of the relations among the sectors of society and the need for an alternate general view. It is the author's judgment that Marx's framework for relating economic, social, and political factors has found its way much more deeply into Western academic thought than most practitioners are aware. Its harshness and oversimplicity is, of course, often softened by *ad hoc* references to moral, idealistic, and individualistic "factors" that operate in history or in particular situations. Nevertheless, if political analysis, social analysis, and economic analysis are to be made to converge on a given problem, the issue of dynamic causation in society cannot be thus evaded.[19]

Ironically, the fact that many of the elements of Rostow's model of economic growth resembled both the conceptual and structural features of Marxist theory troubled his attempt to stake a claim of academic novelty within the field of macroeconomics. As one reviewer of *The Process of Economic Growth* put it, in reaction to Rostow's comments about the importance of addressing the "issue of dynamic causation" in Marxism: "Although Mr. Rostow inveighs against the oversimplified Marxian analysis, his schema is equally subject to the charge that it exhibits a strong bias in favor of economic determinism."[20] Another reviewer elaborated further on the similarities between Rostow's model and Marxist theory:

> Just as Marx, starting from the keen but narrow insight of Ricardians, made a lens that did penetrate the secrets of history even while it distorted them; so in these days someone might arise who would turn modern macroeconomics into as notable a tool of historical interpretation. If that really should happen, how profound might be its effect! Rostow has seen this vision and has been inspired by it; but something has stood in the way of its fulfillment. . . . The historian knows that all these patterns are oversimplified; "models" are not merely uncongenial to him—they are shocking to his sense of historical fact. Thus it takes a rather reckless historian to derive as much advantage from models as he could in fact get. Rostow, in his historical work, has shown that he has this

> quality. . . . But when, in this book, he sets up as a theorist, the historian comes over him; and he shivers upon the brink.[21]

The conceptual "brink" to which the reviewer referred was the methodological border between the disciplines of history and macroeconomics—the site of a potential leap from a chronological narrative of economic growth to a comprehensive theory of the process of economic evolution. In this sense, the significance of Rostow's theory of economic growth rested on his mastery of modeling as an economic historian. M. M. Postan has argued that when one considers the distance the economic historian must travel between historiography and macroeconomic modes of inference, the critics' comparisons of Rostow to Marx were justifiable, for both sought, as historians, to transform "a mere chronological sequence of past experiences into an evolutionary progression of related social situations."[22] Both Rostow and Marx, in framing their respective models of development, hoped to avoid the pitfalls of raw determinism by leaving fully developed conceptions of the state to the side at the outset of their theorizing. As S. G. Checkland has observed, they deferred the assimilation of the concept of the state, "to think in terms of the spontaneous forces generated by individual or group actions, and then, at a later stage, to insert the state into the model."[23]

Leaving the state to the side at the outset of their theorizing did not eradicate a need for either Marx or Rostow to postulate an assemblage of societal units in their models of economic growth. In fact, it was the assumption of group identities that permitted the eventual political ordering and taxonomizing of larger national structures in the Marxist and Rostovian theories. For Rostow, the process of assembling his concept of the liberal democratic, capitalist state allowed him to envision movements within that economic system that set the framework within which its social life and concepts evolve. He wrote in *The Process of Economic Growth:* "These long-run economic influences, through the workings of the social system, also play back on the economy, either reinforcing or retarding the trend of its development."[24] In reference to the "play back" of social influences on the economy, he inserted opportunities for the economist and policy maker to intervene in the development of the state. He argued:

> [I]t might, ideally, be possible for the economist to prescribe the optimum proportions of resources that might be devoted to fundamental science, applied science, etc,, which would maximize the rate of growth of the real national income, as the economist defines that term.[25]

In addition to identifying these conventional areas of economic policy planning, Rostow went further with his ideas for social intervention by specifying the possible scope of what he referred to as the economist's "proportioning of effort and behavior" in a society. The areas of intervention included

> the premium to be placed on leisure as opposed to work, present consumption as opposed to material advance, security as against risk, the weight given to the full complex of motives for having children as against an economically optimum population growth, and so on.[26]

By pushing the parameters of his theory beyond the conventional scope of macroeconomic planning, Rostow expanded the operational premises of his model from the fiscal inducement of economic evolution to a comprehensive version of capitalist social engineering. He argued that the promotion of capitalist development in the third world and the eviction of Marxism from Free World academic thought would not be accomplished solely by theorizing; instead, these goals could be realized only by making them priorities in U.S. foreign aid policy. His view was that the policy maker's influence on the economic actor (as an atomistic element of any society) would set the terms for an aggregate response which would define the social, economic, and political framework of the state. Rostow recognized that the policy maker's recommendations would never be "socially neutral or antiseptic." Of this observation, he remarked:

> This, perhaps, is one way of stating the greatest lesson to be learned from the American postwar experience in seeking to accelerate economic development in various regions of the world, and of defining the challenge of future policy in this area.[27]

Human Motivation in Rostovian Theory

Both Rostow and Marx considered the individual economic actor to be the agent who would set the terms for the modernization of whole societies, and it was their respective conceptions of the nature of human motivation and how to influence it that engendered their opposing visions of the evolution of the state. Robert A. Nisbet has characterized the Rostovian perspective on human action as "a more sophisticated, more diversified, and complex conception of man the actor in human history; granted that Rostow's conception of the nature of economic behavior, its principal incentives, motivations, and ends, differs from Marx's."[28] More than any other theoretical construct Rostow developed in *The Process of Economic Growth,* his image of the economic actor set the stage for his renunciation of Marx's idea of the alienation of labor in capitalism. His "nonrational" view of human motivation supplied the grounds for his rejection of the classical economic assumption of the profit motive of individuals, in which human behavior is viewed as being driven by the rational desire to optimize gain and minimize loss. Rostow's abdication of the assumption of profit maximization in human motivation carried with it iconoclastic connotations for his economic and political theories.

Rostow wrote of a "tripartite Platonic-Freudian view of the human personality," defined in Platonic terms by "the 'spirited' side of man, 'appetite,' and 'reason,'" and he argued that "Freud's id, ego, and super-ego can, for these purposes, be regarded as roughly analogous."[29] Three hypotheses he drew from his Platonic-Freudian perspective on human motivation illuminated his conception of the human actor as both a product and producer of the societal collective, who contributes to and receives from society a set of psychological propensities for economic growth. First, "man is caught up in an effort to balance different and often conflicting impulses and aspirations, in the face of the environment he confronts."[30] Next, "at any particular moment, then, the citizen viewed collectively appears to want most of what he has least."[31] Third, "man is a social animal in the quite specific sense that ties to others are an inherent characteristic of his individuality, a proposition that runs from Aristotle to Freud."[32]

Rostow's third hypothesis, concerning the communal character of human beings, was the one concept he considered essential for guiding the economist's contributions to public policy in a democracy. He derived the supposition that humans are inherently communal creatures from one of the master narratives of societal evolution in the Western tradition. Found in Aristotle's *Politics* and elsewhere, the idea is that the state, by nature, is prior to the individual, in the genetic sense that a seed is the first stage of a completed organism of which it is a part. In this view of the evolution of the state, the individual and society are not seen as alienated, conflicting forces, as in the dialectical materialist philosophy attributed to Marx by the Soviet Communists, whom Rostow claimed "set Hegel right side up again."[33] Instead, society and the individual are viewed as a communal force, caught up, as an interacting organism, in shared contradictions generated by the material and incorporeal desires of the collective, which the state always is struggling to balance.

For Rostow, the way to balance the internal contradictions of the state and the desires of its individual citizens was to apply policy measures to proportion the efforts and behaviors, or what Aristotle termed the "formal causes" of the collective society, by distributing political power as widely as possible. In this manner, Rostow argued, public policy could provide the means for balancing the conflicting impulses of the political, social, and economic sectors of the national environment. The balancing of power would perform the function of inducing democracy and adjusting dynamic causation in the economy in the direction of capitalistic development.

By reconfiguring the classical perspective on societal speciation for twentieth-century applications, Rostow garnered something of a modern version of Aristotelian "motor causes" of the evolution of the state. He wrote of

> six propensities which reflect the behavior of a given society in certain particular directions: the propensity to develop fundamental science; to apply science to economic ends; to accept the possibilities of innovation; to seek material advance; to consume; and to have children.[34]

Rostow argued that his framework of the six propensities, which reflected the aggregate response of individuals to the character of a society, designated a set of determinants that pointed toward "one possible method for introducing social and political forces into the analysis of economic growth."[35] He claimed that these propensities were the formal causes of "movements within the economic system" that "set the framework within which social life and its concepts evolve, pursuing on the whole a sluggish life of their own."[36] Rostow regarded the propensities as the mechanisms in society that united theory and practice, or the ideologies and methods of governance. He wrote:

> The long-run impulses have their main impact on politics, having worked through the social structure, where they have been generalized, built into institutions, associated with non-economic aspirations, and crystallized into ideas and particular, often structural political objectives, often of a fundamental, constitutional character.[37]

Rostow set the operational dynamics of his six propensities against the practico-materialist determination of theory and culture pioneered by Marx. Supporting an alternate picture of theory-practice relations in the transformation of society, he countered the Marxist conception of historical agency as an expression of an incipient revolutionary self-consciousness of the proletariat within the emerging class struggle of bourgeois society. Instead of depicting contemporary history as the site of an open struggle between an emerging proletariat and the forces opposed to it, he subscribed to a much less turbulent theory of sociological modernity, which Timothy W. Luke has described as a discursive framework that speaks of gaining "control of the physical and social environment, building a liberal democratic state, participating in world culture, and joining the scientific revolution."[38] This discourse of social scientific explanation, Luke has observed, portrays the developmental process, in theory, as

> a largely voluntary and fully progressive inner transformation of society's naive potential to accommodate greater social complexity, which follows from economic, political, and social policies adopted by its more than willing leadership and/or actions by its more than willing populace.[39]

The problems Rostow faced in modeling the evolutionary process of societal modernization in reference to the six propensities for economic growth he specified were at least threefold: (1) the problem of justifying the appropriateness of his list of propensities, (2) the problem of rationalizing the method by which he made his selections, and (3) the problem of defining precisely the conceptual term "propensity," both as a psychological inclination of a society for economic growth and as a functional mechanism that influences the growth process. These three problems taxed Rostow's obligation as an economic theorist to demonstrate the generalizability of his new framework of the propensities, a task to which he devoted approximately half of the volume of *The Process of Economic Growth.*

Unlike Marx, who discerned no cure for the alienation of the individual economic actor within the capitalist system, Rostow assumed that his Platonic-Freudian view of the relationship between human propensities and economic growth could assist the economist in compensating for conflicts within the capitalist state by bringing public policy to bear on both individual and societal propensities for economic growth in developing countries. The political dilemma Rostow faced in his approach to policy formulation was that by placing so much stock in economic intervention by U.S. policy makers, he risked pushing his argument too far in the direction of a socialistic centralization of state power. To circumvent conservative criticisms of his ideas concerning the question of the breadth and depth of U.S. intervention in the economies of developing nations, Rostow confronted the issue on pragmatic grounds, as he had done in defense of other aspects of his theory. He thus argued:

> The need to develop this form of analysis is heightened by the probable institutional evolution of many of the underdeveloped areas. It has been a minor irony of the postwar experience of the United States that its agents, both in Europe and in underdeveloped countries, have found themselves urging an increased role for government planning in the economies of the areas where the American interest was engaged. This was the consequence of no conspiracy among New Dealers or Socialists who found their way into American foreign operations. This was a realistic response to the nature of the societies where a sustained rate of economic development was sought in the American interest.[40]

In his effort to justify U.S. economic intervention designed to strike a balance between the "appetite," "spirit," and "reason" of the people of third-world countries, Rostow systematically revealed inadequacies in the short-term orientation of U.S. foreign aid policy. In a 1952 review of *The Process of Economic Growth,* George Soule succinctly paraphrased the political position Rostow expressed in his exposition of the six propensities for economic growth:

> [I]n the administration of President Truman's Point 4, it is a major difficulty that many cultures which strongly exhibit the sixth propensity [to have children] lack the first three [to develop fundamental science, to apply science to economic ends, and to accept the possibilities of innovation], sometimes the fourth [to seek material advance], and occasionally even the fifth [to consume].[41]

Rostow's argument for the need to reconfigure U.S. foreign aid policy as a way of countering Marxism and appealing to the economic propensities of the people of the third world was based almost entirely on his analysis of the British industrial revolution—the first case of capitalistic modernization in world history. He interpreted the historical precedent of the British case in a way that supported both his call for techniques of minimum direct economic intervention and his denunciation of the control apparatus of communist central planning. Trends in British economic growth during the eighteenth century served as the foundation of Rostow's argument that his economic growth theory and policy prescriptions could direct the economic propensities of third world societies away from communism and toward the fruits of capitalistic modernization. It was the British industrial revolution that underpinned Rostow's vision of economic evolution, his policy proposals, and his refutation of Marx's perspective on the rise and fall of bourgeois capitalism.

Narrating the Propensities for Economic Growth: The Paradigm Case of the British Industrial Revolution

Rostow rationalized the selection of his six societal propensities for capitalistic growth by compressing prior research on economic growth, structuring a narrative of the British industrial revolution as the first case of capitalistic modernization in world history, and prescribing development policy for third world modernization on the basis of his historical narrative.

The first step Rostow took in arguing for the validity of his view of the six propensities for growth was to synthesize research conducted by contemporary developmental economists in order to derive explanatory power for his own theoretical framework. Susan Peck MacDonald has provided an explanation of why Rostow would take such a step by suggesting that a researcher's disciplinary community is a source of rational decision-making, and, as such, it "entails a notion of possible progress on disciplinary problems."[42] To achieve progress in specifying his six propensities for economic growth, Rostow cited J. J. Spengler,[43] who had compiled nineteen determinants of economic development, Shepard Clough,[44] who had formulated six determinants that differed from Rostow's, and James S. Duesenberry,[45] who had emphasized the social and psychological bases of economic growth. Rostow exploited the ideas of the three theorists to delineate and authorize his own methodology by proposing to clarify Duesenberry's emphasis, extend Clough's analysis, and compress Spengler's wieldy list of determinants (which Rostow claimed did not actually constitute formal determinants, but rather determinants of the primary Rostovian set).

Having outlined a path to progress within the disciplinary community of developmental economists, Rostow next identified a proper object of historical inquiry, the British industrial revolution of the late eighteenth and early nineteenth centuries. Reasoning chronologically, he devoted little time to supporting a causal relationship between the British experience and its long-range influence on the establishment of his six propensities. He simply claimed:

> The British industrial revolution . . . certainly had important social consequences, including, in the first instance, a reinforcing effect on the propensities, as did the industrial revolutions which have taken place in other parts of the world over the past several centuries.[46]

Once he had designated the British experience as the fount of modernization, Rostow identified the six propensities for economic growth as a product of the European historical context and defined each in psychological and functional terms, as both an inclination and a process. His narrative of the British industrial revolution animated each propensity for growth, lending each one substance in historical time and predictive power by extension. In an allusion to a decline in the British death rate during the mid-eighteenth century, for instance, Rostow attributed the phenomenon to a rise in the propensity to accept innovation. He wrote:

> one must look back to the first development and the slow spread of the modern scientific attitude, with its implication that the physical world was governed by laws which made it capable of manipulation; one must look to the evolution of ways of looking at the world which placed a new importance on the individual and his fate; one must look to the economic and social process by which increasing numbers of men were prepared to view their environment

> in terms which led, on balance, to new dispositions of talent and other resources. Nothing less than the great interacting historical passages we designate as the Renaissance, the Reformation, and the emergence of commercial capitalism is directly relevant.[47]

By presenting a series of similar historical explications, using the framework of his six propensities as an interpretive tool, Rostow generated what Nash has described as "a template, a guide, a model, or a goal of the developing nations."[48] As Nash has argued, the general and central assumptions behind this style of modeling were that the European experience of modernization was inevitable, unilinear, universal, and irreversible. The schema fell within the purview of what Franco Ferrarotti has termed a "myth of inevitable progress," which spans human thought from classical antiquity and espouses

> a theory which implies a synthesis of the past and a prophecy of the future, that is based on an interpretation of history in which society slowly but ineluctably progresses in a desirable direction [a process that will continue indefinitely].[49]

Rostow's version of the progress myth was steeped in a style of technocratic rationality native to the American "policy sciences" of the early cold war era. From the "policy sciences" perspective, first set forth by Lerner and Lasswell, social scientists such as Rostow attempted to represent and incorporate the apparatus of a burgeoning Keynesian welfare state into the engineering and management of bureaucratic tasks that were growing ever more complex and extensive. Viewing the path of progress as an irreversible product of British antecedents, Rostow saw the Anglo-American version of economic growth as being applicable to the development prospects of the third world. Yet, the path to progress was not immune to perversion. For Rostow, such an aberration was exemplified by the Soviet route to modernization, which he considered to be a turn in European-inspired development that achieved modernity with an abhorrent coercion/consensus ratio. Interpreting the elements of communist modernization in light of the propensity to consume, Rostow compared the Soviet conditions of growth to the psycho-social inclinations of "traditional societies," which lack the stabilizing influence of an established middle class. He wrote:

> [I]n a Communist state, devoting its resources heavily to capital development and armaments, the propensity to consume is a function of the full range and effectiveness of the control apparatus rather than the aggregate response of atomistic individuals. If the psychological bases of the propensity to consume or the fundamental value judgments incorporated in it are allocated to any individuals, they must in this case be allocated to those making the central plan

> and administering it—although the effectiveness of the administrative machinery for achieving the distribution of resources laid down by the plan, as between consumption and investment, would also be relevant. Similarly, in a relatively backward society, characterized by extremes of wealth and poverty, the propensity to consume would reflect the actual distribution of resources and the tastes and value judgments of those actually disposing of current income, rather than the behavior which might be observed with a different distribution of income and if the will of the majority were effectively consulted in tax policy and in other fundamental institutional arrangements.[50]

The Rostovian perspective on economic growth, with its foundations in a legacy of eighteenth-century liberalism, found no advantage in the communist plan to maintain social, political, and economic equilibrium by centralizing the mechanisms of modernization in the functions of the state. Rostow argued that when state control of modernization concentrates too far to the left or right of the political spectrum, societal structures shift toward despotism and tyranny. To offset such dangers, he claimed that the state must adjust constantly to the "appetite," "spirit," and "reason" of aggregate individuals, according to the will of a representative government that takes its mandate from the natural rights, human liberty, and civic engagement of the people. In this respect, it is suitable that Rostow began his chronology of economic growth at the age of John Locke, David Hume, and Adam Smith, whose liberal philosophies he furthered in a cold war modality with his arguments concerning the proper course of political and economic modernity in the second half of the twentieth century.

Rostow also echoed Wilsonian precepts of moral idealism, which he claimed set the tone for the twentieth century, but which were not particularly popular in the political climate of the United States during the early 1950s. He forecast, with an assurance alien to the majority of economic historians of his day, a triumph in the third world of the Anglo-American model of peaceful development over methods of Sino-Soviet modernization and its Marxist derivations. Rostow engaged the cold war issue of third world modernization with an American credo of social reform based on a combination of liberal democratic principles and a fervent anticommunism. The "Rostow Doctrine" of foreign aid policy, as it would later come to be known, would become ingrained in academic and political thought in America in less than a decade.

Conclusion

What emerged from Rostow's "biological" model of societal evolution in *The Process of Economic Growth* was a countertheory to Marxism that contested both the dominant neoclassical paradigm in macroeconomics and the norms of U.S. foreign aid policy during the early years of the cold war. As part of an American genre of social scientific discourse devoted to contrasting democracy and communism, Rostow's modernization theory sought to achieve academic novelty with an anti-Marxist rationale for altering macroeconomic assumptions and methodologies. Rostow offered an alternate view of human motivation to the classical economic model of profit maximization, upon which Marxist theory was based, and he presented a rival interpretation of the British industrial revolution that was intended to serve as the basis for a blueprint for the capitalistic modernization of developing nations.

Rostow's theoretical perspective on economic growth arose from an exceptionalist view of the social structures and functions of American society, a view of U.S. civic life that would later be articulated by Seymour Martin Lipset in his widely read book, *Political Man:* "It is the good society itself in operation."[51] The irony of the ethnocentric and politically inspired elements of Rostow's theory was that his concepts concerning economic growth were promulgated during a period in American academic history when various intellectuals proclaimed the "end of ideology" in the social sciences.[52] Even as Rostow and other social scientists aspired to a neutral, positivistic, and instrumental vision of the social sciences, the cold war provided global exigencies that compelled them to join the ranks of ideological and political forces in a concerted effort to fight communism in the unaligned regions of the third world.

Rostow presented his theory as practical knowledge for conducting economic warfare with foreign aid in a protracted test between communist and capitalist methods of modernization. As a disciplinary innovation in developmental economics, Rostovian theory challenged the dominance of short-term macroeconomic analysis and Marx's theory of the effects of dynamic causation in capitalism. In responding to the operational differences between invention and inquiry in the processes of policy formulation and social scientific inquiry, Rostow adapted his theory to the divergent epistemological grammars of both sets of practices. Rostovian theory addressed the rudiments of macroeconomics and foreign aid policy by setting forth criteria of legitimacy that featured the descriptive and predictive power of a "biological" analysis of postwar economic phenomena, development assistance policy, global industrial competition, and strategies for phasing out the cold war.

As an economic historian, Rostow provided a rationale for his focus on long-term economic growth on the grounds of its relevance to the protracted nature of the cold war, which he perceived not only as a military and economic contest, but also as a prolonged conflict between the moral imperatives of the East and those of the West. His effort to produce an alternative view of societal evolution to that of Marxist theory absorbed rival perspectives in macroeconomics by conceiving of a long-term intellectual and economic containment of communism. At the same time, his study systematically demonstrated the deficiencies of rival macroeconomic perspectives in failing to arrest Marxist doctrine in Western thought and fiscal practices. Rostow's general strategy in this respect was to relate the shortcomings of neo-Newtonian macroeconomic thought to the U.S. mutual security assistance program's failure to provide direction for free social and political structures in developing regions.

Rostow's alternative model of economic growth combined historical narration and economic theory for purposes of predicting future economic trends in developing societies. His prescriptions for inducing economic growth and democracy provided a technical and ideological template for the path to progress of developing nations, and, in doing so, they functioned to naturalize the European experience of industrialization and liberal democratic capitalism. In keeping with the institutional mission Rostow and Max F. Millikan had established for the CENIS forum they founded at MIT in 1951, Rostow sought to frame developmental theory in *The Process of Economic Growth* for application to cold war foreign policy. The contribution of the study, as Rostow saw it, resided in its effort to

> accommodate within its structure the process by which major production functions were generated and diffused; to offer a "credible explanation for trend periods, longer than conventional business cycles"; to provide a "credible linkage of conventional business cycles to the process of growth"; and to supply a "mechanism for introducing non-economic factors into the analysis of economic growth."[53]

Among the novel theoretical contributions in *The Process of Economic Growth*, one concept that appeared in the text—the notion of a "take-off" in developing societies heading toward sustained growth—went virtually unnoticed during the early 1950s as an idea that would later generate the systematization of Rostow's well-known "stages-of-growth analysis." While the 1952 analysis stood as the basis for Rostow's theorizing throughout the 1950s and beyond, his subsequent elaboration of the "take-off" stage of economic growth spawned a revolutionary debate in macroeconomics, which thrust Rostovian theory to the forefront of dynamic economic growth analysis. In policy circles, Rostow's "take-off" concept was the idea that eventually fueled a radical reassessment of U.S. foreign aid policies and foreshadowed the implementation of new foreign aid programs in the late 1950s and 1960s.

CHAPTER 3

Ideas in Action: *A Proposal: Key to an Effective Foreign Policy*

During President Dwight D. Eisenhower's first term of office, the strategic objective of U.S. policy in the third world was not to promote modernization with development aid, but rather to minimize the cost of containing communism by reducing the American financial burden with bilateral and regional military pacts. The Mutual Security Agency supported treaty organizations that emerged from these pacts with military and technical assistance designed to influence the political, social, and economic order of developing regions. The American position toward instability in Africa, Asia, Latin America, and the Middle East was to view the unrest not as the result of rapid postwar decolonization and modernization processes, but instead as the product of Soviet-inspired communist aggression. The American foreign policy response took the form of military alliances modeled on the North Atlantic Treaty Organization (NATO) undertaken in Europe.

Adopting a position opposed to the prevailing concept in U.S. foreign policy circles that the Soviet Union was primarily responsible for third world turmoil, proponents of development aid, such as Rostow and the CENIS group at MIT, argued that Mutual Security provisions of mainly military and technical assistance to impoverished regions epitomized a fundamental misunderstanding of the revolutionary conditions activated in emerging societies by the collapse of European- and Asian-based colonial empires. They criticized security pacts and charged that, in light of the transitional nature of the political and economic conditions of developing nations, military alliances could prove to be counterproductive, by destabilizing national systems with an excessive flow of arms. The resulting situation, they surmised, would provide communists with opportunities to manipulate subversives and instigate "brushfire" conflicts that would involve the United States in its role as an alliance partner committed to the defense of unstable countries occupying containment rims in various areas. John Kenneth Galbraith summarized the objections of development aid activists to what they labeled the "pactomania" of the Eisenhower administration, or the precarious emphasis that was placed on security groupings in developing areas during the 1950s:

> Our foreign policy in recent years has been dominated by a remarkable tendency to make the maximum use of our weakest weapons. Of personal diplomacy we have had a plethora. . . . We have also gone in for military pacts at a time when . . . there are grounds for debate whether they can possibly do as much harm as good. All the while economic aid for which our capacity is inherently vast, has been parceled out with great and seemingly increasing reluctance.[1]

The development aid advocates' dissatisfaction with the Eisenhower administration's stance on foreign aid policy spread during the middle to late 1950s, not just among academics, such as the members of the CENIS group at MIT, but also in the Congress, and especially among Senate Democrats. In particular, critics of the priority accorded by the Eisenhower administration to establishing defensive perimeters to contain communist expansion pointed to India, Indonesia, and Egypt as telling cases. A military pact signed with Pakistan in 1954 resulted in a protest by India that led to a declaration of diplomatic neutrality. Similarly, Indonesia refused to enter into an alliance and also remained neutral. Yet perhaps the most persuasive evidence used to indict the Eisenhower policy for neglecting the strategic potential of foreign aid came with the Suez crisis in Egypt in 1956, which critics claimed was the result of a failure to enlist nationalist leader Gamal Abdal Nasser's loyalty with foreign aid after his rise to power in 1954. The criticisms of Eisenhower's approach to the third world led to the commissioning of a dozen or so studies and research reports on the issue of foreign aid policy by congressional committees, presidential commissions, and other bodies.

Among the various studies, the Eisenhower administration's official position on foreign aid was expressed in the 1954 Randall Commission Report, which summarized the views held by conservatives in the administration, especially those of Joseph M. Dodge, chairman of the Council on Foreign Economic Policy, George M. Humphrey, secretary of the treasury, and Herbert Hoover Jr., undersecretary of state. The report recommended that U.S. foreign policy should seek to encourage economic growth in developing nations by liberal trade policies with unrestricted long-term capital and convertible currencies. In lieu of development aid, the Randall Commission advised that U.S. technical assistance should serve as the most effective means for encouraging worldwide modernization.

The idea that private investment would solve the economic ills of developing nations was the theme most often sounded by President Eisenhower, John Foster Dulles, and other administration officials when they referred to the fiscal crises in India, Latin America, and a host of other regions of the third world.[2] When the president spoke to the Congress about foreign economic policy on 30 March 1954, he concurred in no uncertain terms with the conclusions of the Randall Commission when he enumerated U.S. priorities for promoting global development. Eisenhower listed:

Aid—which we wish to curtail
Investment—which we wish to encourage
Convertibility—which we wish to facilitate
Trade—which we wish to expand[3]

Publicly, Eisenhower and Foster Dulles voiced their agreement with the terms of the Randall Report, but as the French struggle in Vietnam reached a crisis in the spring of 1954, the secretary of state became troubled by events in Indochina. Foster Dulles's anxiety was heightened by the acceleration of a Soviet economic and political offensive enunciated in Moscow at the Twentieth Party Congress in February 1954 that aimed to extend communist power and influence into unaligned areas of the third world through various forms of foreign assistance. Acting on his apprehensions, Foster Dulles privately sought the advice of C. D. Jackson, who was leaving a post as assistant to the president for psychological warfare[4] to return to his position as the vice president of Henry R. Luce's magazine empire, Time, Inc., and as the publisher of *Fortune* magazine. Jackson agreed to develop a report outlining a "World Economic Plan" as a final contribution to the administration.

In late March, 1954, Jackson turned to Millikan and Rostow at CENIS for assistance in organizing a meeting of figures from economics, banking, industry, labor, and government, to be held at the Princeton Inn in Princeton, New Jersey, on 15 and 16 May 1954. The purpose of the "off-the-record conference," sponsored by Luce's Time, Inc., was to convene a working meeting to generate the beginnings of a world economic plan without the burdens of organizational commitment or media publicity. Millikan and Rostow were commissioned to produce a proposal from the conference proceedings, which they finished on 25 May 1954 and forwarded to President Eisenhower on 23 July 1954 along with a speech draft penned by Rostow and John K. Jessup of *Life* magazine, in case the president became enthusiastic enough to launch the program.[5]

Despite the coordinated efforts of the Princeton Inn group and CENIS, along with the support of Foster Dulles and others, President Eisenhower, who was concerned primarily with budgetary expenses and congressional resistance, rejected the report and remained committed to what Rostow described as "a policy of short-run military and political alliance designed to frustrate direct Communist aggression."[6] However, even with the president's reluctance to support a world economic plan in 1954, the Princeton Inn report, which served as the basis for what later came to be known as the Millikan-Rostow thesis, had not seen the end of its circulation.

Between 1954 and 1957, with a series of events that shifted public perceptions of the nature of the cold war in the third world, the political significance of the Princeton Inn proposal became apparent to an audience outside of the Eisenhower administration. Millikan and Rostow redrafted the 1954 proposal for a world economic plan twice, once in 1956, and again in 1957. The second draft of the report, entitled "A Proposal for a New United States Foreign Economic Policy," was circulated in Congress in 1956, where it was discussed in the course of a heated debate on the issue of development aid. One year later, Millikan and Rostow produced a third draft as a book, entitled *A Proposal: Key to an Effective Foreign Policy*, which was published in 1957.[7] The book version of the proposal condensed five years of formal research on development undertaken by members of CENIS and combined it with the unofficial proceedings of the Princeton Inn Conference to make public the arguments of development aid activists who had participated in debates on foreign aid policy during the middle to late 1950s.

The development of the Millikan-Rostow proposal for a world economic plan, which began as a synopsis of the Princeton Inn proceedings of 1954, represented a collaborative process of social scientific advocacy. In drafting the proposal, the two economists confronted not only the schism between supporters and opponents of development aid but also the tension created by an intertwining of the values of self-interest and idealism that coexisted within the tradition of American realism in the 1950s, and particularly in the area of American economic diplomacy. As social scientific rhetoric intended to describe, structure, and promote a new approach to U.S. foreign aid policy, Millikan and Rostow's proposal for the disbursement of development aid to third world nations generated a global interdependence narrative that linked the humanitarian means of promoting social welfare abroad and the pragmatic ends of achieving a balance of power in the self-interest of the United States. Instead of envisioning a world order balanced by military power, the economists argued that a multi-hegemonic world would emerge from the development aid-induced process of global modernization.

The Millikan-Rostow narrative relied on the assumptions of a value system that can be termed "realistic idealism," which is a part of the American national character that combines the rational calculations of the paradigm of realism and the moralism of democratic internationalism, and that seeks to justify the means of foreign policy on the basis of its ends. The paradoxical nature of "realistic idealism," as a discourse that presented both affirmations of and objections to the cold war, arose from attempts by U.S. policy makers to steer a rational course in the nuclear age, while doing the "right thing" as humanitarians to avoid a global catastrophe.

The Millikan-Rostow proposal adhered to the value system of realistic idealism by expounding the authors' belief that both the pragmatic and the moralistic ends of domestic welfare, democratic internationalism, and national security could be met through a single means of diplomacy—a comprehensive U.S. development aid policy. In this regard, the proposal sought to induce a value reorientation in U.S. foreign policy circles by introducing a new set of guidelines for "competitive coexistence" in the Free World and the communist bloc. Millikan and Rostow argued that a positive change in America's image in the unaligned third world, caught in the struggle between the United States and the Soviet Union, would occur only if policy makers were willing to meld the sometimes conflicting values of realism and idealism in a world economic plan. In this way, the United States could pursue its own self-interest in global affairs by promoting liberal democratic capitalism in developing nations.

The Princeton Inn Conference of 1954: Rhetorical Invention in Foreign Aid Policy

The thesis of the Millikan-Rostow proposal stated the argument for a U.S. development aid program succinctly: "[A] much-expanded long-term program of American participation in the economic development of the underdeveloped areas can and should be one of the most important means for furthering the purposes of American foreign policy."[8] The proposal's conclusion reinforced the economists' call for the United States to become proactive in producing a world order based on security, social progress, democracy, and economic optimism—one that would eventually bring about the end of the cold war. They wrote:

> The fundamental task of American military and foreign policy is to maintain a world environment for the United States within which our [democratic] form of society can continue to develop in conformity with the humanistic principles which are its foundation.[9]

When the Princeton Inn Conference convened in 1954 to begin making the case to the Eisenhower administration that the goal of national security in the cold war, as Millikan and Rostow later stated it, should be "the problem of protecting not merely the nation's real estate but also its basic values as a society,"[10] the major obstacle the group faced was the fact that the issue of foreign aid, with its idealistic tendencies, historically had been a matter of great contention within the prevalent paradigm of realism.[11] This was true because, in the moral reasoning endemic to the advocacy of foreign aid programs during the 1950s, proponents often were at odds to demonstrate how the initiatives could serve national security interests. The issue of appraising the means and ends of a foreign policy relevant to current conditions in the world without conflating what was desirable and the power to carry it out was one that always had been at the center of the strategic calculus of realism.

G. Thomas Goodnight, in an analysis of Hans J. Morgenthau's classic 1951 statement of the principles of realism, *In Defense of the National Interest,* has described the realists' problem with idealistic foreign policy rhetoric that Morgenthau termed "sentimentalism," or "that discourse which excites moral principles without attention to the pragmatic course which successful action pursues."[12] Goodnight has characterized Morgenthau's position on the "sentimental" approach to foreign policy as follows: "When the pathos of moral appeal overmatches practical concerns with the efficacy of policy, bad decisions result—and imprudent conduct invites more of the same."[13]

Development aid activists of the 1950s were especially vulnerable to charges of "sentimentalizing" their rhetoric to the point of creating a set of policy expectations that could not be satisfied, either at home or abroad. In discussing the basis of realists' skepticism toward the arguments of development aid activists, Lucian W. Pye explained the aversion that Morgenthau and other theorists held for "sentimentalism" in foreign aid policy in general: "Realistic reasoning and refined policy calculations, the accepted guides for all other tools of foreign policy tend to be obscured in foreign aid by the scope given to fantasy and emotions."[14]

Armed with an awareness of the realist biases harbored by prominent members of the Eisenhower administration and the Congress toward foreign aid, participants in the Princeton Inn Conference of 1954 were determined not to give the impression of being "given to fantasy and emotions" in their deliberations over a world economic plan. In a memorandum to Foster Dulles dated 9 April 1954, C. D. Jackson invoked the value system of realistic idealism as he explained the humanitarian purpose of the proceedings in light of the available resources for carrying out the objectives of a world economic plan. He wrote to Foster Dulles:

> What the United States needs, in the development of its foreign policy, in its successful counter to Soviet expansion, in its determination to roll back Communism by peaceful means, is a bold, imaginative plan embracing not just one,

> but all, of the possible elements involved. The essential element of such a World Economic Plan is that it will *work*. It must contain things to be done—things that can be done. We have had tons of theory, but hardly more than ounces of action. If a World Economic Plan is developed on this basis, it will then have sufficient dramatic appeal to be understood by *people* everywhere. And if *people* want it, *governments* will want it. . . . What is needed is not another report, but an imaginative synthesis of much that already exists, to which should be added a large number of action items which up to now Washington has either shied away from or which have become lost in the mass of papers after getting some kind of formalized policy approval.[15]

Jackson's emphasis on the synthesis of ideas and action in the formulation of a world economic plan signaled his desire to bridge contending institutional vocabularies and practices that had divided those who had been labeled realists and idealists in past policy disputes over foreign aid. He hoped to arrive at a consensus at the Princeton Inn Conference on how the United States might use a world economic plan to ensure "the fact that the grass is indeed greener on freedom's side of the fence will cease to be merely an American statement, and become a reality."[16] In Jackson's view, one way to convey America's message of freedom through economic diplomacy was to eradicate the division frequently made by policy makers between domestic and foreign politics. With this goal in mind he asked participants at the Princeton Inn Conference to address four major questions: (1) What national purposes might a world economic plan serve? (2) What was the Free World's economic problem in broad terms? (3) What could the United States do to stimulate and maintain a "partnership for growth"? (4) What could the Princeton Inn group do to induce policy action and continuity of action on a world economic plan?[17]

On Saturday, 15 May, the first day of the Princeton Inn Conference, Jackson invited the participants to engage in an unrestricted discussion of the four questions he had posed, telling them: "[D]on't consider the political feasibility of things, because if we start getting bogged down now on the political feasibility, this is just going to be just another group of 'do-gooders' coming out with a nice report which will hit the archives with a dull thud."[18] Despite Jackson's caveat that the group should remain open to all ideas, lines of division emerged quickly during the deliberations over the four questions, particularly on the issue of what the national purpose of a foreign economic policy should be, and whether the United States already had a viable policy in place.

General Robert Cutler, special assistant to the president, assumed the role of the orthodox realist in the group, and insisted that matters of both domestic and foreign politics be clarified in discussing the question of national purpose as one related to the United States alone, or as one related to the position of the United States as the leader of the Free World. Playing devil's advocate, Cutler pressed the other members on the issue of whether a world economic plan should operate in conjunction with or independently of military policy. Millikan and Rostow, who were commissioned to produce a draft report from the proceedings, answered Cutler's inquiries by insisting that the plan should be one that would encompass both the domestic welfare of the United States and that of developing nations. They argued that, although the operations of the initiative should be kept separate from those of the military in order to ensure that the Soviets could not label it a new form of imperialistic aggression, the initiative would serve the ends of national security. Rostow made the case as follows:

> It is that quite aside from our literal security interests in the world, quite aside from our literal economic interests in the world, there is, if you like, an authentic American ideological interest in the world, and it is that other societies develop not in the image of the United States, but according to some version of the humanistic tradition which is appropriate to their culture. . . . But we do have faith that if men are making their choices without economic frustration, without social frustration and without military danger—we have a faith, and there is a lot to back us—that they will opt for societies which can live congenially with ourselves and give it an environment in which we don't become a democratic garrison. And this is a real interest.[19]

Professor Edward S. Mason of Harvard University stated the terms of the question of how a world economic plan would serve the national interest as a humanitarian endeavor most explicitly when, early on, he stated: "[A]ny discussion of Foreign Economic Policy ought to start with the primary notion that there aren't any ends in this area; you are only talking about means to some end that lies outside of the field of economics and lies really in the realm of politics and security."[20] The group's discussion of the abstruseness of the ends of a world economic plan led to a consensus that the initiative could strengthen national security in a nonmilitary way by serving as a means to achieve political alliances in a "partnership for growth." The "partnership" idea, they argued, would appeal to Americans on the domestic front as a program in which all participating countries would be expected to contribute to an investment pool to fund development projects. This conclusion was not novel, for Rostow had made the same claims as early as 1952, in a set of CENIS "Notes on a New Approach to U.S. Foreign Economic Policy," written to further the interests of development aid advocates during the presidential election year.[21] What was exceptional about the 15 May Princeton Inn discussion was the recognition by all of the participants of the need to clarify the plan so that the details could be communicated persuasively to the American people and to peoples abroad as a supplement to American psychological warfare efforts.

Harold E. Stassen, director of the Foreign Operations Administration, spoke of the group's challenge in furthering foreign economic policy in the United States: "I think that this is the place where Foreign Economic Policy has to be stated down in specific terms, and there is a tremendous educational job internally that needs to be done. I think your approach of getting the phrases and the specifics of Foreign Economic Policy is a step in that process."[22] In terms of the message to be spread outside of the United States, labor leader David J. McDonald, president of the United Steelworkers of America, spoke candidly about the necessity of linking foreign economic policy and American propaganda:

> No matter what the basis [of a world economic plan] is, we cannot win unless we have a Manifesto (if that is what you want to call it) or a statement of principles that the people of the world can understand, a Manifesto that we can use to train people to go out and preach, and train them in foreign lands along our way of thinking, so as to put over our ideas in the minds of the people. We must let them know, at least, what our ideas are.[23]

By the end of the first day of the conference, agreement was reached that a global initiative in support of development—a "partnership for growth"—was necessary, and that effective communication of the U.S. position and ideology on the world economic plan would have to be implemented in order for the program to function on the proposed international scale.

On Sunday, 16 May, the group turned to the task of commenting on a draft document produced by Millikan and Rostow, which was based on the previous day's proceedings. Many of the participants from Washington had departed on Saturday, including General Cutler, CIA director Allen Dulles, Harold Stassen, and Gabriel Hauge, administrative assistant to the president.[24] Without the input of some of the Washington group, the remaining members discussed what should be included in the final version of the Princeton Inn proposal to be forwarded to the president.

Rostow suggested that the document should not be an academic paper in tone and content, but should exploit the theme of a "partnership for growth." He also stressed the need to include a discussion of salient crises in Southeast Asia to provide a statement of immediate context for policy makers who were concerned with short-term goals, even though the proposed world economic plan would function as a long-term approach to foreign economic policy. He argued:

> That present situation . . . should include a statement of the underlying persistence of the dollar gap, the struggle and inadequate successes of the growth process in underdeveloped areas, plus all these things coming to a head around Japan's balance of payments, and the whole thing in Southeast Asia. That would all be part of a statement of context.[25]

The topics Rostow identified were ones that concerned policy makers who were in agreement with the recommendations of the 1954 Randall Commission Report, and who would have to be convinced of the expediency of the Princeton Inn group's "partnership for growth" initiative. Millikan concurred with Rostow's idea that the proposal would have to have a "political flavor," but he questioned whether the opening emphasized self-interest to a sufficient degree. Robert Garner, vice president of the International Bank, argued that the opening did not say enough about the economics of the plan. Dr. Lloyd V. Berkner, president of Associated Universities, Inc., made the point that "the framework [of the papers] must have symbols that appeal very deeply to the beliefs and hopes of people, such as 'a partnership for growth,' 'peace through cooperation,' 'atomic energy for peace,' and so on."[26] Berkner's view, which concurred with the McDonald proposal to exploit the propaganda value of a world economic plan, emphasized the need to recapture the "benign words" from the Soviets.

In the end, it was agreed, as Rostow phrased it, that the Princeton Inn document would have to "get at least some operating concepts aside from the *ad hoc* ones in the Free World to match up against this over-simple and powerful force in the Soviet Union."[27] In the final moments of the conference, Millikan clarified the challenge the Princeton Inn group faced in addressing foreign economic policy makers in the United States:

> The submission of another report is not the answer. The real problem of American foreign economic policy is how you manage to get done the things that almost all sensible men would agree need to be done. That is not just the problem of presenting the President with a document, or the problem of getting a sense of what needs to be done infused by the Government. It is a problem of identifying the kinds of resistances and roadblocks to action in the United States. A large part of these spring from public understanding—not necessarily understanding of the public in the mass sense, but certainly in a leadership sense.[28]

The first draft of the report that emerged from the two days of proceedings of the Princeton Inn Conference identified national security as the most important purpose of a world economic plan.[29] As Rostow and Millikan had suggested, both short- and long-term goals in support of the American self-interest were emphasized in the opening. The two economists argued, in the mode of "realist idealists," that the world economic plan would serve both economic and security purposes, as well as humanitarian ends. More importantly, they called for policy makers to abandon the practice of arbitrarily dividing the paradigms of realism and idealism when engaging in strategic calculations concerning economic diplomacy. They wrote:

> [T]hese aims [of the world economic plan] make clear how false is the dichotomy between selfish and altruistic considerations motivating our actions. Every one of the above objectives [presented in the opening of the Princeton Inn report] serves what is in the broad sense a selfish end. But we believe our long run objectives to be in fact identical with those of others. Insofar as there are wellsprings of American energy, in the missionary tradition, seeking opportunities for world service, they can find an outlet in this set of policies. But our purposes will be clearer to our partners if they understand the depth of our conviction that our own national interest is fundamentally involved.[30]

The long-term view of American economic diplomacy Millikan and Rostow advocated in the Princeton Inn report involved helping developing countries to achieve a degree of steady economic progress in order to confront the difficulties of the transition to self-sustaining growth. The world economic plan relied on the idea of a "partnership for growth," to cultivate feelings of goodwill and respect among the peoples of the Free World. The "partnership," Millikan and Rostow argued, would extend beyond the cash nexus of development loans to the exchange of students, teachers, technicians, farmers, businesspeople, and others, as well as the use of America's chronic food surpluses to gain "political and ideological leverage."[31]

The idea of exchanging peoples under the partnership arose from David J. McDonald's argument that the United States needed to "construct an apparatus to reach the minds of the ordinary people of the free and captive worlds."[32] Millikan and Rostow added the McDonald proposal to the Princeton Inn report as an appendix, in which it was argued that Americans who traveled abroad under the partnership must be "educated and re-educated to advance in every corner of the world our foreign policy and our political and economic principles."[33] "The basic ideas which they are to advance," they wrote, "are stated in the Atlantic Charter. It is the frame within and upon which can be built a complete ideological structure."[34] In particular, the articles of the Atlantic Charter calling for "freedom from fear and want," for economic collaboration among nations, and for the right of all peoples to choose their own form of government were themes that would lend support to the political and ideological message that the "partnership for growth" would reinforce with material incentives.[35]

From the Princeton Inn Proposal to the Millikan-Rostow Thesis: Keeping Up the Fight

Millikan and Rostow expanded the initial draft of the Princeton Inn proposal to a fifty-two-page paper by 23 July 1954, and sent it to President Eisenhower. As Rostow has recalled, "The paper went from the White House to [Foster] Dulles, who in turn gave it to his new Undersecretary of State, Herbert Hoover, Jr."[36] Hoover, Secretary of the Treasury George M. Humphrey, and Chairman of the Council on Foreign Economic Policy Joseph M. Dodge—all zealous fiscal conservatives—rallied against the proposal. In the face of the strong opposition within the administration, C. D. Jackson appealed directly to the president to make an unambiguous command decision on the world economic plan. Eisenhower refused, and took the position that a subordinate in the administration should pull together a consensus on the issue. The logical figure to build such an agreement was Foster Dulles, who had contacted Jackson to draft the Princeton Inn proposal in the first place. However, even though the secretary of state supported the plan as an anticommunist initiative, he refused to lead a confrontation on the issue against Hoover, Humphrey, and Dodge, as well as a host of opponents in Congress.[37] By the autumn of 1954, the defeat of the proposal for a world economic plan was imminent.

Rostow attributed the conservatives' success at routing the Princeton Inn proposal to the influence of adverse elements in the larger political environment of 1954:

> Eisenhower was not prepared to overrule his opponents within the administration—notably Humphrey, Hoover, and Dodge; and he was not prepared to take on the opposition in the Congress, much of it within his own party.[38]

In December 1954, Rostow wrote Jackson to encourage him to continue to fight for the proposal, and he expressed a special concern for Dodge's rejection of the plan as the head of Foreign Economic Policy. Rostow characterized what he referred to as the "Dodge-Humphrey view" as follows:

> Any fool knows that the men in these underdeveloped countries are only too ready to talk and act as if U.S. dough will solve their problems when, in fact, they have to solve them at home. Let us help them with technical assistance.

> Let them learn that capital is other people's money which must be respected and put to use only under conditions which will yield a solid return.[39]

Rostow argued that, with respect to countries such as India, Indonesia, Japan, and communist China, Dodge and Humphrey failed to grasp the dynamics at work in the developing world and the benefits that the United States could derive from an investment offer in modernization projects. "I don't think we should give up on this one," he wrote to Jackson, "partly because it's right, partly because the problem of economic development is so new that good men can misunderstand the possibilities."[40]

During 1955 and 1956, the Eisenhower policy toward the third world continued to focus on the developing countries' relations to communist military power, and, in the fiscal year 1955, most military aid and defense support grants went to Indochina, Korea, and Taiwan, with smaller grants going to Pakistan, the Philippines, and Thailand. Only 15 percent of the total aid was made available to countries outside of the framework of military pacts, including such strategically important nations as Egypt, India, and Indonesia.[41] In 1956, Millikan and Rostow continued the battle begun by Jackson, circulating a second draft of the Princeton Inn proposal in Washington during a Senate examination of the foreign aid issue in December hearings of the Subcommittee on Foreign Economic Policy of the Joint Economic Committee. The proposal received favorable comment in the press, so the economists decided to publish it with Harper & Brothers of New York in order to reach an audience beyond Washington. The timing was propitious, for by 1957 some of the opponents of foreign aid were withdrawing from Washington, and the advocates of an enlarged, long-term development aid policy were gaining supporters.

Modeling Democracy: The "Diffusion of Power" and Development Aid Policy

The foreign policy perspective of the Millikan-Rostow thesis presented in the 1957 book *A Proposal: Key to an Effective Foreign Policy* was premised on the claim that, with the arrival of the 1960s, a new phase of the cold war would bring about a diffusion of political, social, and economic power among nations, which would be unavoidable but potentially manageable by U.S. policy makers. This idea of an emerging multipolarity marked by an ever-widening balance of power was based on realist precepts compatible with those of Morgenthau. Yet, instead of concentrating on a mechanism of successful competition between nations in the area of military power, Millikan and Rostow supported a plan that relied on the modeling of liberal democratic capitalism to achieve strategic results in the developing world. Their thesis abandoned a conventional cold war disjunct in which the Soviet Union and the United States were viewed as the principal antagonists and controlling powers in world affairs. That logic had set the terms for such Eisenhower-era phraseology as "monolithic communism," "massive retaliation," "brinkmanship," and, with respect to the unaligned nations, "agonizing reappraisal." In lieu of embracing the ingrained vocabulary of many of the cold warriors of the 1950s, Millikan and Rostow worked to merge the concepts of both realists and idealists by theorizing not with an eye toward the terms of a bipolar world balanced by nuclear weaponry but with a logic and discourse grounded in the image of a multi-hegemonic global system based on economic interdependence.

The Millikan-Rostow thesis highlighted the significance of emerging forces in the unaligned countries of Asia, Africa, the Middle East, and Latin America. The economists conjectured that the progress of third world states in these regions would bring about a "diffusion of power," which would result in the end of the cold war. As to the dynamics of this "great transition," they argued that the foreign aid policy of the Eisenhower administration had been little more than a regressive response to "the awakening of formerly static peoples," and that the continuation of such a policy would pit the United States against a large portion of the world's population in the decades to come. They wrote:

> The danger is that increasing numbers of people will become convinced that their new aspirations can be realized only through violent change and the renunciation of democratic institutions. . . . The United States has not presented a consistent and persuasive alternative in terms of the democratic process. It is the unpleasant truth that the United States has come to be regarded increasingly in the uncommitted areas of the world as a power at best neurotic and at worst aggressive, preoccupied with military preparations and with a game of international power diplomacy which has no meaning for the newly awakened ordinary citizen. We are no longer identified, as we once were, with the aspirations of people for social and economic improvement or with their Utopian image of a society designed to satisfy those aspirations.[42]

In a world that Millikan and Rostow viewed as becoming ever more fragmented, but increasingly interdependent, their conception of an effective deterrent for global conflict and nuclear war rested not on the force of military pacts, but rather on long-term economic solutions that would bind together nations in free market networks. Their vision of a devolution of global power was founded on a complicated image of the dynamics of the cold war, in which they recognized a connection between sources of third world nationalism and the activities of communists who preyed on the rising expectations of decolonized peoples. To prevent the communists' exploitation of the desire of third world peoples for modernization, Millikan and Rostow argued that an effective projection of U.S. power would have to consist of a more intricate set of strategic and symbolic actions than those prescribed by the "self-help" imperatives advocated by the 1954 Randall Commission Report and similar official documents on foreign aid.

With the advent of a multi-hegemonic world, Millikan and Rostow reasoned, the enlargement and maintenance of U.S. military power and alliances was but one national priority. A more future-oriented precedent was to assist in the economic, social, and political transformation of struggling nations, to promote "the evolution of a world in which threats to our security and, more broadly, to our way of life are less likely to arise."[43] Millikan and Rostow insisted that, in the context of postcolonial patterns of global growth, the integration of realistic and moralistic approaches in U.S. foreign aid policy would avert an estrangement of the uniqueness of the history of American society and its potential for inspiration and replication as a model for "awakening" areas.

To advance their case for the implementation of an expansive development aid program to promote the U.S. self-interest abroad, Millikan and Rostow combined estimates of world economic growth and appeals to international responsibility in order to convince Americans of the expedience of assisting the third world.

By merging patriotic entreaties with their social scientific arguments, which attempted to demonstrate a causal relationship between capitalistic economic growth and democracy, the economists charged conservative opponents of development aid with harboring "isolationistic tendencies." These tendencies, they claimed, were inherently "un-American," and would allow the pressures imposed by the "garrison-state" of the Soviet Union to "threaten our most cherished values."[44]

The American exceptionalism[45] Millikan and Rostow exhibited in their policy proposal was supplemented by both a rejection of the classical model of the rational economic actor[46] and the adoption of an antirevolutionary and legalistic worldview endemic to the principles of moral idealism.[47] Their position on the imperatives of America's global mission was as follows:

> Our great opportunity lies in the fact that we have developed more successfully than any other nation the social, political, and economic techniques for realizing widespread popular desires for change without either compulsion or social disorganization. Although our techniques must be adapted to local conditions abroad if they are to be effective there, they represent an enormous potential for steering the world's newly aroused human energies in constructive rather

> than destructive directions. Moreover, deep in American society, hankering for effective expression, capable of mobilization, is a dedication to the fundamental principles of national independence and human liberty under law. In their largest sense the proposals in this book are designed to give fresh meaning and vitality to the historic American sense of mission—a mission to see the principles of national independence and human liberty extended on the world scene.[48]

The conviction expressed in the Millikan-Rostow proposal—that America's ethos, political culture, and economic system of capitalism stood as models for the rest of the world—exhibited a crude ethnocentrism, for which the thesis frequently has been indicted.[49] On an operational level, the proposal elucidated a cold war program for establishing ideological and institutional mechanisms to extend Western influence into every aspect of the national lives of developing countries. Millikan and Rostow's thesis envisioned the propagation of liberal democracy through the use of U.S. development aid and by "restating systematically and promulgating widely the values of Western democratic liberalism in a form which would be irresistibly persuasive to peoples everywhere."[50] In distinguishing their development aid strategy from Mutual Security initiatives, military pacts, and other contemporary policies, the economists made clear their belief that their plan would pacify the third world. They wrote:

> underlying the proposals in this book is the conviction that we have put relatively too much emphasis in recent years on pacts, treaties, negotiation, and international diplomacy and too little on measures to promote the evolution of stable, effective, and democratic societies abroad which can be relied upon not to generate conflict because their own national interests parallel ours and because they are politically healthy and mature.[51]

Millikan and Rostow advocated development aid in humanitarian terms, but theorized that American offers of aid would produce a sweeping psychological commitment to the type of liberal democratic capitalism sanctioned by the United States. They argued that development aid policy would prove superior to the construction of an American military monopoly within the edifice of the cold war, attempted in the late 1950s, because the modernization of the third world would bring about patterns of global growth favorable, over the long run, to the self-interest of the United States. Most significantly, Millikan and Rostow claimed that development aid would hasten the end of the cold war by allowing for the dissemination of a liberal ideology designed "to counter and expose systems of thought like communism which have a built-in commitment to violence as an instrument of change."[52]

"Peaceful Revolution" and the Stages of Economic Growth

Rostow's "stages of economic growth" model, its nonrational view of economic agency, and its vision of "peaceful revolution" through capitalistic progress served as the grounds for Millikan and Rostow's call for U.S. legislators to endorse an expansive development aid policy.

Central to the economists' argument that development aid was an effective instrument for convincing third world leaders of the advantages of Euro-American capitalism was Rostow's idea that patterns of economic maturation in different countries could be arrayed and isolated to render a common model of the "stages of economic growth." As a taxonomical device, the "stages" framework offered indices for ranking the evolutionary status of the economies of developing nations. In their proposal, Millikan and Rostow emphasized the usefulness of the "stages" model for identifying nations that were advanced enough, in their propensities to accept and apply fundamental science and other means of modernization, to absorb and exploit development aid efficiently.[53] The economists invoked the disciplinary ethos of developmental economics to provide a pragmatic rationale for applying the "stages" schema in the process of planning and implementing development aid policy. They wrote:

> [T]here is emerging from the intensive work of social scientists on the development problem a recognition that there are common elements in the patterns of development of different countries which have implications for development policy everywhere.[54]

The three stages of economic growth that Millikan and Rostow presented in the 1957 version of their proposal served as the foundation of their analysis of the modernization process and as the basis for their argument that development aid could be used to induce and reinforce free market values in emerging societies. The mixed biological-aeronautical metaphor they used to hypothesize an ascending curve of economic and technological growth in a capitalist society was that of a "take-off into self-sustaining growth." The stages of growth curve included an initial period, "during which the preconditions for economic progress are established,"[55] a "take-off" stage, "during which the country makes the complex transition to a position where sustained economic growth becomes possible,"[56] and a third stage of "self-sustained growth," in which "comes the long period of regular if fluctuating progress."[57]

The "stages" model that appeared in the Millikan-Rostow proposal was an early version of a more thoroughly elaborated theory of five stages of economic growth that Rostow offered in 1960. Even though Rostow had not completed his theory in 1957, the three stages of growth he and Millikan identified that year as the "key to an effective foreign policy" had political appeal as a way of analyzing the prospects for development in various countries. In particular, the categorization of developing societies according to their level of economic evolution was seen as a step toward appeasing the demands of conservative legislators, since policy makers would have a mechanism to ensure that U.S. aid to third world nations would be distributed efficiently and not be open-ended. In the developing world, Millikan and Rostow argued, the stages of growth model also held the potential to reassure political and economic leaders that modernization could be inevitable if transformations of the economy proceeded by rational design.

In summarizing all of the benefits of the stages model, Millikan and Rostow were emphatic that the U.S. development aid program would be limited if the governments of developing nations could be convinced to adhere to a planned effort to move from the preconditions, through the take-off, and into self-sustaining growth. They wrote:

> In the light of this analysis it is essential to note that the proposals set forth in this paper do not open the United States up to an endless, open-ended, world-wide claim on its resources. The American purpose would be to assist countries in establishing the preconditions for growth (mainly through technical assistance) and to assist them with capital, notably in the decisive period of transition. The objective is not to redistribute income as between the industrialized and underdeveloped nations: the objective is to help the underdeveloped nations into the stage of self-sustained growth. When a country has passed the transition, it should be in a position to operate on its own with help only from normal international capital market institutions.[58]

The case made by Millikan and Rostow, that the demand for U.S. allocations of development aid would be transitory, was necessary for the economists to support their fiscal argument that such a program would be less costly and more constructive than military escalation, "as the arms race in major weapons moves into what may be a protracted stalemate."[59] This set of claims distinguished their plan from past arguments for development aid. A "banking-desire" metaphor served as the basis for Millikan and Rostow's case that the United States would be able to apply the stages model of economic growth to determine the appropriate extent of U.S. investment in developing nations. They claimed that the exact allocation of American funds would depend on a country's ability to demonstrate its propensities to absorb the capital. The "banking principle," as they characterized their proposed loan system, would be based on the stages framework and would function according to accepted standards of domestic lending institutions in America. They explained:

> A banker does not list all his potential customers and then try to decide how to allocate his loanable funds in such a way as to be fair to each. He sets certain criteria for the soundness of loans and then welcomes all customers who can satisfy him that they meet the criteria.[60]

The criteria that guided Millikan and Rostow's banking principle for the disbursement of development loans were conceived by the economists with the assumption that the nomenclature of the stages of economic growth would allow for the empirical calculation of the soundness of U.S. investments by identifying the level of development of recipient nations.

It was also assumed that once the amount of a development loan was determined, the promise of foreign aid would induce a desire in the government of a developing nation to formulate a country program for modernization to demonstrate that the aid could be absorbed in a manner consistent with American standards of liberal democratic capitalism. The evolutionary taxonomy of the stages model dictated that a country determined by policy makers to be in the "preconditions" stage could absorb only technical assistance to establish infrastructure that would support future economic growth. If a country was deemed to be advanced enough to be categorized as in the "take-off" stage, disbursements of capital could facilitate and maintain growth. The withdrawal of U.S. grants and loans could safely ensue upon a nation's achievement of the stage of "self-sustained growth."

The categories of the stages of growth model, which under Millikan and Rostow's proposal would determine the size and substance of development aid, were derived from a 1956 article by Rostow entitled "The Take-off into Sustained Growth." The macroeconomic hypotheses Rostow had set forth the year before he and Millikan published their policy proposal in 1957 provided the rationale for their "banking principle" and the empirical basis of its applications. Rostow wrote in 1956

> that the process of economic growth can be usefully regarded as centering on a relatively brief time interval of two to three decades when the economy and the society of which it is a part transform themselves in such ways that economic growth is, subsequently, more or less automatic.[61]

He claimed that the take-off requires

> a society prepared to respond actively to new possibilities for productive enterprise; and it is likely to require political, social, and institutional changes which will both perpetuate an initial increase in the scale of investment and result in the regular acceptance and absorption of innovations.[62]

Rostow argued in his 1956 article that, in the general historical case, "the achievement of preconditions for take-off required major change in political and social structure, and, even, in effective cultural values."[63] This hypothesis led to Millikan and Rostow's conclusion in 1957 that U.S. development aid would serve as an external catalyst to bring about societal change in the third world and instill in the minds of the peoples of developing nations the idea that economic progress was both possible and desirable. Rostow's nonrational view of economic agency, with which he had challenged the precepts of classical economic theory in the early 1950s, supported the concept that economic growth could not occur without concurrent changes in the noneconomic propensities of a nation. Rostow declared:

> the economic motives for seeking economic progress converge with some noneconomic motive, such as the desire for increased social power and prestige, national pride, political ambition and so on.[64]

Rostow's emphasis on the significance of the noneconomic bases of modernization in the Millikan-Rostow proposal helped to make the case that material incentives provided by the United States to developing nations could stimulate the kind of social and political motivations that would reinforce American values in the course of donor-recipient transactions. As a blueprint for American foreign aid policy, the Rostovian "take-off" concept supported the premise that economic growth would create an ideological conduit through which to channel nationalist sentiments in third world countries toward liberal democratic capitalism. If American policy makers could use development aid to turn the rising expectations of the peoples of emerging nations toward the promise of economic independence, then communists would not be able to exploit the fatalistic attitudes of transitional societies—a problem that Rostow claimed was a major cause of economic stagnation. The idea that third world countries could achieve the economic independence they desired held strong appeal for fiscal conservatives in the United States, for once societies moved through the stages of growth, the United States could look forward to being a trade partner rather than an aid donor. Rostow explained what he saw as the appeal of his stages of growth model to citizens of the developing nations as follows: "In your own lifetime [as a citizen of a developing nation] you couldn't imagine getting as rich as the Americans, but if the nature of growth had this lift in it, then you're on your way."[65]

By generating their banking principle of development aid disbursement from the taxonomy of Rostow's stages of economic growth model, Millikan and Rostow amplified the operational advantages of their proposal for harnessing the forces of nationalism in the developing world. In their view, development aid was vital, "to provide maximum incentives to the governments of the underdeveloped countries to take the steps necessary to promote development and thus make their countries eligible for assistance."[66] The Western nations supplied the model of economic and political modernization that Millikan and Rostow considered worthy of emulation by developing nations—the ideal that could serve as an inspiration for countries to achieve an "economic industrial revolution" as they emerged from "the present revolutionary phase of history."[67] In the self-interest of the United States, development aid policy would offer "a positive answer to the immediate threat posed for us by the current political, economic, and psychological offensive of the Communist bloc."[68] The antirevolutionary orientation of the Millikan-Rostow proposal for development aid has been described by Bruce Miroff as "a massive ideological screen, which shut out all hints of imperialism; where others might recognize exploitation, they [Rostow and Millikan] mainly saw beneficence."[69]

As Miroff has suggested, Millikan and Rostow's "ideological screen" was intended to overcome a third world hostility toward a heritage of Western colonial domination that might hamper the effectiveness of U.S. development aid policy. To offset anti-American sentiments in developing nations, the economists emphasized what they saw as the exceptional ethical bases of the American experience. In their view, the American experience compelled the United States to support free countries and to propagate its secular spiritual values in bringing about political, social, and economic progress throughout the world. They wrote:

> From the revolutionary beginnings of our history the United States has, on balance, acted in loyalty to the conception that its society has a meaning and purpose which transcend the nation. Down to the present day the peoples of the United States and of the world have not wholly lost the sense that this nation represents a continuing, unique experiment in the development of free societies. If over the coming decades the United States should turn its back on the great revolutionary transformations going forward in the underdeveloped countries, devoting itself almost exclusively to domestic chores and objectives, American society will progressively lose some of those basic spiritual qualities which have been historically linked to the nation's sense of world mission. The nation will risk the long-run danger of helping bring about, by its own spiritual decline, a kind of self-enforced isolation which would further damage the military and non-military bases of national security.[70]

Millikan and Rostow's brand of American exceptionalism added a moral component to their realist conceptions of the pragmatism of development aid policy by emphasizing the significance of nationalism in the domestic politics of developing nations, and the nonrational bases of economic growth. The economists' notion that America had "a sense of world mission" in promoting global democratization confronted a problem associated with the disinterest of orthodox realist theorists in "non-rational" influences on international relations. As Tony Smith has argued:

> By the same token that it discounts ethics and the role of the irrational in world affairs, realism likewise accords little importance to the domestic base of the state in its concern to explain the pattern of international relations. Hence, the tremendous change in the structure of domestic politics that has swept over the world in the last two centuries with the rise of nationalism and corresponding changes in the structure of the state . . . would necessarily be of no more than secondary interest to realists, any more than such issues as whether a country were capitalist or Christian would matter.[71]

By applying criteria of moral idealism and legalism to economic analysis, Millikan and Rostow worked to expand the strategic focus of the paradigm of realism beyond that in which, as Robert Hariman and Francis A. Beer have described, "nation states calculate and compare benefits and costs of alternative policies, and rank each other according to their power, which is measured primarily in terms of their material, and especially military, capabilities."[72] Rostow's stages of economic growth model was attuned directly to the structure and functions of domestic affairs in the third world and the influence of those factors on relationships among the industrialized and developing nations. Rostow's system of analysis supplemented the realist concentration on the material capacities of nations by ranking countries on the basis of their nonmaterial propensities to "take off into self-sustaining growth." Unsatisfied with the practice of isolating only external variables in rendering policy calculations, Rostow introduced a number of internal variables to the analysis of economic evolution, which complicated the process of foreign policy planning. He explained:

> When the stages of growth are . . . linked systematically to the eternal triangle of problems [of welfare and constitutional issues, security issues, and the process of growth itself] with which governments must deal, one does not get a closed, logical system in which all is neatly determined and the politics of all nations at all times fall into neat patterns. But one does have a dynamic framework within which those clamorous competitors—security, welfare, and growth—can be related not merely to the resource mobilization and allocation process but also to pressures for change in the constitutional system and its balance. And suggestive patterns of human and societal experience do naturally emerge, without violating the inherent elements of uniqueness in the cases.[73]

The consideration of nonrational forces in the Millikan-Rostow proposal led the economists to deny any possibility that the United States could hope to achieve and maintain a cold war balance of power on purely military terms. The proposal argued that, in fact, the Soviets' recognition of the limitations of conventional and nuclear weapons was a motivating factor behind the Russian economic offensive in the third world, to which America had failed to respond in effective ways. Millikan and Rostow explained:

> By means that are either subtle or unsubtle, as occasion demands, Moscow is telling American allies and potential allies that American military strength can no longer protect them; that should major war come, the United States could not prevent their national destruction with Soviet weapons. Therefore, Moscow argues, the only rational course for other countries is to disengage from alliances with the United States, an argument of some evident persuasiveness from Iceland to Ceylon. . . . It has gained considerable force from the fact that it is accompanied by a psychological, political, and economic policy that is designed not merely to make association with the United States unattractive, but also to make association with Moscow more attractive.[74]

Millikan and Rostow argued that, in many ways, official Soviet communist philosophy, with its dialectical materialist theory of history, was more congruent with the ideological transformations occurring in the decolonized areas than was American-style liberal democratic capitalism. Even worse, they claimed, was the fact that U.S. policy makers frequently misinterpreted the motives of third world trendsetters due to a paradox that "lies in the meanings of key words [about economics and politics]," which led to "semantic problems" for Americans when key figures were judged by what they said rather than by their economic policies and initiatives. Millikan and Rostow claimed that when American policy makers succumbed to the illusion created when third world leaders talked like communists but acted like capitalists, those planners of U.S. policy weakened efforts to influence leaders in developing countries by preventing them from receiving foreign aid. For development aid policy to function properly, obstacles of language would have to be overcome in order to persuade leaders, on a case-by-case basis, of the benefits of democracy and the free market. If this was not accomplished, Millikan and Rostow warned, the process of capitalistic growth could be aborted by policy makers responding to revolutionary tendencies in the third world with intolerance and rigidity. They wrote:

> [W]e believe that crude attempts to force a free private enterprise philosophy on recipient countries as an explicit or implicit condition for aid are almost certain to be self-defeating; on the other hand we believe there are good

> reasons for expecting countries now avowedly socialist but determinedly democratic to move toward greater reliance on private enterprise as their development proceeds. . . . To connect our assistance with a frontal attack on socialist ideology will result in all probability in a refusal of aid and a vigorous reassertion of socialist principles.[75]

Millikan and Rostow's argument that the cold war was, on balance, a stage in "the great transition" of the global diffusion of power prompted their call for more flexible techniques for implementing development aid programs. Their concern for creating effective strategies to influence and transform the economies and politics of developing nations focused on a long-term goal: namely, the preservation of U.S. power in what inevitably would become a post–cold war world. Their answer to Moscow's strategy for associating itself "with the aspirations of the people of the Free World for peace, economic progress, and political independence"[76] was for U.S. policy makers to be more proactive in confronting the global devolution of power. The strategy required a logic and vocabulary of "realistic idealism" that treated the maladies of developing countries as endemic to the stages of economic growth.

Conclusion

The three-year development of the Millikan-Rostow proposal represented the culmination of a collaborative rhetorical effort by the participants of the Princeton Inn Conference of 1954 and members of CENIS at MIT. The purpose of the Princeton Inn Conference was to convince the Eisenhower administration that U.S. development aid could prevent the Soviets from capitalizing freely on an escalating nationalism in the third world as part of a psychological campaign against the West. The self-interest of the United States, Millikan and Rostow argued, was not confined to the military containment of the Russians, for even if communism withered away as a force in the world, developing nations might move through the stages of economic growth "along lines hostile to the West and the Western tradition."[77] From a realist perspective, the economists' advocacy of development aid policy was grounded on the premise that, in the late 1950s and early 1960s, the United States was poised to influence the directions of the diffusion of power that would result in a multi-hegemonic balance of power in a post–cold war world. In a speech at the Naval War College in 1956, Rostow argued that development aid policy was not a purely idealistic concept, but a rational instrument of nonmilitary warfare, which would help to defeat the Soviets and to gain allies in the third world:

> [W]e need a foreign policy designed squarely to meet and defeat our avowed enemies in the political, ideological, and economic conflict now taking place. This requires, in particular, a program designed to accelerate economic growth in the underdeveloped areas of the Free World capable of aligning the United States with the positive aspirations of the bulk of the world's population who live in these areas and of channeling off their acute, rampant nationalist feelings and ambitions into constructive domestic channels. The achievement of this purpose is far more than a problem in economics; but a new economic foreign policy is an essential missing tool.[78]

Millikan and Rostow's idea that the cold war, much like the stages of economic growth, was a global process that proceeded in phases supported their claim that a new foreign economic policy would be a long-term investment to ensure the United States a secure position in the post–cold war world. The diffusion of political, social, and economic forces that would occur with the progression of the cold war into the 1960s, they felt, would demand that policy makers be prepared to look to America's exceptional past as a model of liberal democratic capitalism for the developing nations of the third world. By pursuing a "world mission" of global development, Millikan and Rostow argued, the United States would benefit not only materially but also spiritually as formerly static nations emerged from a Western-influenced course of economic growth as allies and open markets in the Free World.

The value system of "realistic idealism" inherent in the Millikan-Rostow thesis generated a global interdependence narrative that was prescient in its encouragement of "competitive coexistence" among established and emerging powers during the 1950s. At the end of 1958, Congress created a Development Loan Fund (DLF) on a small scale. The International Development Association (IDA) was formed in 1959, along with the Inter-American Development Bank (IDB), which would provide a critical component of President John F. Kennedy's Alliance for Progress program to develop Latin America. Millikan and Rostow's efforts as lobbyists were instrumental in the passage of these initiatives, but it was not until the 1960 presidential campaign that Rostow's theory of the stages of economic growth would take its place at the center of American foreign aid policy.

CHAPTER 4

Narrative Reason in Rostow's *Stages of Economic Growth: A Non-Communist Manifesto*

From 1958 to 1959, Rostow took a sabbatical leave from CENIS at MIT to lecture and write at Cambridge University. Rostow described the series of eight lectures he delivered during the year he spent in England as: "An economic historian's way of generalizing the sweep of modern history."[1] In his Cambridge lectures, which served as the basis for Rostow's 1960 magnum opus, *The Stages of Economic Growth: A Non-communist Manifesto,* he elaborated his hypothesis that the process of economic growth since approximately 1700 has been marked by five clearly defined stages in each of the nations that have gone through it. He also specified ways that policy makers could apply the stages of economic growth to distribution of foreign aid and persuasion of developing nations to adopt the tenets of liberal democratic capitalism in lieu of socialism and communism.

In Europe Rostow's Cambridge lectures were well received, and, in 1959, he was invited by the Institute of World Economy and International Relations in Moscow to speak on the topic of "The Stages of Economic Growth and the Problems of Peaceful Co-existence." On 25 May 1959, he told the gathering of Soviet economists in Moscow that his stages of economic growth model was an "alternative to the system of historical analysis developed by Karl Marx,"[2] and that "the sequence of the stages of growth gives to the Soviet Union and the United States a common interest and a common responsibility to end the arms race."[3]

One year after his Moscow speech, Rostow's book, *The Stages of Economic Growth,* was published, and, as Aidan Foster-Carter has observed, his theory of economic growth became "the most widely known model both within the profession [of developmental economics] and beyond."[4] Rostow's "non-communist manifesto" continued to garner international acclaim after 1960, and was issued in two subsequent editions in 1971 and 1990. Perhaps the greatest testimonial to the prominence of Rostow's stages of economic growth came in 1982, when

Charles P. Kindleberger and Guido di Tella edited a three-volume Festschrift in celebration of the theory.[5]

The dialogue engendered by Rostow's *Stages of Economic Growth* has moved well beyond the disciplinary boundaries of developmental economics. Few texts have disclosed as overtly the rhetorical conventions of cold war economic diplomacy in America, and few have been more instructive as to the ways economists use rhetorical appeals to propagate and institutionalize their concepts in academia and public policy. Rostow conceived of the idea of combining historical narrative and economic theory by observing the economic instability of third world nations and their vulnerability to what he termed a "diffusion of power" during the cold war. By applying a traditional methodology of economic history, which had been displaced in the mid-nineteenth century by statistical models of analysis, Rostow was able to mount a convincing challenge to the dominant neoclassical paradigm of macroeconomics, and to Marxist theory, which shared the narrative basis of his theorizing. The production of a rival narrative to that of Marx allowed Rostow to align his theory of the stages of economic growth with U.S. foreign aid initiatives that confronted an economic competition with the Soviet Union that began in the early 1950s. The economic cold war strategy was as important to U.S. policy makers as the nuclear arms race, but was far less visible to the American public.

An examination of the narrative rationality[6] of Rostow's developmental economic theory in his *Stages of Economic Growth* reveals that he worked through his stages of economic growth as a frame narrative of capitalistic evolution that contained embedded narratives of human motivation, social organization, and societal change.[7] Rostow's stories within a story competed directly with the elements of Marx's narrative of the rise and fall of capitalism and offered U.S. policy makers a template for using development aid to ensure the triumph of liberal democracy in a post–cold war world.

Responses to *The Stages of Economic Growth*

By the time Rostow published *The Stages of Economic Growth: A Non-communist Manifesto* in 1960, his approach to the study of development had become archetypal within the paradigm of modernization theory.[8] His theoretical lexicon and five stages of economic growth—the traditional society, the preconditions for "take-off," the "take-off" stage, the drive to maturity, and the age of high mass-consumption—provided an analytic "bone structure" that was widely cited and applied by scholars and government officials, in the United States and abroad.[9] Diane B. Kunz has written of the "stages of economic growth" thesis, which became known in foreign policy circles as the "Rostow Doctrine":

> This doctrine offered an intellectual counterweight to Communist ideology and a seemingly easy way to fight communism's spread. If the United States provided some seed money, the developing world's path to non-Communist economic development seemed inevitable.[10]

Rostow's argument that all nations pass naturally through the same phases of development convinced U.S. policy makers to homogenize their methods of economic interventionism in the third world, although that view of the evolution of liberal democratic capitalism tended to mask conflict and emphasize the continuities of the development process. Above all, the anticommunist pretext of *The Stages of Economic Growth* made its logic, lexicon, and narrative structure amenable to the discourse of development aid advocates, who referenced it to advocate and implement counterrevolutionary initiatives throughout the world.

Rostow labeled *The Stages of Economic Growth* "both a scientific effort and a tract for the times."[11] The 1958 Cambridge lectures from which the book emerged were presented at a time when international affairs had been deeply affected by the image of the launching of the first Soviet Sputnik satellite a year earlier, and by what appeared to be a rising momentum in Mao's China, then in the grip of the Great Leap Forward. A rising sense of economic and technological confidence in the communist world was met in the West by a fear of falling behind. This state of affairs generated both a space race and an economic competition between the United States and the Soviet Union. As a result, even before its publication *The Stages of Economic Growth* provoked furious international debate, after Rostow expounded it to the official organization of Soviet economists in Moscow, and when the London *Economist* praised it as "the most stimulating contribution made to economic and political discussion by an academic economist since the war."[12] The theory drew the wrath of Yuri Zhukov, the head of Russia's State Committee for Cultural Relations with Foreign Countries, who officially denounced it in *Pravda* for "digging in old rubbish dumps" in an effort to discredit Marx and deny the sanctity of the class struggle as the moving force in history.[13] A comparable diatribe printed in *Kuang-ming Jih-pao,* a Chinese-language newspaper in Beijing, reproved the book as "reactionary theory," and labeled Rostow a "knight" of the cold war, "in service with the U.S. ruling elite."[14]

Along with the international political controversy over Rostow's bid to frame a developmental economic theory worthy to rival that of Marx, his work elicited both bemusement and veneration in U.S. academic circles. American critics dismissed his tale of the previous 150 years of economic evolution as an emulous and primitive exercise in materialistic historicism.[15] Admirers deemed *The Stages of Economic Growth* "a basic text for a world that is preoccupied with the problems and competition for growth."[16]

The Frame Narrative of *The Stages of Economic Growth*

The first major hypothesis Rostow set forth in *The Stages of Economic Growth* was as ambitious as it was uncomplicated:

> It is possible to identify all societies, in their economic dimensions, as lying within one of five categories: the traditional society, the preconditions for take-off, the take-off, the drive to maturity, and the age of high mass-consumption.[17]

With this hypothesis, Rostow signaled his intention to bridge historiography and macroeconomics as a method to analyze the stages of economic growth. This form of modeling relied on a mastery of detail in historical narration as well as economic theory. By proposing to recount and establish connections between a series of economic stages in narrative form, he reached back to a deeply rooted historiographical tradition of economic history that had guided analysts of development from Adam Smith to J. S. Mill and Marx. In his first book, a 1948 analysis of the British economy of the nineteenth century, Rostow clarified his method of combining historical narration and economic theory: "The purpose of the narrative is to mobilize the evidence in such a way as to make it capable of generalization, while presenting the movements within the economy as an essentially unique sequence of events."[18]

Rostow's reliance on narrative as a method of economic analysis made his theorizing comparable to the discourse of his intellectual nemesis, Marx. M. M. Postan has observed that both, as historians, sought to transform "a mere chronological sequence of past experiences into an evolutionary progression of related social situations."[19] As narrators of economic growth, both Marx and Rostow attempted to use modern macroeconomics as a lens to interpret economic principles of history, to forecast the future of capitalism, and to advise economic and social policies to further their respective political positions. However, despite similarities in the narrative structures of their theories, the teleological bearings of the theories deviated; Rostow envisioned the "organic" growth of capitalism, while Marx foretold its demise.

To account for how he and Marx had arrived at antithetical conclusions about the fate of capitalism through similar narrative frameworks, Rostow used his first major hypothesis concerning the universality of the stages of economic growth as a frame narrative, or a story that contained embedded narratives of the five phases of capitalistic development and related themes. Of the oppositional nature of his stories within a story, he wrote: "As against our stages—the traditional society; the preconditions; take-off; maturity; and high mass-consumption—we are setting then, Marx's feudalism; bourgeois capitalism; Socialism; and

Communism."[20] As a self-described "economist-biologist," he rejected what he considered to be Marx's depiction of politics, society, and culture as "mere superstructure built upon and derived uniquely from the economy."[21] He sought to avoid economic determinism in his own account of the five stages of the development process by integrating the interaction of human motivation, social structures, and societal change into his narration of a sequence of growth that was analogous to the stages through which a maturing human passes. In conveying his "biological" picture of capitalistic growth, he acted as an intrusive narrator by self-consciously commenting on what he called "Marx's basic errors." Rostow's explanation of the rise of liberal democratic states consisted of vastly different assumptions about capitalists, workers, human behavior, and social organization than those of Marx.

His frame narrative, which he supported with his mixed biological-aeronautical metaphor of the "take-off" of capitalism into "sustained growth," offered what he claimed to be a more pertinent mode of inquiry for investigating the myriad forces that influence the growth of a real economy. In addition, it prescribed a homogeneous set of remedies for the economic problems of third world nations in each stage of economic maturation.

What appealed to U.S. policy makers, who adopted the Rostovian narrative as a template for cold war foreign aid programs, was its denial of Marx's account of the role of proletarian revolution in the decline of bourgeois capitalism. Instead of depicting contemporary history as an open struggle between an emerging proletariat and the bourgeois forces opposed to it, Rostow's story of societal development invoked a less turbulent theory of modernity. Timothy W. Luke has described this style of theorizing as a discursive framework that speaks of gaining "control of the physical and social environment, building a liberal democratic state, participating in world culture, and joining the scientific revolution."[22] It was for these reasons that Rostow's vision of "peaceful revolution" came to pervade the counterrevolutionary rhetoric of what President Kennedy proclaimed the "Decade of Development" of the 1960s.[23]

Embedded Narratives in *The Stages of Economic Growth*: The Dynamics of Cold War Modernization

Rostow presented a frame narrative of five stages of economic growth that anticipated modernization without revolution, in which the ideological conversion of economic actors into capitalist entrepreneurs would lead to an aggregate transformation of entire societies into liberal democratic states. Three embedded narratives concerning human motivation, social organization, and generational changes in national character allowed him to refute Marx's economic-technological explanation of the development process and substitute his own biological account. In that account, he likened society to an interacting organism comprised of a complex balance of social, political, religious, and psychological factors. The combination of his biological perspective and the three embedded narratives of the dynamics of economic growth yielded his conception of the cold war as a diffusion of power away from Washington and Moscow, as well as his argument for using U.S. development aid to grow the economies of third world nations in order to cultivate allies.

The Embedded Narrative of Human Motivation

Rostow outlined his first embedded narrative in the second major hypothesis of *The Stages of Economic Growth* by focusing on the issue of dynamic causation in the economy as the basis of his refutation of Marxism:

> [W]e accept from the beginning the perception on which Marx, in the end, turned his back and which Engels was only willing to acknowledge wholeheartedly as a very old man; namely that societies are interacting organisms. While it is true that economic change has political and social consequence, economic change is, itself, viewed here as the consequence of political and social as well as narrowly economic forces. And in terms of human motivation, many of the most profound economic changes are viewed as the consequence of non-economic human motives and aspirations.[24]

Whereas Marx portrayed economic change as having political and social consequences, Rostow reversed the direction of the causal relationship and depicted economic transformation as being the consequence of political and social forces. This reversal of dynamic causation in the movements of the economy supported his objection to Marxist theory as "a set of more or less sophisticated logical deductions from the [classical] notion of profit maximization."[25] He drew a distinction between Marx's acceptance of the classical premise of profit maximization, which attributed human motivation to a rational drive to maximize gains and minimize losses, and his own biological view of nonrational, noneconomic agency,[26] which viewed human motivation as a balancing act among conflicting desires. On one level, his idea of nonrational motivation was an attempt to escape charges of economic determinism (a pitfall that has continued to plague models of economic development), and on another, it was a means by which to focus on a different set of agents, acts, and events in his narrative of the evolution of capitalism.

By rejecting profit maximization as the motive of economic actors, Rostow refuted Marx's depiction of the character of the industrial laborer as a self-interested agent pitted against bourgeois capitalists in the setting of a class struggle that represented the moving force of history. He wrote:

> The most important analytic assertion in Marx's writings is the assertion in the Communist Manifesto that capitalism "left no other nexus between man and man than naked self-interest, than callous cash payment." In the stages-of-growth sequence man is viewed as a more complex unit. He seeks, not merely economic advantage, but also power, leisure, adventure, continuity of experience and security; he is concerned with his family, the familiar values of his regional and national culture, and a bit of fun down at the local.[27]

Rostow's emphasis on the worker's sense of community and the role of reactive nationalism in the modernization of traditional societies was drawn from his observations of the process of global decolonization following World War Two. In contrast, Marx's inferences about the course of a proletarian revolution were based on his insights about the nineteenth-century British middle class and the profit motive. Consequently, Rostow questioned the generalizability of Marx's data and argued that the oracle of communism was misguided in making the industrial worker the downtrodden protagonist of his dialectical prophecies and in overemphasizing the economy as "the anatomy of society." His disparagement of Marx's view of the worker as the vanguard of the communist revolution related to his second embedded narrative of economic growth.

The Embedded Narrative of Cold War Social Organization

Rostow's contention that the capitalist entrepreneur, and not the proletarian, is the decisive agent who establishes the preconditions for the capitalistic transformation of a society constituted the most significant variation of his theory from Marxism. For Marx, early capitalism created requisites for the destruction of the system by laying the groundwork for the onset of stagnant real wages for labor and the pressure of competition to find markets for industrial capacity. In the face of the severe unemployment that would result, the proletariat would react to the contradictions brought about by the capitalists' pursuit of profit by seizing and transferring ownership of the means of production to the State.

By substituting the capitalist for Marx's worker as the protagonist of his developmental narrative, Rostow envisioned the preconditions for "take-off" not as the death knell of capitalism but rather as "the great watershed in the life of modern societies."[28] He portrayed the industrial entrepreneur not as the enemy of labor but instead as an enlightened social engineer who overcomes traditional resistances to steady economic growth by building compound interest into the habits and structure of society. He argued that the capitalists' utilization of compound interest would annul the probability of a Marxist revolution, since all classes would benefit from that accelerator of growth. Compound interest would enable the population to exploit modern science and to bring cost-reducing inventions into capital stock, and would allow innovating entrepreneurs to borrow money on a long-term basis. Given ideal conditions in which, politically and sociologically, the capitalist superseded the traditional landed elite to begin building a modern society, the stages of economic growth would naturally emerge in a system caught up in the "take-off" power of compound interest.

The credibility of Rostow's theory depended in part on whether it could account for the existence and relation of the communist state to the stages of growth. Rostow was able to account for the rise of communism by applying his biological-aeronautical metaphor to explain how the political, social, fiscal, and technological "take-off" mechanisms that influence societal speciation may become vulnerable to the temporary malady of a "disease of the transition," namely, communism itself. He wrote: "It is in such a setting of political and social confusion, before the take-off is achieved politically and socially as well as economically, that the seizure of power by Communist conspiracy is easiest."[29] With this argument, he sought to refute Marxism on a pragmatic level by attributing the rise of communist states, and in particular the Soviet Union, not to a Marxist version of economic determinism, in which ownership of the means of production decides everything, but to a "power determinism," in which a well-disciplined minority commandeers political authority in an ill-organized society. "Lenin and his successors have, in effect, turned Hegel back on his feet; and they have inverted Marx,"[30] he wrote, as he considered the irony of the Soviets' reversal of Marx's narrative: "the political dictatorship of the [communist] elite over the majority, operating in terms of its own interests, is a fair approximation of what Marx believed to be the political confrontation of capitalism, where those with property ruled."[31]

Rostow's portrayal of communism as a "disease of the transition," spread by a purposeful minority who expropriate from innovative capitalists the "take-off" mechanisms to dictate production functions in a society, allowed him and other members of the U.S. security establishment of the 1960s to explain America's counterrevolutionary struggle against communism as essentially a biologically curative operation. The potency of the disease metaphor made it amenable to the rationales of America's two-pronged strategy to stem communist expansion in the third world by applying development aid programs as disease treatment and the antiguerrilla warfare initiatives of Kennedy's "flexible response" security policy as prevention.[32] As Rostow told the graduating class of the Army Special Warfare School at Fort Bragg, North Carolina, in 1961:

> My view is, then, that we confront . . . a systematic attempt by the Communists to impose a serious disease on those societies attempting the transition to modernization. . . . I salute in particular those among you whose duty it is—along with others—to prevent that disease, if possible, and to eliminate it where it is imposed.[33]

The Embedded Narrative of the "Buddenbrooks" Analogy

Rostow's comparison of communism to a disease afflicting transitional societies supported his third embedded narrative—a literary analogy to Thomas Mann's novel, *Buddenbrooks*, about three generations of a merchant family. From Mann's novel, he drew the phrase "Buddenbrooks dynamics" to account for generational changes in the national characters of societies that affect the course of economic growth. He wrote:

> In Thomas Mann's novel of three generations, the first sought money; the second, born to money, sought social and civic position; the third, born to comfort and family prestige, looked to the life of music. The phrase ["Buddenbrooks dynamics"] is designed to suggest, then, the changing aspirations of generations, as they place a lower value on what they take for granted and seek new forms of satisfaction.[34]

The Buddenbrooks dynamics was a key explanatory device in Rostow's economic discourse, and it helped him to elaborate his view that the configuration of the post–cold war world would be determined, to a great degree, by the character and changing ambitions of the populations of the United States and the Soviet Union, and by the ends toward which reactive nationalism was channeled in developing nations. His interpretation of the Buddenbrooks dynamics of various nations supported his vision of the post-1955 phase of the cold war as a "diffusion of power" to developing countries, away from the United States and Russia. The narrative logic of the Buddenbrooks dynamics represented an ideological obverse of the bipolar strategy of nuclear "brinkmanship" that was articulated during the Eisenhower years. The analogy allowed him to privilege the third world as the vital ideological arena of the cold war within the narrative frame of his stages of economic growth, and it promised a productive approach to global development issues, rather than the risk-laden calculations of maintaining a nuclear balance of power.

In interpreting the Buddenbrooks dynamics of the Soviet Union, Rostow's idea was that the third generation of Russians, having been born into a society in which the communists had achieved economic maturity while staving off the age of high mass-consumption, would seek new satisfactions in the form of enlarged social welfare and consumer goods and services. The communist system, geared toward strict regulation of consumption, agriculture, and heavy industry, would not be able to provide for the demands of the populace, nor would it be able to cultivate allies through economic relationships in the global marketplace. In a society based on the maintenance of the regime's internal control and the expansion of Soviet power into developing areas, the economy would collapse from a lack of diversification and from the weight of social discontent. The policy challenge for the United States would be to convince developing nations of the benefits of liberal democratic capitalism, while waiting for the Buddenbrooks dynamics in Russia to move forward, generation by generation, toward their logical conclusion. This cold war waiting game would not be simple, however, for the Buddenbrooks dynamics of the United States posed internal threats to the American way of life that were inverse to those of the Soviet Union.

In predicting the future character of American society, Rostow sketched a converse Buddenbrooks narrative that predicated changes in the national character almost exclusively on the problem of boredom with consumption. Whereas the third generation of Soviets would covet consumption opportunities denied to them by the communists, the American population, born into an age of high-mass consumption, would cease to find in the production and consumption of durables and services worthy outlets for the expression of their "energies, talents, and instinct to reach for immortality."[35] As the Buddenbrooks dynamics moved on, mass boredom would set in and Americans might lapse into spiritual stagnation, superfluous warfare, or a detached, suburban version of the eighteenth-century country lifestyle, he explained, "in some mixture of the equivalent of hunting, shooting and fishing, the life of the mind and the spirit, and the minimum drama of carrying forward the human race, sufficient frontiers to keep for life its savour."[36] The result of the American indifference to the fortunes of capitalism would be that, with the combined pressures of a rising population, a deficit in social overhead capital, and a costly arms race, the American economy would be strained by a rocketing "dependency ratio," or the number of dependent persons one hundred members of the working force must support.

The effect of an American ennui on the nation's future alarmed Rostow, and for the United States to resist the onset of civil narcissism and isolationism, he argued for a "global reconciliation of the human race."[37] This prescription was rich in policy implications for advocates of U.S. development aid programs. His argument was that as global power diffused away from Washington and Moscow due to their respective Buddenbrooks dynamics, the challenge of forging constructive, nonaggressive relations with developing countries would be the key to sustaining either democracy or communism in a post–cold war world. As the influence of "middling" powers in the third world increased, generation by generation, they would identify their emerging prosperity with the nations who had assisted them in moving through the stages of economic growth. On the basis of this prediction, Rostow and other development aid advocates argued that a fundamental realignment of U.S. foreign policy would be required to contend with the Buddenbrooks dynamics of developing countries. This new approach would turn national resources away from the nuclear arms race, with its emphasis on the destructive capabilities of science and technology, and toward what Rostow described as the "great act of persuasion": "We must demonstrate that the underdeveloped nations—now the main focus of Communist hopes—can move successfully through the preconditions into a well-established take-off within the orbit of the democratic world."[38]

The Buddenbrooks dynamics of the developing world would complicate U.S. economic diplomacy, however, for the national character of many third world nations had been shaped by a colonial history that had cultivated a xenophobic nationalism among the masses. Depending on the history of the colonial, quasi-colonial, or other invasive relationship a country had had with an imperial power, nationalism might be turned outward to right real or believed past humiliations on the world scene (as in the Russian case); it might be held in and focused on political consolidation of the victory won by national over regional forces (as in China); or it might be turned toward economic and political modernization obstructed by former colonial powers (as in the United States). If the United States hoped to channel the reactive nationalism of developing nations toward democratic values, Rostow argued, policy makers would have to slowly lift "the horizons of expectation" of the masses by demonstrating that America's colonial history had produced a liberal democratic creed devoid of imperialistic intent and guided by the promise of "peaceful revolution." "[B]y articulating persuasively a vision of where we would like everyone to fetch up," he argued, America's promotion of democracy in developing countries eventually would convince even the Russians "to accept and absorb the implications of the new world of diffused power."[39]

The quixotic optimism of Rostow's economic rhetoric, with its solutions to nuclear stalemate and prescriptions for inducing modernization and democracy in the third world, belied the shortcomings of its taxonomical narration of the historical development of the West. By engaging in a selective historiography that stressed a lack of conflict in the stages of economic growth, Rostow collapsed his story of capitalistic evolution into a single transition that obscured the unique fiscal problems of individual nations. Nevertheless, Rostow's model remained influential in academe and U.S. foreign policy circles throughout the 1960s, and as late as 1985, Howard J. Wiarda wrote of the persistence of Rostow's rhetoric: "[A] great deal of our economic assistance program is still based, more implicitly than explicitly by now, on the 1960 book by W. W. Rostow, *The Stages of Economic Growth,* a key book that helped shape the Alliance for Progress and all subsequent U.S. aid efforts."[40] By 1989, *The Stages of Economic Growth* had come to appear more prescient than it had in the 1960s, as the Soviet empire collapsed in the manner Rostow had anticipated with his Buddenbrooks analogy. A year later, Cambridge University Press reprinted his book in a third edition.

Conclusion

Rostow's discursive strategies in his 1960 magnum opus, *The Stages of Economic Growth,* were designed to reestablish historical narration in the methodological tradition of economic history, to refute Marxist theory in order to achieve academic and political legitimacy for his ideas during the cold war, and to link his theory to foreign aid policies that responded to the global decolonization that had occurred in the wake of World War Two. By relying on a textual analysis of *The Stages of Economic Growth,* this chapter has demonstrated how national policy imperatives can affect the discourse and intellectual development of social scientific theory and how theory may, in turn, influence policy. In a personal interview conducted by the author on 16 November 1995, Professor Rostow made it clear that, in his view, no real distinction exists between the world of ideas and political action. His studies of communism, he stated, were always "highly operational," and the "communicative clarity of the stages of growth framework led to a greater circulation of the theory in policy."[41]

Rostow managed his challenge to Marxism and his prescriptions for using development aid as an instrument of cold war through the use of a frame narrative of the five stages of economic growth and a set of embedded narratives that revolved around themes of human motivation, social organization, and changes in national character that were the consequence of what he termed the "Buddenbrooks dynamics." His frame narrative bore a structural resemblance to Marx's developmental theory, but his embedded narratives systematically refuted the four stages of a communist revolution, one by one. His embedded narratives also refuted the major assumptions behind the Marxist view of economic growth; namely, the profit motive of the worker, the social causes of proletarian revolution, and the future character of communist states. To counter Marx's story of the decline of capitalism, he offered a five-part narrative of "peaceful revolution" that substituted a nonrational conception of human motives, a biological view of society as an interacting organism that requires scientific and technological stimulation for healthy development, and a futurism based on his vision of a generational march toward globalization in a post–cold war world.

CHAPTER 5

Advocating the Alliance for Progress: Rostow, Kennedy, and the Rhetoric of Peaceful Revolution

In 1961, newly elected President John F. Kennedy set out to achieve the policy goals of the "Rostow Doctrine" of foreign aid policy by launching the Alliance for Progress program to promote noncommunist modernization in Latin America. The new president was determined to pursue American interests in the Western Hemisphere through economic diplomacy, rather than with military measures alone. The challenge for Kennedy and his advisers was to secure legislative and budgetary authority for the Alliance program in the United States, and, as Arthur Schlesinger Jr. wrote, to "capture the imagination of the masses"[1] in the Americas. During the early months of Kennedy's administration, a flurry of policy planning and rhetorical activity occurred on behalf of the Alliance, and as Jerome Levinson and Juan de Onis have observed, "Reformist political ideas, concepts of economic planning, and a host of other notions that had been confined to the fringes of inter-American discussions suddenly found wide audiences."[2]

Rostow, whom Kennedy appointed as deputy special assistant for national security affairs and later as chair of the Policy Planning Council of the State Department, played a key role in persuading the president to make the 1960s an "economic development decade." In December 1960 he wrote to Kennedy, "It is crucial to the Free World position that the first days of the Kennedy administration be used for a breakthrough on the question of aid to the under-developed nations."[3] Regarding Latin America, Rostow predicted that with the benefit of U.S. aid, countries such as Brazil, Colombia, Mexico, and Venezuela would reach the "take-off" stage of development by 1970. He argued that within ten years, more than 80 percent of Latin America's population would "be drawing from special international sources either no capital or much diminished volumes of capital."[4]

Despite the optimistic economic projections of what the Alliance for Progress would achieve in the Americas, Kennedy's motives behind initiating the program were not purely altruistic, for he, Rostow, and other New Frontiersmen were convinced that Latin America had become a primary cold war battleground. Kennedy had received a stern warning in 1960 from his Task Force on Immediate Latin American Problems that, "In Moscow and Peiping revolutionary seizures of parts of Latin America appears [*sic*] to have been agreed on as an early target in the 'Cold War' now active in the Caribbean littoral."[5] On 6 January 1961 Nikita Khrushchev seemed to confirm the misgivings of the task force when he delivered a lengthy speech in Moscow that was studied closely by Kennedy's foreign policy team. Rabe has provided an account of how the speech was interpreted by Kennedy's advisers:

> NSC official Walt W. Rostow surmised that Khrushchev intended to promote guerrilla warfare. Ambassador to Brazil Lincoln Gordon decided that Khrushchev, by backing wars of national liberation, had signalled his intention to use Cuba as "a base for military and intelligence activities against the United States" and for further "opportunistic conquests in Latin America."[6]

As a result of Kennedy's suspicion of Khrushchev's intentions in Cuba, the evolution of his Latin American policy during the early months of his administration reflected the rise of a two-pronged approach for dealing with problems in the Western Hemisphere. The strategy involved a combination of initiatives aimed at "counterinsurgency" and "peaceful revolution," to be pursued both militarily and with U.S. foreign aid policy to promote the economic, political, and social development of Latin America. The purpose was to produce a rival model of modernization to the Castro example in Cuba. As Rostow reported on the scope of the administration's primary tasks in the developing world:

> By our military dispositions, we must continue to make either major or limited war an irrational undertaking for Communists. On this basis, we must use our economic resources to the full in doing what we can to insure that the nations of Asia, the Middle East, Africa and Latin America remain independent and move through their difficult transitions to modernization in ways that open the possibility of democratic evolution for their societies.[7]

In his advocacy of the Alliance for Progress, Kennedy's references to the motifs of "counter" and "peaceful" revolution registered Rostow's influence on his rhetoric. The economist's hand in the president's speech making carried over from his work with Kennedy in the Senate during the late 1950s and during the 1960 presidential campaign. In the new administration, Rostow's contributions to speech writing continued in two of his functions as a policy maker. As a member of the National Security Council, he was charged with planning "antiguerrilla" military strategies. He was assigned a role in designing development aid policy because of his expertise in the area of economic "take-offs." Drawing on his model of the stages of economic growth, Rostow theorized that planned industrial revolutions carried out by the urban middle class of developing nations would prevent Marxist-style rebellions against capitalism. He and others in the administration encouraged President Kennedy to include in his Alliance for Progress rhetoric appeals to "democratic-progressive" figures in Latin America, such as Romulo Betancourt of Venezuela, Jose Figueres of Costa Rica, Arturo Frondizi of Argentina, Alberto Lleras Camargo of Colombia, and Victor Haya de la Torre of Peru, whom the New Frontiersmen saw as leaders capable of spearheading economic "take-offs" in the hemisphere.

The "action intellectuals" of the Kennedy administration considered the urban middle class of Latin America and the democratic-progressive leadership of various nations to be the natural agents of modernization. Kennedy's Task Force on Immediate Latin American Problems identified specific areas of the hemisphere in which a "democratic-progressive front" could be established as a bulwark against communism.[8] Rostow and others believed that such a front would emerge from middle sector groups' acceptance of Western liberal values and rejection of dictatorships. As Wiarda has observed of the Latin Americans who participated in the establishment of the Alliance program:

> The Latin Americans who helped set up the Alliance were a particular kind and generation of Latin Americans. Many had attended U.S. universities, they had read [Seymour Martin] Lipset and Rostow, their writings were full of citations of the newest developmental literature. The U.S. participants were also a special group . . . believers (like their Latin American counterparts) in state-led and -directed development, often determinists who assumed that economic development would inevitably lead to political development.[9]

The Kennedy administration's belief that Latin Americans would model their institutions after U.S. economic and political systems was sustained by what Abraham F. Lowenthal has explained as the New Frontiersmen's "'Western Hemisphere idea,' that the states of North and South America are bound together by their common background and aspirations in a special and close relationship."[10] Kennedy alluded to the "Western Hemisphere idea" and the "Rostow Doctrine" of foreign aid policy in his Alliance for Progress rhetoric to make the program appear applicable to all Latin American nations, regardless of the differences in culture, attitudes, aims, and interests among those nations. In the end, the Kennedy administration's misguided belief in the harmonious nature of the Americas and the tendency of Rostow's modernization theory to make area studies less relevant to U.S. foreign aid strategy impeded an effective implementation of the Alliance program. Nevertheless, the topics of centralized planning of development projects and economic consolidation of Latin America made for powerful rhetorical appeals, both to members of the U.S. Congress interested in immunizing the Western Hemisphere against communism and to Latin American leaders eager to receive foreign aid money during the 1960s.

Mobilizing the Alliance for Progress, 1961

In a 1961 memorandum to the president's assistant special counsel Richard Goodwin, Lincoln Gordon defined the central theme of the Alliance for Progress as a "sustained effort for economic development and social progress, combining vigorous measures of self-help with the provision of complementary outside resources under the guidance and stimulation of greatly strengthened agencies for regional cooperation."[11] The Rostovian concepts of self-help and coordinated economic planning that Gordon evoked in his synopsis of the Kennedy administration's conception of the Alliance program could be initiated only with the swift acquisition of U.S. congressional support and Latin American enthusiasm. The obstacles to an effective beginning were twofold. In the United States, skeptics in Congress might resist funding requests, since President Kennedy had begun speaking in terms of billion-dollar aid for a decade of economic development and social reform. In addition, the Task Force on Latin America had warned the president of cynicism in the Americas concerning the Alliance: "Latin American apprehension exists that the incoming Administration, while justifiably upgrading Asia and Africa, may continue to leave Latin America a step-child."[12]

Kennedy and members of his transition team moved quickly to remove domestic and inter-American doubts about the Alliance program by emphasizing during the first three months of the new administration the importance of the initiative to U.S. foreign policy. Goodwin and members of the Task Force on Immediate Latin American Problems, along with Rostow and others who helped to design the development aid component of the Alliance program, worked to frame messages that would appeal to both the national security concerns of U.S. legislators and the social idealism of the democratic-progressive leaders of Latin America. The resulting campaign on behalf of the Alliance was carried out in a series of speeches delivered by Kennedy early in 1961, including the president's inaugural address of 20 January, his State of the Union Message of 30 January, his Alliance for Progress keynote address, delivered in the East Room at the White House on 13 March, and his "Special Message to the Congress on Foreign Aid" on 22 March.

Kennedy's Rhetorical Campaign for the Alliance: Sequence of Speeches, 1961

The security and humanitarian goals of the Alliance for Progress, both of which President Kennedy hoped to advance with his early advocacy of the program in 1961, were supported by Rostow's conception of the process of modernization in his theory of the stages of economic growth. Rostow's ideas inspired the president's characterizations of the Alliance program as an anticommunist initiative at home and as a humanitarian agenda abroad. To merge the themes of counter- and peaceful revolution, Kennedy exploited Rostow's view that antiguerrilla security measures could assist, and indeed were an essential part of, a developing nation's peaceful movement through the stages of economic growth. Furthermore, as Rostow's involvement in speech writing and other functions became more direct, the ideas he had first developed during the 1950s about channeling "reactionary nationalism" into modernization goals, disbursing aid on a "banking principle," and linking economic, political, and social transformations to induce a capitalist "take-off into self-sustaining growth" in developing nations appeared in policy rhetoric that Kennedy aimed at either domestic or foreign auditors, depending on the occasion.

Inaugural Address, 20 January 1961

In his inaugural address, Kennedy sought to signal to Latin Americans the seriousness of his commitment to the Alliance for Progress by speaking of it as if it were a break with past policies, although the foundations of the program already had been set in place by such Eisenhower era initiatives as the Social Progress Trust Fund. He followed the counsel of Rostow and other policy planners by touting the Alliance program at the earliest possible juncture as the basis of a new philosophy of American social revolution. Kennedy's reference to the Alliance in his inaugural address sought to confront what was seen in his administration as the failure of the ideology of liberal democratic capitalism to rival that of Marxist revolution in Latin America, which had inspired Castro's transformation of Cuba.[13] In appeals directed to American legislators, Kennedy stressed the idea that the U.S. strategy to counter the communist threat in Latin America demanded a "New Look"—a more imaginative response than had ever been attempted in the Western Hemisphere.

Kennedy's reference to the Alliance for Progress in his inaugural address alluded to the "Western Hemisphere idea" of the program by describing it as a cooperative enterprise based on the imperatives of human freedom and social and economic well-being; namely, a "peaceful revolution." He said:

> To our sister republics south of our border, we offer a special pledge—to convert our good words into good deeds—in a new alliance for progress—to assist free men and free governments in casting off the chains of poverty. But this peaceful revolution of hope cannot become the prey of hostile powers. Let all our neighbors know that we shall join with them to oppose aggression or subversion anywhere in the Americas. And let every other power know that this Hemisphere intends to remain the master of its own House.[14]

By linking in his inaugural address the idea of nonviolent social transformation in the Americas and the anticommunist objectives of U.S. foreign policy, Kennedy prepared the grounds for the extension of those distinct appeals in his State of the Union Message, his Alliance keynote speech, and his "Special Message to the Congress on Foreign Aid," which contained the rationale for funding the Alliance program at an unprecedented rate of four billion dollars for the 1962 fiscal year.

Annual Message to the Congress on the State of the Union, 30 January 1961

In his State of the Union message, Kennedy cast the international position of the United States in crisis terms, and he described his speech as one delivered "in an hour of national peril and national opportunity."[15] Seeking the acquisition of a larger federal budget, Kennedy explained the Alliance program as an anti-Castro measure, and he argued that the initiative was tied to the national interest as a means of advancing both the diplomatic integrity of the United States and the mobility of the armed forces in the struggle against communism in the Western Hemisphere. In this vein, Kennedy promoted the Alliance program as a component of his "flexible response" security strategy in Latin America, which he argued would require several types of congressional funding in addition to military expenditures.

In an attempt to distinguish his foreign aid policy from the Mutual Security emphasis that had guided the Latin American initiatives of the Truman and Eisenhower administrations, Kennedy stressed to the Congress the need for "central policy direction" in military, economic, and humanitarian functions in order to coordinate programs that he said "overlap, conflict or diffuse our energies and resources."[16] He insisted that by bringing together many bureaucratically fragmented operations under a unified security policy, foreign aid programs, such as the Alliance for Progress, could help to create a more effective defense structure to stop the expansion of communist forces in the south. By combining his appeal for funding to bolster military readiness with his argument for supporting Latin American modernization as a way of stemming the spread of communism, the Alliance for Progress was presented to Congress as an expedient package for addressing what Rostow had identified in his model of the stages of economic growth as the "organic interplay" of economic and noneconomic motives that influence the evolution of developing societies. The Alliance program would serve as a vehicle for channeling the forces of reactionary nationalism in Latin America away from associations with Castroism and toward the open markets of the Free World. Kennedy claimed that his new foreign aid initiative required:

> more flexibility for short-run emergencies
> more commitment to long-term development
> new attention to education at all levels
> greater emphasis on the recipient nation's role, their effort, their purpose, with greater social justice for their people. . . .
> and orderly planning for national and regional development instead of a piecemeal approach.[17]

Kennedy reminded the Congress of the pledge he had made in his inaugural address "to our sister republics to the south," that "our goal is a free and prosperous Latin America."[18] However, to balance the idealism of his Alliance promise with a measure of pragmatism, he projected several of Rostow's concepts concerning the "banking principle" of development aid disbursement, or the idea that, in order to acquire loans, nations should be able to demonstrate their "absorptive capacity" to utilize the capital for development projects. For the purpose of securing sufficient foreign aid funding from the Congress, Rostow suggested to Kennedy that he quote an inflated figure to legislators so that enough capital would be allotted to ensure that democratic-progressives in Latin America could meet the goals of their "country programs" for modernization. In a memorandum to the president entitled "The Strategy of Foreign Aid," Rostow wrote:

> Although actual absorptive capacity [of the developing nations] on serious developmental criteria might justify [requesting a lower figure], there is a strong case to be made for shooting high to maximize the psychological and political effect in the under-developed areas as well as to hedge against Congressional trimming.[19]

The president accepted Rostow's advice and made it clear to the Congress in his State of the Union message that:

> The problems of achieving this goal [of constructing a sound and expanding economy for the entire noncommunist world] are towering and unprecedented—the response must be towering and unprecedented as well, much as Lend-Lease and the Marshall Plan were in earlier years, which brought such fruitful results.[20]

Kennedy compared the goals of the Alliance for Progress to the ones that had motivated America's role in the postwar reconstruction of Europe in order to acquire congressional budgetary support for a decade-long commitment to Latin America. As Rostow has explained, the fact that the president defined his foreign aid policy as both an anti-Communist crusade and a transitory commitment of ten years made it more palatable to fiscal conservatives than the prospect of funding and conducting limited wars in developing areas.[21] In contrast to the situation in Africa and other regions of the third world, policy makers who considered Latin America as being on the verge of a Rostovian "take-off" had a less difficult time making the case that development aid would bring about "sustained growth" and increased inter-American commerce.[22] Still, some administration officials were wary of Kennedy's comparison of the Alliance program to the Marshall Plan. As Lincoln Gordon wrote to Richard Goodwin:

> The concept of a long-term development program for Latin America inevitably brings to mind the post-war European Recovery Program. Many people, indeed, have spoken of the need for a "Latin American Marshall Plan." In most respects, this is a misleading analogy. The problems of overcoming an ancient heritage of poverty, widespread illiteracy, and grave social, economic, and geographical imbalances in the developmental process are fundamentally different from those of engendering economic recovery in industrially advanced nations temporarily crippled by war.[23]

As Gordon suggested, Kennedy's Marshall Plan analogy did exaggerate the claim that the Alliance for Progress would yield quick modernization in Latin America, which, in turn, would give rise to a democratic-progressive front against Castro, but the comparison was key for promoting the program at home in his State of the Union message.

Address at a White House Reception for Members of the Congress and for the Diplomatic Corps of the Latin American Republics, 13 March 1961

To make his case to auditors abroad in his Alliance keynote address, delivered at a White House reception for the Diplomatic Corps of the Latin American

Republics on 13 March, Kennedy turned his focus away from the theme of "counterrevolution," which he had developed in his State of the Union message, and concentrated instead on the notion of "peaceful revolution." Although Kennedy's keynote speech went largely unheard in the United States, it was transmitted throughout Latin America via electronic media and in printed form. The president's words were translated and broadcast in Spanish, Portuguese, and French, as well as in English, to the nations of the south by the Voice of America.[24]

Speaking in the East Room of the White House, Kennedy evoked the administration's "Western Hemisphere idea" by explaining to sympathetic members of the U.S. Congress and the Latin American Diplomatic Corps that the peril of communist expansion in the Western Hemisphere was not simply a military threat to the United States, but also a danger to the national identities of all of the countries of North and South America combined. In an attempt to elicit a shared understanding of the meaning of the phrase "American revolution" in relation to the cold war, Kennedy appealed to the nationalistic aspirations of the Latin Americans in order to salve bitter memories of U.S. domination, embodied, historically, by the Monroe Doctrine and, in the more recent past, by the policies of the Truman and Eisenhower administrations. In a significant departure from his earlier Alliance rhetoric, the president avoided uttering the word "communism" altogether in his keynote speech, and instead suggested that the actions of Castro and the Soviets were an extension of the imperialism imposed on the Americas throughout history. He said:

> [We] confront the same forces which have imperiled America throughout its history—The alien forces which once again seek to impose the despotisms of the Old World on the people of the New.[25]

Arguing for a new regionalism, Kennedy repeated Rostow's call for a combination of self-help and inter-American cooperation within the Alliance program to preserve the national integrity of countries receiving development aid and to bring about a "peaceful revolution of hope" throughout the Americas. Rostow had written in *The Stages of Economic Growth* that "a reactive nationalism—reacting against intrusion from more advanced nations—has been a most important and powerful force in the transition from traditional to modern societies."[26] On this basis, Rostow suggested to Kennedy that when he explained his new foreign aid plans to potential Free World partners, he should speak of the initiatives in "less national terms" than those with which earlier programs had been launched.[27] The president adopted Rostow's strategy of appealing to Latin Americans' pride and patriotism in his Alliance keynote address by speaking of the initiative as a momentous event in the shared history of colonial resistance in North and South America, and by recalling a heritage of "peaceful revolution" in which north and south had been united by a uniquely American process of social, political, and economic transformation.

By linking the ideology and tradition of American revolution in the Western Hemisphere, Kennedy portrayed the Alliance program as a new phase of an ongoing struggle, "to free our people for the spiritual and intellectual fulfillment which has always been the goal of our civilization."[28] He spoke of the destiny of the Americas to become a model for the world, not by recalling the North American Puritan metaphor of a "shining city on a hill," but instead by invoking the visions of the Venezuelan patriot and statesman Simon Bolivar[29] and the defiant Mexican president Benito Juarez[30] to identify with the revolutionary traditions of his Hispanic auditors. He said:

> One hundred and thirty-nine years ago this week the United States, stirred by the heroic struggle of its fellow Americans, urged the independence and recognition of the new Latin American Republics. It was then, at the dawn of freedom throughout this hemisphere, that Bolivar spoke of his desire to see the Americas fashioned into the greatest region in the world, "greatest," he said, "not so much by virtue of her area and her wealth, as by her freedom and her glory." . . . And across vast, turbulent continents these American ideals still stir man's struggle for national independence and individual freedom. But as we welcome the spread of the American revolution to other lands, we must also remember that our own struggle—the revolution that began in Philadelphia in 1776, and in Caracas in 1811—is not yet finished. . . . For our unfulfilled task is to demonstrate to the entire world that man's unsatisfied aspiration for economic progress and social justice can best be achieved by free men working within a framework of democratic institutions. If we can do this in our own hemisphere, and for our own people, we may yet realize the prophecy of the great Mexican patriot, Benito Juarez, that "democracy is the destiny of future humanity."[31]

William D. Rogers has written of Kennedy's Alliance keynote speech: "The address was a watershed. U.S. relations with Latin America entered a new phase. . . . The United States was taking on the role of social revolutionary."[32] Not only had Kennedy joined the revolutionary legacies of North and South America under the guiding philosophy of the Alliance for Progress, he also had gone a great distance to assure Latin Americans that the United States intended to make good on overdue promises by joining in "a vast cooperative effort . . . to satisfy the basic needs of the American people for homes, work and land, health and schools—*techo, trabajo y tierra, salud y escuela.*"[33] In this respect, the president downplayed the themes of self-help and reform that Rostow had identified as the major determinants of the success of developing nations in achieving "sustained growth." The impression Kennedy gave to the Latin Americans was that the United States would distribute development aid freely to galvanize hemispheric support for the Alliance program, in a manner that, Rogers has suggested, "many in the Eisenhower Administration [would have] thought an ill-disguised form of socialism."[34] Simon G. Hanson has written that Kennedy's address led the Latin Americans to believe that money could solve all of their problems; in the words of Kennedy's secretary of state, Dean Rusk, it was "dollar diplomacy modern style."[35] Yet, as the Alliance keynote was being translated, transmitted, and printed into pamphlets to be distributed across Latin America, congressional funding had yet to be secured for even the first year of the massive initiative.

Special Message to the Congress on Foreign Aid, 22 March 1961

Kennedy recognized the need for expedient action to insure that the promise of foreign aid he had repeated to Latin Americans on numerous occasions during the first three months of his administration would to some degree be fulfilled. He therefore scheduled a "Special Message to the Congress on Foreign Aid" to be delivered nine days after his Alliance keynote speech. According to Rostow, speechwriter Theodore Sorensen failed to produce a satisfactory speech draft for the 22 March occasion, so the president turned to Rostow to execute the task, as an expert in development aid policy.[36] In scripting the speech, Rostow introduced Kennedy's budgetary request by having him urge the Congress to recognize three "facts" about foreign aid in 1961: the inadequacy of existing foreign aid programs for meeting the needs of the developing world; the disastrous consequences to national security that would ensue as the result of the economic collapse of developing countries; and the temporary nature of the U.S. commitment, which would lead to a day when the developing countries would "no longer have to depend on outside assistance."[37]

Rostow had Kennedy repeat the petitions for foreign aid funding he first had made to the Congress in his State of the Union message, and, in particular, his request for an unprecedented amount of money to repel economic and political assaults by communist forces on the developing world. Rostow wrote for Kennedy: "The ability to make long-range commitments has enabled the Soviet Union to make developing nations economically dependent on Russian support—thus advancing the aims of world communism."[38] In crafting Kennedy's appeal for his foreign aid budget request, Rostow recognized the need to garner bipartisan support in order to gain congressional approval of the four billion dollars the president was seeking for the fiscal year 1962. Rostow therefore had Kennedy, for the first time in the president's advocacy of his foreign aid program, recall the importance of Truman's and Eisenhower's aid initiatives to fight international communism and demonstrate the fiscal power of democracy. Also, in an effort to project both the security and humanitarian rationales for the foreign aid program in order to intersect with the sentiments of both liberals and conservatives on the issue, Kennedy told members of Congress:

> [I]n our time these new nations need help for a special reason. Without exception they are under Communist pressure. In many cases, that pressure is direct and military. In others, it takes the form of intense subversive activity designed to break down and supersede the new—and often frail—modern institutions they have thus far built. But the fundamental task of our foreign aid program in the 1960's is not negatively to fight Communism: Its fundamental task is to help make a historical demonstration that in the twentieth century, as in the nineteenth—in the southern half of the globe as in the north—economic growth and political democracy can develop hand in hand. . . . The 1960's can be—and must be—the crucial "Decade of Development"—the period when many less-developed nations make the transition into self-sustained growth—the period in which an enlarged community of free, stable, and self-reliant nations can reduce world tensions and insecurity.[39]

Calling the United States "the single largest counter to adversaries of freedom,"[40] Rostow sketched a reallocation of foreign aid funds in which military support would be reduced and development aid increased to further the aims of democracy in developing nations ($1.6 billion for military spending and $2.4 billion for economic assistance). The key to Kennedy's appeal to Congress, as Wiarda has argued, was the rationale for the aid program provided by Rostow—that as a cold war strategy, the plan would bring about "humanitarian and social and political reforms . . . apparently with the advancement of U.S. security interests."[41] The approach framed by Rostow and other economists in Kennedy's brain trust, the "Charles River School," as Arthur Schlesinger Jr. named the group, "represented a very American effort to persuade developing countries to base their revolutions on Locke rather than Marx."[42] Schlesinger described the Charles River economists' idea of foreign aid policy as follows:

> [F]oreign aid, instead of being a State Department slush fund to influence tactical situations, should aim at the strategic goals of a stronger national independence, an increased concentration on domestic affairs, greater democracy and a long-run association with the west.[43]

In the end, as Robert A. Packenham has observed, "Congress accepted Kennedy's plea for a 'historic demonstration that economic growth and political democracy can go hand in hand,' incorporating that exact language into the Foreign Assistance Act of 1961."[44] The mobilization phase of Kennedy's advocacy of the Alliance for Progress was successful in securing first-year funding for the program and the support of democratic-progressive leaders in Latin America. By the end of 1961, the impression of the Alliance program Kennedy had left with Congress was one of a unilateral strategy for dealing with communist expansion in the Western Hemisphere within the framework of his "flexible response" security policy. In the manner Rostow had conceived, antiguerrilla forces would confront short-term emergencies in Latin America, while annual disbursements of development aid would serve to influence the long-term modernization of nations within the Alliance network.

In a different vein, Kennedy had publicized the multilateral functions of the Alliance program in Latin America by speaking of U.S. development aid as if it would be the primary catalyst for the economic unification of the hemisphere. While there is little doubt that the Latin Americans understood the anticommunist imperatives of the Alliance, Kennedy's accent on the aid money in his public statements compelled democratic-progressive leaders to acquiesce to the cold war conditions of the program as the price for obtaining loans. As Alberto Lleras Camargo of Colombia commented, the cross-strains of counter- and peaceful revolution in Kennedy's rhetoric distorted international views about what the Alliance program could achieve. Kennedy's dissimilar representations of the program to foreign and domestic auditors blurred perceptions of its goals in Latin America and the United States. Of the confusion about the Alliance, Lleras Camargo wrote:

> Ask any American from, say, the Middle West what the Alliance is, and he will tell you, if he happens to be exceptionally well-informed, that it is a policy toward Latin America which imposes new burdens on him as a taxpayer but which, properly handled, may serve to stop the Latin Americans from falling under the power of Communism, as Cuba fell. To what extent is this extraordinary distortion the work of those who have had an interest in making the movement attractive? To a great extent, certainly. The truth is that such misrepresentations and oversimplifications were powerful enough to make the very authors of the policy lose sight of its original meaning, its importance, its direction.[45]

Conclusion

The mixed messages Kennedy communicated in the United States and in Latin America concerning the Alliance for Progress were, to a great degree, the product of inconsistencies in Rostow's economic theory, which undergirded the design of the program and the content of the president's rhetoric. Rostow purported to recognize the uniqueness of the process of modernization from nation to nation, but it was Europe and America that had provided the model of development in his theory of the stages of economic growth. Rostow's Anglo-American template of modernization fed into the Kennedy administration's "Western Hemisphere idea" that North and South America shared a common bond in geography and history, and that the nations of Latin America could be made into a harmonious community to unite the hemisphere against Castro and the Soviets.

The counterinsurgency aspects of Rostow's thinking, which were based on his classification of communism as a "disease of the transition" in nations progressing toward the stage of self-sustaining economic growth, helped to form Kennedy's Alliance rhetoric. Rostow argued that if a nation could succeed in channeling its forces of reactionary nationalism into the centralized planning of development goals, then protection from foreign sabotage of those plans would shield the society's "growth" activities from the larger cold war. The problem with this argument, as it was used to advocate the Alliance program to Latin Americans, was that in many cases the military forces that were trained to serve as a kind of national police and corps of engineers became an instrument to repress the very middle class they were expected to protect. In this respect, Kennedy's pairing of the themes of counter- and peaceful revolution in his explanations of the Alliance program may have helped to sow the seeds of a broader oppression in Latin America. As William O. Walker III has argued, by obsessively opposing the radical Left, the United States may have encouraged the forces of the Right, for "in the first five years of the Alliance there were nine military coups against constitutional, civilian governments."[46] When asked if the Alliance program might have contributed to the emergence of Latin American militaries as right-wing agents of repression, Rostow stated, "Military coups are endemic to Latin American politics," and he added that he did not believe the aid program had had anything to do with the collapse of Latin American democracies during the 1960s.[47]

Despite its drawbacks, the "Rostow Doctrine" was convincing as the foundation for Kennedy's Alliance rhetoric, with its generic account of the economic evolution of developing nations. The type of "peaceful revolutions," or industrial "take-offs into self-sustaining growth," that Rostow envisioned for developing nations such as those in Latin America made no provisions for a variety of variables, including the fact of foreign ownership of key resources and industries. Under such conditions, industrialization was unlikely to occur as long as the terms of trade for primary exports and opportunities for manufactured exports from Latin America remained poor. The Charter of Punta Del Este, the founding document of the Alliance for Progress, outlined no measures to block foreign competition and it provided little incentive for domestic investment in the nations of the Latin America. For these and other reasons, the Alliance program began to falter within one year of its inception. Kennedy and Rostow's homogenous interpretation of the course of third world development masked differences among Latin American nations, as well as between those nations and the United States.

CHAPTER 6

From Punta Del Este and Back: The Alliance Fades

Two months after President Kennedy delivered his Alliance for Progress keynote address in the East Room of the White House on 13 March 1961, the Council of the Organization of American States (OAS) resolved to convene a special meeting of the Inter-American Economic and Social Council at ministerial level, at Punta del Este, Uruguay, from 5–17 August 1961. The purpose of the meeting was to draw up a multilateral agreement among Latin American nations on the specifics of the Alliance program. However, during the three months over which the meeting was planned, United States-Latin American relations deteriorated in the aftermath of the aborted Bay of Pigs invasion of Cuba on 17 April 1961, in which President Kennedy gave approval for a brigade of Cuban exiles under the direction of the CIA to be set ashore to spark a general uprising against the Castro regime. For many Latin Americans, the counterinsurgency motive behind the Bay of Pigs discredited Kennedy's promise of "peaceful revolution" under the Alliance for Progress. The fumbled operation, as Bruce Miroff has written, "remained [in Latin America] a powerful object lesson in the U.S. response to social revolution in the hemisphere."[1]

Kennedy's ill-timed effort to depose Castro tarnished his Alliance pledge that the United States would deal with the Latin Americans as "partners in progress," and, for a time, his popularity waned among democratic-progressive leaders in the Western Hemisphere. The subterfuge at the Bay of Pigs represented for many an abrogation of Kennedy's commitment to the principle of self-determination in the partner nations of the Alliance for Progress, which the president had extolled as a cornerstone of his foreign aid policy. Lincoln Gordon has recalled the less than ideal setting in which the details of the Alliance program were formalized at Punta del Este:

> [O]nce the Bay of Pigs took place, it was not the most agreeable atmosphere for anyone to get involved in. There were a great many pieces of broken china

> to be picked up all over the hemisphere as a result of that. This was probably the single greatest error of the Kennedy administration, and my impression is that President Kennedy felt that way himself. He never made any bones about recognizing this as having been an error.[2]

While the humanitarian side of the Alliance initiative, which Kennedy had promoted so painstakingly in early 1961, had been sullied by the Bay of Pigs, it was clear to U.S. officials that the Latin Americans harbored no desire for the program to vanish. The OAS delegates to the Punta del Este meeting were unwilling to accept Kennedy's explanation that the Bay of Pigs invasion had been an attempt, in the spirit of the Alliance program, to promote liberal reform elements against Castro's betrayal of middle-class revolution in Cuba. Nevertheless, the allure of the U.S. foreign aid money Kennedy had promised on various occasions in 1961 remained a powerful incentive for Latin American leaders to embrace the Alliance. Realizing this fact, Secretary of the Treasury C. Douglas Dillon struck a conciliatory tone on the first day of the Punta del Este meeting by telling the ministers in attendance that the United States was prepared to accept practically all that responsible leaders of the hemisphere had proposed during the past eight years.[3] Dillon's words were well received by the delegates, with the exception of Ernesto "Che" Guevara, whom Castro had dispatched to head the Cuban delegation.

In the tense diplomatic environment of the Punta del Este meeting, which was exacerbated by the anti-United States rhetoric of Che Guevara and the Cubans, the establishment of the Alliance for Progress as an operational policy was plagued by the OAS ministers' hostility toward the United States, which had hampered inter-American relations during the first half of 1961. In an atmosphere charged with Latin American animus, the founding documents of the Alliance program—"The Declaration to the Peoples of the Americas" and "The Charter of Punta del Este"—were debated and approved by the OAS delegates on 17 August 1961. The content of the documents, as they were drafted by Kennedy's advisers and sanctioned by the OAS ministers, inaugurated the program with such unrealistically high expectations that one Kennedy adviser, Bill Hadded, was moved to write to the president, only months after the Alliance had been established, that despite all of the talk by Rostow and others about long-term economic planning, the program had become a "play it by ear" operation.[4] After Kennedy's assassination in 1963, Hadded's phrase, "play it by ear," would resonate as an apt description of the Alliance for Progress, as the attentions of President Lyndon B. Johnson and Rostow, who was appointed national security adviser in 1966, were turned away from Latin America and toward the escalation of war in Vietnam.

The First Punta Del Este Meeting, 1961

On 6 August 1961, the second day of the Punta del Este meeting, Che Guevara declared to the OAS ministers that the Alliance for Progress was nothing more than a "soft" strategy of neoimperialism on the part of the United States, in the tradition of the Monroe Doctrine. Guevara condemned the program as a thinly disguised ploy to domesticate the peoples of the Hemisphere to the orders of the United States, and he sought to capitalize on the Bay of Pigs incident to convince the delegates that they were deluding themselves to think the United States would lend them money without strategic intent. The Cuban's diatribe against the Alliance program provided a moment of drama during the course of the proceedings. Rogers has recounted the incident:

> Che Guevara, who in fatigue uniform was leading the Cuban delegation, launched into the attack everyone had been waiting for. His delegation, he said, was in agreement with only one point in the expert's preparatory report: that a new stage was beginning in the relations of the American peoples. That new stage was beginning because of Cuba. The Conference owed all to Cuba, he declared, whether the beneficiaries liked it or not. The Bay of Pigs had followed the March 13 Alliance address by a month. The Alliance was nothing more than a reaction to the Cuban Revolution. And the Alliance was bound to fail.[5]

In reality, the shortcomings of the Alliance for Progress were less attributable to the program's anti-Castro intent than they were to the unachievable aims and expectations written into its founding documents. "The Declaration to the Peoples of the Americas" articulated Kennedy's goal of consolidating democratic governments in the nations within the Alliance. "The Charter of Punta del Este" elaborated no less than ninety-four specific goals to be achieved during the 1960s. The complementary texts, as Jack Heller and Miguel S. Wionczek have observed, were "perceived as a fundamental redefinition or rewriting of the 'constitutional' ground rules of the inter-American system."[6]

The founding documents of the Alliance for Progress were so specific in delineating the constitutional terms and conditions of the program that, when put into action, they limited the latitude for interpretive adjustments and modifications in policy planning as the program ensued. In June 1961, Rostow assisted Special Assistant to the President Richard Goodwin in drafting the Alliance documents for the August meeting at Punta del Este. Rostow encouraged the specificity of the objectives of the charter and suggested to Goodwin that its preamble "should contain statistics on illiteracy, slums, living standards, etc. It should in effect, state the operational targets against which the Alliance for Progress is aimed."[7]

Rostow contributed seven of the twelve general objectives of the Alliance program that appeared in the charter, which called for "comprehensive and well-conceived programs for economic and social development, to be carried out [and] formulated in accordance with democratic principles."[8] These "country programs," as they were called, required recipients to formulate long-term development plans of at least ten years before they could qualify to receive any portion of the $20 billion in U.S. aid promised in the "Declaration to the Peoples of the Americas." The stipulation of country programs, which arose from Rostow's conception of a "banking principle" of foreign aid disbursement, resulted in U.S. congressional insistence that each nation's performance in meeting the charter's goals be monitored to determine the loan-worthiness of the petitioning government.

The meticulous language of the document made it clear that the review process would set a rigorous standard for loans, which became a barrier for the less developed nations. The charter was unequivocal in specifying the measures of loan-worthiness that Alliance officials would take into account:

> In evaluating the degree of relative development, account will be taken not only of average levels of real income and gross product per capita, but also of indices of infant mortality, illiteracy, and per capita daily caloric intake.[9]

The problem with the charter's stipulation that Latin American countries be held strictly accountable for their progress in development in order to qualify for U.S. foreign aid was that the poorest nations, which needed assistance the most, were the ones that lacked the resources, experts, and technical staff to formulate and evaluate long-term country programs for modernization. In effect, the banking principle that Rostow conceived as a safeguard against spendthriftiness in U.S. foreign aid disbursement denied small and individually weak Latin American republics emergency funding for the urgent troubles facing their populations. The dilemma concerning "country programs" was an issue of great contention at the Punta del Este meeting, where, as Levinson and Onis have written, the delegate from the host country, Uruguay, along with those from Ecuador and Paraguay, threatened to walk out if they were refused immediate assistance: "President Eduardo Victor Haedo of Uruguay threatened to denounce the Alliance 'if we don't get some money fast.'"[10]

The conflict among the delegates at the Punta del Este meeting over the issue of country programs was not the only one initiated by Rostow's contributions to the charter. Rostow had theorized, as early as 1952, that a country would have to maintain an annual rate of economic growth of a minimum of 2.5 percent for no less than ten years in order to achieve the "take-off into self-sustaining growth."[11]

In his contributions to the charter, Rostow emphasized to Goodwin that the figure of 2.5 percent annual growth should be included as a goal of all nations in the Alliance for Progress. In the final draft of the charter, Rostow's growth figure appeared prominently among the general objectives of the program, as follows:

> It is recognized that, in order to reach these [general] objectives within a reasonable time, the rate of economic growth in any country of Latin America should not be less than 2.5 per cent per capita per year, and that each participating country should determine its own growth target in the light of its stage of social and economic evolution, resource endowment, and ability to mobilize national efforts for development.[12]

The charter's stipulation of Rostow's 2.5 percent annual growth figure as an Alliance goal failed to take into account the numerous impediments to development that the economies of many Latin American nations had confronted during the period preceding the launching of the Alliance for Progress, which included difficult balance-of-payment situations, adverse terms of trade, high unemployment, and a scarcity of foreign financial resources beyond Kennedy's promise of U.S. aid. Well before the Alliance program was conceived of by Kennedy's advisers during the 1960 presidential campaign, Argentinian economist Raul Prebisch, of the United Nations Economic Commission for Latin America (ECLA) had pointed out that foreign competition and the small size of domestic markets in Latin America served to deter significant industrial development in the Western Hemisphere. Prebisch and other structuralist economists argued that the type of "take-offs" into industrial development that Rostow envisioned were unlikely to occur as long as the conditions of trade for primary exports remained poor in Latin America.

Goodwin's quotation of Rostow's 2.5 percent annual growth figure as an expectation in the general objectives of the Alliance charter ignored Western penetration into Latin American markets and made no provisions for the fact that many key industries and resources in the hemisphere were owned by foreign corporations. Prebisch and other members of the ECLA accused Rostow of conflating economic growth and development by failing to distinguish between the significance of per capita growth and the diversification of production factors, which increases labor productivity. In the end, the ECLA's call for the diversification of the economies of Latin American nations was not incorporated into the objectives of the Alliance charter, and the document did not outline measures to block off foreign competition in order to provide incentives for domestic investment. The rates of annual growth in the majority of Latin American nations in the Alliance for Progress fell far below 2.5 percent during most of the 1960s.

One item that Rostow stressed to Goodwin for inclusion in the Alliance charter, and one that held real revolutionary potential for the modernization of Latin America, was the need for agrarian reform, as Rostow argued, "To bring to agriculture and to rural life the benefits that modern technology can provide, changing systems of land tenure which stand in the way of this objective."[13] Rostow and others recognized that agrarian reform was crucial for realizing all of the other objectives of the Alliance for Progress. The reason for this, as Scheman has written, was because the Latin American equation contained "a dispossessed and impoverished landless peasantry—which injected a political element far more volatile than in other Western nations."[14]

At the Punta del Este meeting, agrarian reform was the one objective of the Alliance for Progress that the U.S. delegates pressed firmly on the OAS ministers, and it contributed greatly to the perception of Latin American leaders that the program was a unilateral initiative by the United States. Resistance to changes in ownership of land and farming techniques came from an array of economic and political forces in Latin America, and this made the problem of agrarian reform the most controversial objective of the Alliance program. Tony Smith has observed that, because of the insurmountable objections of the Latin Americans to the agrarian reform called for in the Alliance charter, the Kennedy administration backed away from full support of it soon after the Punta del Este meeting:

> The chief concerns were political, stemming from a growing fear that the kind of transformation called for in agriculture might well play into the hands of local communists (a worry vigorously fanned by the established Latin landed elite, who would not cooperate with Washington's initiatives).[15]

Due in part to the Kennedy administration's failure to persuade the OAS delegates to go along with agrarian reform, agriculture had the poorest showing during the 1960s among all of the twelve objectives spelled out in the Alliance charter. Tax reform ran a close second, as the tax systems in many Latin American nations remained inefficient and favored the landed elite and cattlemen who represented the constituencies of the traditional oligarchs in various countries. In many instances, the tax burden was shifted to the very industrialists and industrial laborers whom Rostow and the founders of the Alliance viewed as the vanguard of the kind of modernization the program envisaged. By the end of 1963, after President Kennedy was assassinated, many in the United States and Latin America declared the Alliance for Progress dead, for the program had become so closely associated with the young president that it was hard to imagine how it could continue without his advocacy and support.

Return to Punta Del Este: The Alliance during the Johnson Years

Before Kennedy's death in November 1963, the president had realized that the Alliance program was going badly, with poor economic statistics and the rise of military coups against the constitutional governments of the Dominican Republic and Honduras. After 1963, the Alliance for Progress lived on, but President Lyndon B. Johnson paid relatively little attention to Latin American affairs during most of his years as president. A National Security Agency report on the state of the Alliance program when Johnson assumed office found that the per capita gross national product for Latin America had dropped from 2 percent in 1960 and 1961 to 0.5 percent in 1962 and 1963, and that political extremists and communists had made headway in several key nations, including Brazil, Chile, and Venezeula.[16]

At the urging of his first national security adviser, McGeorge Bundy, President Johnson responded to the decline of the Alliance program by creating the position of assistant secretary of state for inter-American affairs. Bundy believed that the establishment of the new, high-level position would help to revitalize Latin American policy. Johnson made the controversial appointment of Thomas Mann to the post. Mann, who was a fervent anticommunist, sided with U.S. business interests in advocating the protection of foreign investments in the nations of the hemisphere. In his first speech on the Alliance program, in March 1964, Mann listed four principles of the new Johnson policy in Latin America (or the "Mann Doctrine," as it was later called). The policy priorities Mann identified in his address were the promotion of economic growth, the protection of U.S. investments, nonintervention in Latin American internal affairs, and a strict anticommunist agenda.

Some who had served in the Kennedy administration interpreted Mann's 1964 address as the definitive end of the Alliance program, but Mann himself stayed on as assistant secretary for only one year. The Latin American position changed hands three more times during Johnson's time in office, with one former member of the Kennedy administration, Lincoln Gordon, assuming the post from 1966–67. Johnson met infrequently with the officials involved in the Alliance for Progress, with the exception of Rostow, who became his national security adviser in 1966.

In the State Department, where Rostow served as chair of the Policy Planning Council from 1961 to1966, he attempted, on several occasions, to propose ways of reorganizing U.S. foreign aid policy and saving the Alliance for Progress.[17] President Johnson appointed Rostow as U.S. representative on the Inter-American Committee for the Alliance for Progress (CIAP) in May 1964, citing the high regard of Latin Americans for Rostow's economic scholarship and his pioneering approaches to Latin American development as reasons for the commission.[18] By that time, the Agency for International Development (AID) had initiated efforts to revitalize foreign aid policy in the third world with what was termed the "national market concept" of modernization. The national market concept was based on the view that developing countries should move their efforts at economic growth from the confines of cities to the rural areas, where abundant land could be made into a more efficient source of both agricultural and industrial production. On 19 June 1964, Rostow wrote to the administrator of AID, David Bell, that in regard to the Alliance for Progress, "some of the most promising exercises will consist in trying systematically to apply the national market concept to a specific region within a country."[19] He recommended that AID set up a special marketing technical assistance unit and technical assistance teams for the devising of regional marketing programs. Rostow's advice for inducing Latin American development on a regional basis within nations represented a backing away from his idea of country programs, which had bedeviled the founding of the Alliance program with the demand for Latin Americans to produce modernization blueprints on a comprehensive, national scale.

Even before 1964, and in light of the failures of the Alliance program near the end of the Kennedy years, Rostow had begun shifting his position on the benefit of country programs toward the national market concept of rural development. In a speech entitled "How to Make a National Market," delivered on 1 October 1963 at the Seventieth Annual Convention of the Farm Equipment Institute in New Orleans, Louisiana, Rostow expressed his change in thinking. Before an audience of farm equipment dealers, who were more than eager to export their goods to the rural communities of Latin America, he asked:

> What greater reality could the Alliance for Progress have than if it began to yield a sharp drop in food costs to the urban consumer; a shift in rural production to new, higher quality and higher productivity agricultural products; full utilization and rapid expansion in industrial plants; and a flow of cheap farm equipment and cheap industrial products to the villages? . . . It is possible that private and public authorities might decide to work together intensively—on an experimental basis—in a particular region. The aid resources available to the Alliance for Progress might be woven into the scheme where such special financing was required.[20]

By the time President Johnson appointed Rostow as national security adviser in 1966, the economist had conceded completely to the opinion of other members of the administration with regard to the Alliance program that the best route to Latin American modernization was to promote increased U.S. private investment in the region. Indeed, as the CIAP representative, Rostow had written to Johnson two years earlier, concerning his advocacy of the increased involvement of private enterprise in the Alliance program:

> I am sure you will be particularly interested to know that we have decided to undertake a major effort to define the guideline of conduct and performance on the part of both foreign private enterprise and the Latin American nations which would lead to an expanded flow of private capital and technology into Latin America.[21]

Along with their support of U.S. private investment in Latin America, Rostow and others in the Johnson administration counted "the growing movement towards constructive regionalism in Latin America" as part of their record of progress on the world scene.[22] The regional approach to foreign aid in Latin America, Rostow wrote to the president in 1966, "forces the local people to take greater responsibility for self help . . . and makes clear to the Congress that many institutions and nations are in fact sharing the assistance burden."[23] Despite the emphasis on self-help that Johnson and Rostow sought to further by advocating the construction of regional markets within the Alliance framework, however, they recognized the need for an increase in development resources to back the U.S. commitment to Latin America under the program. This demand called for a congressional allocation of a sum of approximately $500 million in 1967, by Rostow's estimates,[24] which led the Johnson administration to initiate a Joint Resolution to the Congress to support the Alliance for Progress and to orchestrate an OAS Summit in 1967, at Punta Del Este, the birthplace of the Alliance. The summit site in Uruguay was chosen to amplify the symbolism of the Johnson administration's efforts to intensify inter-American economic integration among the Alliance partners and to reaffirm the charter of Punta del Este, which had established the program in 1961.[25]

Early in 1966, Rostow advised Johnson that the Vietnam crisis had "dominated the public image of the President and his foreign policy," and that the administration should act to focus public attention on his foreign policy achievements, "for example, accelerating the Alliance for Progress and extending it into the 1970's."[26] As an attempt to highlight Johnson's concern for inter-American relations, the 1967 OAS Summit was designed to serve multiple purposes. Rostow hoped that the summit would generate positive publicity for the president in the U.S. media as a way of counterbalancing the negative coverage of the crises in Vietnam.[27] The meeting also would serve as a way to pressure Congress to pass the Joint Resolution for additional funding for the Alliance program in 1967. Ultimately, it was hoped that the Johnson administration's willingness to convene such a high-level conference in Latin America would improve U.S. relations with the foreign ministers of the OAS, many of whom believed that Johnson had violated the spirit of inter-American cooperation in the Alliance for Progress in 1965 by ordering twenty thousand troops to invade the Dominican Republic and put down a democratic movement labeled "communist" by the administration, in order to restore Juan Bosch to the presidency.

Planning for the 1967 OAS Summit began in April 1966, after President Johnson gave strong support to the Latin American economic integration movement in an address at the dedication of the Lincoln Statue in Mexico City. In July 1966, Rostow sent Johnson a status report on preparations for the summit with a target date of November or December 1967. In a speech on the fifth anniversary of the Alliance for Progress on 17 August 1966, the president gave a broad outline of what he had in mind for the summit program. The three principal elements of Johnson's summit package included a request that the Latin Americans reduce tariffs in exchange for an increased U.S. contribution to fund physical integration of the region through the International Development Bank (IDB). An appeal was made that the Latin Americans agree to higher growth targets in agriculture and education in exchange for increased U.S. funding of those sectors. Finally, a petition was put forth that the OAS ministers agree to a modern investment code as a way of stimulating increased U.S. private investment in individual nations.[28]

By the end of 1966, Johnson and Rostow were dissatisfied with the Latin American leaders' positions on the summit package, and, in particular, their refusal to accept the self-help commitments that U.S. officials demanded as a condition for increased foreign aid. In early 1967, Lincoln Gordon and others traveled abroad to shore up support for the summit in the hemisphere, while Johnson worked at home to enlist the backing of members of Congress for the Joint Resolution to support the Alliance for Progress. On 13 March 1967 Johnson delivered a message to Congress on the summit and requested an increase in aid to Latin America of up to $1.5 billion over five years. After the speech the Latin American response to the idea of the summit remained mixed, but the odds of gaining passage of the Joint Resolution to increase funding for the Alliance increased when the House of Representatives approved the measure in late March.

President Johnson was disappointed by the Latin Americans' reactions to his 13 March message concerning the summit, so he decided to use a scheduled visit to his Texas ranch by Latin American ambassadors as an occasion to garner support for his proposals. Rostow was concerned that Johnson might look upon the barbecue solely as a social event, rather than as a working session, so he generated a set of talking points and dinner remarks to keep the president on message at all times, specifically, that the summit "is a test of the proposition that the Alliance for Progress is largely a Latin American enterprise in which the United

States is a junior partner."[29] Johnson and Rostow wanted the Latin Americans to establish a common market, embark on multinational projects, and eliminate unnecessary military expenditures. Many of the Latin American leaders who attended the Texas barbecue saw the Johnson administration's demands as both a withdrawal of the U.S. commitment to the region and an infringement on their right to self-determination. The common market concept, for many, appeared to be a throwback to the Kennedy administration's misguided "Western Hemisphere idea" that all nations of North and South America were predisposed to harmonious relations by virtue of their common geography.

Before the OAS Summit was convened in Punta del Este, on 12–14 April 1967, the Johnson administration made sure that the U.S. Information Agency (USIA) was taking full measures to stimulate public awareness of the event in Latin America, with film and television productions, as well as written materials and pamphlets printed in the Spanish language, with titles drawn from tested Alliance for Progress themes, such as "Peaceful Revolution in Action."[30] In the United States, administration officials made appearances to discuss the summit on television news shows, such as "Issues and Answers" and "Meet the Press," and they delivered speeches to various audiences, including one before the Overseas Press Club in New York. At a press conference on 6 April 1967, Rostow described the OAS meeting as "an old style summit meeting . . . styled in the sense it is not hurriedly called for cosmetic effect, or to deal with a crisis."[31] "It was called," he explained, "because there was a gradual growing sense that about mid-point in the Alliance for Progress it would be good for everyone to take stock."[32]

Rostow's claims that the Punta del Este Summit Conference was unrushed and not intended for purposes of presidential image making were not entirely forthright. The Johnson administration devoted enormous amounts of energy toward public relations in early 1967. Administration officials pushed for an April conference date in lieu of the original target date of November or December 1967, and they lobbied the major television networks to do hour-long specials on the summit immediately before it was to be convened.[33] In late March, Rostow and others engaged in a highly publicized effort to provide live coverage of the summit via the Communication Satellite Corporation's latest telecommunications satellite, launched from Cape Kennedy, Florida, on 23 March 1967.[34] The satellite transmission was seen as a way to dramatize American technological and political support for Latin America. By the telecommunications standards of the late 1960s, the Johnson administration's attempts to broadcast the OAS Summit from space were unprecedented in the history of inter-American affairs.

At the meeting in Uruguay, President Johnson conferred face-to-face with the twenty other hemisphere chiefs of state on the formation of a Latin American Common Market and the other economic reforms he had called for in his summit package. In a series of casual talks with his fellow presidents, followed by a formal address that was considered vague by many commentators, Johnson's performance at the conference was judged a moderate success that prepared the ground for joint inter-American development through a common market and multilateral projects to improve living standards in the hemisphere.[35] The general reaction of the Latin American press was that the summit goals of economic integration and improved trade relations were positive, but that the decisions made at Punta del Este were not the best means to achieve those ends.[36] Mexican President Diaz Ordaz, for one, decried the Latin American dependence on U.S. benevolence. "The economic integration process," he said, "must be exclusively a Latin American effort. . . . The Conference results 'were not overly important, but sufficiently significant.' "[37]

The "Charter of the Presidents of the American Republics for the People of the Americas," which was the summit declaration that was issued from the Punta del Este Conference, declared that the nations of Latin America would work together to promote democracy, achieve economic integration, and "insure the security of the Continent against direct or indirect aggression without expending precious resources on unnecessary armaments."[38] The pledges were all consonant with what had been the Johnson policy toward Latin America since the time the Mann Doctrine first was announced in 1964. The lack of novelty in the OAS Summit decisions contributed to the Latin Americans' impression that Johnson's commitment to continue the Alliance for Progress into the 1970s was irresolute, and this led to a high degree of apathy toward implementing the summit decisions.

As early as October 1967, Rostow reported to the president that "the achievements during the six months since Punta del Este are not dramatic."[39] The U.S. Congress, too, found little to inspire their support for Johnson's Latin American initiatives. In late 1967, the president's request for an additional $100 million for Alliance funds in the fiscal year 1968 to assist expanded programs in agriculture and education was cut in half by both the House and the Senate. The president never achieved a working rapport with democratic Latin American presidents, and, as Rabe has noted, "in his 596-page memoir, Johnson devoted only four pages to the Alliance for Progress. He blamed the Alliance's shortcomings on the congressional failure to allocate additional funds in 1967."[40]

Conclusion

Over the course of the 1960s, and during both the Kennedy and the Johnson administrations, the incongruities that arose between the Alliance for Progress rhetoric and the realities of the program led to what Heller and Wionczek have labeled "a ten billion dollar misunderstanding."[41] One major cause of the discrepancy between the ambitious talk and the performance of Latin American nations in the Alliance program was the fact that the conceptual basis of the initiative was derived from Rostow's stages of economic growth theory. Rostow's model of economic growth was designed to meet long-term development goals, but could not be adjusted effectively to account for short-term exigencies in Latin America and other third world countries, such as India and Vietnam.

As the chair of the Policy Planning Council in the Department of State, Rostow argued in 1965 that the type of initiative that Kennedy had put in place in Latin America to fight communism through the Alliance program also would work in Southeast Asia. He wrote:

> All our success stories in the underdeveloped areas—whether in Latin America (Mexico), Asia (Taiwan, South Korea), or Africa (Tunisia)—demonstrate that political life begins to take shape and stability when men focus on the practical task of making a modern nation and spend less time debating abstract ideologies. We need in Saigon a small, absolutely top-notch team of American economists to work quietly with a few good Vietnamese economists to produce this plan.[42]

Rostow's belief that development aid could move nations through the stages of economic growth, and serve the ends of American diplomacy and security as a by-product of the process, appeared to be a simple and sensible program of action, whether it was applied in Latin America, Asia, Africa, the Middle East, or Vietnam. The "Rostow Doctrine" of foreign aid policy combined development aid and counterinsurgency initiatives in hopes of promoting democracy and shielding maturing societies from communist subversion, regardless of where the sabotage was occurring in the world. However, by the end of the 1960s it became clear, in Latin America and more acutely in Vietnam, that while Rostow's stages of growth model was a persuasive instrument of social scientific and political advocacy, its totalizing assessment of the economic evolution of developing countries could not be converted into an operational form generalizable from nation to nation. Ideas could not be translated into action. The middle class that Rostow, Kennedy, and Johnson spoke of as the force that would reinvest its earnings in the economies of developing societies to stimulate economic growth simply did not exist in many of the nations of Latin America, Asia, and other regions.

On the cusp of the 1970s, the miscalculations in the foreign aid policies of the Kennedy and Johnson administrations with regard to Latin America could not be glossed over any longer with talk of "regionalism," "self-help," and "economic integration," or allusions to Rostow's "stages of economic growth." A memorandum that Rostow forwarded to President Johnson on 7 February 1968 reflected a sense of high anxiety in the administration that the tide of public opinion, both in the United States and in Latin America, had turned against the Democrats' ways of handling inter-American affairs—so much so that a living symbol of Latin American enmity toward the United States during the 1950s was beginning to appear as the harbinger of a new direction in hemispheric relations.[43]

On 6 February 1968, Richard Nixon was heckled after a speech at the University of Wisconsin at Oshkosh by James Kellerman, a student who told him that he would be branded a liar if he failed to offer specific radical programs for Latin America. Kellerman warned Nixon that if he talked about "another Alliance for Progress," then he chanced "being spit on again by Latin America."[44] Nixon took the attack and turned it into his first presidential campaign policy statement on Latin America. As university officials fidgeted on the platform, Nixon gave a seven-minute answer filled with statistics and recollections of his own trips to Latin America, and he called for fresh policy, to "open up the heartland" with highways, to lift agricultural capacity, and to enhance educational systems across the region. In his memorandum to Johnson on the episode, Rostow accused Nixon of being "behind the times," in "typical Republican fashion."[45] In reality, a new stage of Latin American policy making had taken off on the college campus in Oshkosh, Wisconsin.

Conclusion

Social scientists who wish to advocate particular policy directions in government act as managers of discourse who use argument and rhetorical appeals to propagate and institutionalize their theories in academia and politics. As communicators in the policy process, along with politicians, bureaucrats, media figures, and interest groups, economists and other researchers adapt their work to the contingent circumstances in which they invent theory. Social scientists scrutinize the stock of common knowledge in their disciplines to determine how they can achieve academic novelty for their theories and make social scientific contributions to policy making. When one examines the discursive activities of social scientists, such as those of economic historian Walt Whitman Rostow, one can discern the types of phenomena that Herbert W. Simons has associated with a general understanding of rhetoric "as invention, as argumentation, as figuration, as stylistics, as audience and situational adaptation, and as an art of composition or arrangement."[1]

Rostow's involvement in foreign aid policy deliberations during the 1950s and 1960s epitomized the social scientific turn toward argumentation and advocacy that occurred in the United States after World War Two, with the rise of the cold war in international relations and the advent of the "policy sciences" in colleges and universities. John Morton Blum has written that Rostow's model of the stages of economic growth "came to provide a metaphor for American policy" in the area of economic assistance to third world countries.[2] The same can be said of how leaders of the developing nations, such as those in Latin America, interpreted American officials' applications of Rostovian theory to the U.S. foreign aid program of the 1960s. As Rostow told Richard Neustadt in an interview in 1964,

> In the days when I was in the White House, we had all these fellows from the developing countries coming in to see the President and they almost always made reference to the concept of take-off. We used to wait and see how long it took for the reference to emerge. He once teased me about it, suggesting that

their references had more to do with their interest in aid money than in my virtue as a social scientist—to which I agreed.[3]

While the communicative clarity of Rostow's theory of the stages of economic growth led to its widespread circulation in U.S. policy circles, the limitations of Rostow's virtue as a social scientist were exposed when his ideas were operationalized in foreign aid programs, such as President Kennedy's massive Alliance for Progress to develop Latin America. Rostow's stages of economic growth model was notable for the way it incorporated the oral qualities of a lecture format into the structure and prose of an economic treatise. Admirers and detractors alike espoused the lexicon of Rostow's approach to the study of economic growth, thereby ensuring public notice of the theory as an evolutionary account of modernization. However, as a style of theory building that can be characterized as deductivist and taxonomical, Rostovian theory stressed the commonalities in the evolution of developing nations, but masked significant social, political, and economic differences among nations. In this regard, as Ian Roxborough has observed, Rostow's stages of economic growth suffered from the same shortcomings as other modernization theories of its day in attempting to extend the historical evolution of the West to the third world. Ian Roxborough has written:

> One of the great weaknesses of much modernization theory was not that it was ahistorical, but rather that its account of the actual historical development of the West was a misleading and mistaken one. Not surprisingly, when the third world was examined from this perspective, the distortions were magnified. . . . The historical record simply does not match the picture of Western development one gleans from the works of modernization theorists. That view of Western history stressed the lack of conflict and the continuities of the process; it tended to collapse a complex series of long-term changes into a single "transition."[4]

Only belatedly did U.S. policy makers discover that Rostow's global and homogeneous interpretation of the process of modernization failed to provide a universal set of remedies that fit all developing countries equally well. This was especially true in Latin America, with regard to the Alliance for Progress. Rogers has written of Rostow's influence on the Kennedy administration's "Western Hemisphere idea" of the initiative: "The idea that all nations pass naturally through fairly similar stages of economic growth—which had grown out of the pioneering studies of Walt Rostow—though accurate in broad terms, tended to obscure the special nature of the Latin American problem."[5] The "Rostow

Doctrine" of foreign aid policy served the ends of social scientific and political advocacy of the Alliance program quite well, with its generalized assessment of the economic evolution of developing countries in Latin America, but, as Miroff has argued,

> A reader [of Rostow's *Stages of Economic Growth*] would have no sense at all of the extent to which Western (particularly American) capital dominated the economies of many underdeveloped nations. By ignoring the facts of Western economic penetration into the Third World, Rostow was able to avoid some serious problems in his economic growth model. . . . [B]ut for a liberal Administration intent upon economic interventionism in the Third World it made superb ideology.[6]

As an ideology, Rostovian theory was vehemently anticommunist, and it was applied by the Kennedy administration to the Alliance for Progress in Latin America in response to Fidel Castro's installation of communism in Cuba during 1959 and 1960. Rostow argued that peaceful, industrial revolutions could circumvent Marxist-style rebellions against capitalism in the Western Hemisphere, encourage democracy, and isolate Castro. Best of all, with enough development aid and the support of antiguerrilla, counterinsurgency forces, the stages of economic growth could be replicated anywhere in the world that communist subversion was occurring—in Asia, Africa, and the Middle East, as well as Latin America.

As Rostow saw it, the major challenge for the U.S. foreign aid program was to hold off the "disease" of communism until a developing nation could mature to a secure stage of liberal democratic capitalism. Castro became the "cancer" in Latin America who threatened the course of political, social, and economic evolution in the region; thus, the Alliance for Progress was born. However, the emphasis on centralized economic planning that Rostow contributed to the Kennedy administration's conception of the Alliance and the consequential deferral of attention to immediate crises in Latin American republics stymied the goals of the program and led to sweeping disillusionment with the initiative throughout the Western Hemisphere. The Alliance dissolved over the course of the 1960s, and especially after 1963, when it became apparent to the Johnson administration that the threat of Castroism was not of the magnitude it had appeared in 1961. As Rabe has observed, "[President Johnson] did not share President Kennedy's apocalyptic vision that the Cold War would be decided in Latin America."[7] In the end, as Enrique Lerdau has observed, the developmental initiatives of the Alliance for Progress, which were inspired by the discourse of Rostow's modernization theory, never filled the gap between ideas and reality;

instead, the rhetoric of modernization "lingered on in subsequent years in about the same way as the grin of a Cheshire cat."[8]

In the post–cold war world of today, Rostow's themes of nation building, fiscal interdependency, and macromanagement of the global economy have become commonplaces of policy discourse as the economic fates of nations have been woven together and colored by political, social, and religious nationalism. After 1989, Russia, a major lender of foreign aid during the cold war, became a major recipient of development loans from the International Monetary Fund and other sources. Rostow's prediction of a global "diffusion of power" arrived in the form of a multinational, global economy, rather than the nuclear balance of power that some anticipated during the 1950s and 1960s. What did not come to pass was the Rostovian vision of a world community operating under a credo of liberal democracy and multinational federalism, "to provide for the human race by common endeavor a framework of stable peace, human freedom, and reasonable levels of economic welfare."[9] Just as international economic ties were strengthened during the 1990s, among nations in Europe and other areas, regional conflicts, terrorism, and human rights violations in less stable countries impeded the kind of growth Rostow claimed would "hasten the day when all can share the choices open in the stage of high mass consumption and beyond."[10]

Since the late 1960s, the failures of various government programs, such as the twenty-billion-dollar Alliance for Progress, have fomented a number of challenges to the practice of applying social scientific knowledge to policy making. Social scientists' claims to objectivity have been troubled by epistemological questions concerning methodologies and the applicability of social scientific methods to policy formulation. An ongoing fragmentation of the "policy sciences" has cast doubt on the viability of the interdisciplinary imperative articulated in the original Lasswellian conception of the movement. In fact, the label "policy sciences" has become so thoroughly discredited in academe that social scientists who aim to inform policy no longer refer to themselves as "policy scientists." Instead, they identify their research as "policy analysis" or "consultation." In addition, concerns are raised about the influence of institutions and sectional politics on knowledge production for policy purposes. The demand for social scientists to make their research "relevant" to policy makers is often seen as compromising objectivity.

In light of the many questions surrounding relations of social science and government policy, rhetorical inquiry offers one distinct method for clarifying how and why social scientists employ argumentation and discursive appeals to achieve legitimacy for their theories in knowledge-producing and political-administrative institutions. This study of the role Rostovian theory played in the formulation, advocacy, and implementation of U.S. foreign aid policy has demonstrated what the outcome of social scientific advocacy can be, when theory and rhetoric converge on a grand scale. In studying policy advocacy by social scientists, scholars working in the interdisciplinary rhetoric of inquiry movement will discover successes, along with dire failures, by theorists who inform the decisions of those in power, and rhetorical analysis will continue to further knowledge about relations among social scientific research, public policy, and political authority. In an information age, in which research provides standards for decision making in the governance of nations, rhetorical studies focuses our attention on the need for constant vigilance concerning the scope and limitations of knowledge utilization by policy communities.

Endnotes

Introduction

1. W. W. Rostow, "Ideas and Action, Address Made at the Carnegie Institute of Technology, Pittsburgh, Pa., June 11, 1962," *Department of State Bulletin* 47 (9 July 1962): 60.
2. Representative studies include: Noam Chomsky, *Intellectuals and the State* (Vertaling: Gerda Telgenhof, 1978), *On Power and Ideology* (New York: Black Rose Books, 1987), and *Language and Politics* (New York: Black Rose Books, 1988); Noam Chomsky and Edward S. Herman, *Manufacturing Consent* (New York: Pantheon Books, 1988); Michel Foucault, *The Order of Things: An Archaeology of the Human Sciences* (New York: Pantheon Books, 1971), *The Archaeology of Knowledge,* trans. Sheridan Smith (New York: Pantheon Books, 1972), and *Power/Knowledge: Selected Interviews and Other Writings, 1972–1977* (New York: Pantheon Books, 1980); Anthony Giddens, *Positivism and Sociology* (London: Heinemann, 1974) and *Social Theory and Modern Sociology* (Stanford, Calif.: Stanford University Press, 1987); Antonio Gramsci, *Selections from Prison Notebooks* (New York: International Publishers, 1971); Jürgen Habermas, *Toward a Rational Society: Student Protest, Science and Politics,* trans. Jeremy J. Shapiro (London: Heinemann, 1971), *Legitimation Crisis,* trans. Thomas McCarthy (Boston: Beacon Press, 1975), and *Communication and the Evolution of Society,* trans. Thomas McCarthy (Boston: Beacon Press, 1979); Stuart Hall, *The Hard Road to Renewal* (London: Verso, 1988); Herbert Marcuse, *One-Dimensional Man: Studies in the Ideology of Advanced Industrial Society* (Boston: Beacon Press, 1964); and Paul Rabinow, ed., *The Foucault Reader* (New York: Pantheon Books, 1984).
3. Representative studies include: Martin Bulmer, "Social Science and Policy Making: The Use of Research by Government Commissions," *American Behavioral Scientist* 26 (1983): 553–680, *Social Science and Social Policy* (London: Allan & Unwin, 1986), and *Social Science Research and Government: Comparative Essays on Britain and the United States* (New York: Cambridge University Press, 1987); Hugh Heclo, "Issue Networks and the Executive Establishment," in *The New American Political System,* ed. Anthony King (Washington, D.C.: American Enterprise Institute, 1978), 87–124; Michael Q. Patton, *Utilization-Focused Evaluation* (Beverly Hills, Calif.: Sage Publications, 1978); and Carol H. Weiss, "The Uneasy Partnership Endures: Social Science and Government," in *Social Scientists, Policy, and the State,* ed. Stephen Brooks and Alain-G. Gagnon (Westport, Conn.: Praeger, 1990), 97–111.
4. Representative studies include: Gene M. Lyons, *The Uneasy Partnership: Social Science and the Federal Government in the Twentieth Century* (New York: Russell Sage

Foundation, 1969); Dorothy Ross, *The Origins of American Social Science* (Cambridge, Eng.: Cambridge University Press, 1991); and Peter Wagner, Carol Hirschon Weiss, Bjorn Wittrock, and Hellmut Wollman, *Social Sciences and Modern States: National Experiences and Theoretical Crossroads* (New York: Cambridge University Press, 1991).

5. Representative studies include: Charles W. Anderson, "The Human Sciences and the Liberal Polity in Rhetorical Relationship," in *The Rhetoric of the Human Sciences: Language and Argument in Scholarship and Public Affairs*, ed. John S. Nelson, Allan Megill, and Donald N. McCloskey (Madison: University of Wisconsin Press, 1987), 341–62; Richard Harvey Brown, *Writing the Social Text: Poetics and Politics in Social Science Discourses* (New York: A. de Gruyter, 1992); Carolyn R. Miller, "The Rhetoric of Decision Science, or Herbert A. Simon Says," in *The Rhetorical Turn: Invention and Persuasion in the Conduct of Inquiry*, ed. Herbert W. Simons (Chicago: University of Chicago Press, 1990), 162–84; John S. Nelson, "Stories of Science and Politics: Some Rhetorics of Political Research," in *The Rhetoric of the Human Sciences*, 198–220, and "Political Foundations for the Rhetoric of Inquiry," in *The Rhetorical Turn*, 258–89; Donald E. Polkinghorne, *Narrative Knowing and the Human Sciences* (Albany: Albany State University of New York Press, 1988); and Martin J. Shapiro, "The Rhetoric of Social Science: The Political Responsibilities of the Scholar," in *The Rhetoric of the Human Sciences*, 363–80.
6. See D. N. McCloskey, *The Rhetoric of Economics* (Madison: University of Wisconsin Press, 1985), *The Writing of Economics* (New York: Macmillan, 1987), *The Consequences of Economic Rhetoric* (New York: Cambridge University Press, 1988), *If You're So Smart: The Narrative of Economic Expertise* (Chicago, Ill.: University of Chicago Press, 1990), *Second Thoughts: Myths and Morals of U.S. Economic History* (New York: Oxford University Press, 1993), and *Knowledge and Persuasion in Economics* (New York: Cambridge University Press, 1994).
7. W. W. Rostow, *The Stages of Economic Growth: A Non-communist Manifesto* (Cambridge: Cambridge University Press, 1960), 2.
8. Simon Kuznets is the author of *Secular Movements in Production and Prices: Their Nature and Their Bearing Upon Cyclical Fluctuations* (Boston: Houghton Mifflin, 1930). Rostow wrote of Kuznets's criticisms of his model in the preface to *The Stages of Economic Growth: A Non-communist Manifesto*, 2d ed. (Cambridge: Cambridge University Press, 1971), xl: "Professor Kuznets has led the attack on the stages of growth on this question of the appropriate degree of disaggregation; and, quite properly, his extraordinary scholarship as a statistical analyst of growth has influenced others." The passage refers to the schism in macroeconomics between quantitative and qualitative methodologies in developmental theory.
9. Rostow details the differences between his historiographical methods and the statistical methods of the neoclassical economists in "Reflections on Political Economy: Past, Present, and Future," in *Eminent Economists: Their Life Philosophies*, ed. Michael Szenberg (Cambridge: Cambridge University Press, 1992), 222–35.
10. In his book, *Eisenhower, Kennedy, and Foreign Aid* (Austin: University of Texas Press, 1985), 202–3, Rostow wrote that he and his colleagues at CENIS collaborated in what

he described as "a considerable propaganda activity [on behalf of U.S. development aid policy] conducted by political and academic figures: books, articles, and letters to assorted editors; speeches and symposia; appearances before congressional committees, etc."

11. In 1956, Max F. Millikan and Rostow coauthored a report on development aid policy, "A Proposal for a New United States Foreign Economic Policy," at the request of former Eisenhower White House staffer C. D. Jackson. The report was subsequently converted into a book, which was published to influence the course of congressional debate on aid to India and other countries: Max F. Millikan and W. W. Rostow, *A Proposal: Key to an Effective Foreign Policy* (New York: Harper & Brothers, 1957), 12.
12. After being assigned to the Senate Foreign Relations Committee in 1957, Kennedy decided to take on the issue of foreign aid to India to differentiate himself from conservatives in the Democratic Party so he sought Rostow's assistance on the matter. During Kennedy's 1960 presidential campaign, Rostow served as a foreign policy adviser and speechwriter. He is credited with creating the slogan, "Let's Get America Moving Again," and possibly, "The New Frontier," which is a phrase that appeared in his writings on economic growth. A discussion of Rostow's role in policy planning and speech writing during Kennedy's 1960 campaign can be found in Archibald Cox, "Memorandum to John F. Kennedy Regarding the Organization of the Policy-Formulation and Speech-Writing Side of the Election Campaign, June 17, 1960," Richard Goodwin Working Papers, 1958–60: 1960 Campaign Issues, Box 996, Pre-Presidential Papers, John F. Kennedy Presidential Library (hereafter cited as JFK). Rostow's suggestions to Kennedy concerning foreign aid policy in 1961 can be found in W. W. Rostow, "The Strategy of Foreign Aid, 1961, Dec. 22, 1960," Transition Files, Task Force Reports 1960, Box 1074, Pre-Presidential Papers, JFK.
13. Rostow's prominence as a pioneer in developmental theory is recognized by scholars across disciplines. His "stages of growth" model is celebrated in a three-volume Festschrift: Charles P. Kindleberger and Guido di Tella, *Economics in the Long View: Essays in Honour of W. W. Rostow* (New York: New York University Press, 1982).
14. Daniel Lerner and Harold D. Lasswell, *The Policy Sciences: Recent Developments in Scope and Methods* (Stanford, Calif.: Stanford University Press, 1951), 8.
15. Manning Nash, *Unfinished Agenda: The Dynamics of Modernization in the Developing Nations* (Boulder, Colo.: Westview Press, 1984), 2. The specific texts on modernization theory to which Nash referred are Gabriel A. Almond and James S. Coleman, *The Politics of Developing Areas* (Princeton, N.J.: Princeton University Press, 1960); S. N. Eisenstadt, *Modernization: Protest and Change* (Englewood Cliffs, N.J.: Prentice Hall, 1966); E. E. Hagen, *On the Theory of Social Change: How Economic Growth Begins* (Homewood, Ill.: Dorsey, 1962); A. Inkles and D. H. Smith. *Becoming Modern: Individual Change in Six Developing Countries* (Cambridge, Mass.: Harvard University Press, 1974); Marion J. Levy Jr., *Modernization and the Structure of Society: A Setting for International Affairs,* 2 vols. (Princeton, N.J.: Princeton University Press, 1966); W. A. Lewis, *Development Planning* (London: C. Allen Unwin, 1966); D. McClelland, *The Achieving Society* (Princeton, N.J.: Princeton University Press, 1961); Talcott Parsons,

Societies: Evolutionary and Comparative Perspectives (New York: Prentice Hall, 1966); W. W. Rostow, *The Stages of Economic Growth,* 1st ed.; and Edward A. Shils, "Political Development in the New States—The Will to be Modern," in *Readings in Social Evolution and Development,* ed. S. N. Eisenstadt (Elmsford, N.Y.: Pergamon, 1970), 379–419.

16. C. E. Black, *The Dynamics of Modernization: A Study in Comparative History* (New York: Harper & Row, 1966), 7.
17. For a more complete explanation of the logical structure of Rostovian theory, see Artur Bogner, "The Theory of the Civilizing Process: An Idiographic Theory of Modernization?" *Theory, Culture, and Society* 9 (1992): 23–53.
18. W. W. Rostow, *The Process of Economic Growth* (New York: W. W. Norton, 1952), 257.
19. W. W. Rostow, "The Stages of Economic Growth," *Economic History Review* 12 (1959): 1.
20. W. W. Rostow, "Reflections on Political Economy: Past, Present, and Future," in *Eminent Economists: Their Life Philosophies,* ed. Michael Szenberg (Cambridge: Cambridge University Press, 1992), 273.
21. W. W. Rostow, *Eisenhower, Kennedy, and Foreign Aid,* 36.
22. Sociologist and political scientist Theda Skocpol has argued that critical studies of social scientific advocacy need to be conducted at an intermediate level—between grand theory and "theories of the case"—to get at the "various ways in which governmental structures and activities have affected the intellectual development and social organization of the social sciences themselves, as well as their policy applications." See Theda Skocpol, "Government Structures, Social Science, and the Development of Economic and Social Policies," in *Social Science Research and Government: Comparative Essays on Britain and the United States,* ed. Martin Bulmer (Cambridge: Cambridge University Press, 1987), 42.
23. John S. Nelson, Allan Megill, and D. N. McCloskey, "The Rhetoric of Inquiry," in *The Rhetoric of the Human Sciences: Language and Argument in Scholarship and Public Affairs,* ed. John S. Nelson, Allan Megill, and Donald N. McCloskey (Madison: University of Wisconsin Press, 1987), 3.
24. Bjorn Wittrock and Peter Wagner, "Social Science and State Development: The Structuration of Discourse in the Social Sciences," in *Social Scientists, Policy, and the State,* ed. Stephen Brooks and Alain-G. Gagnon (New York: Praeger, 1990), 117.

Chapter 1

1. Biographical profiles of Eugene and Walt Rostow are available in "Rostow, Eugene V.," in *Current Biography 1961* (Bronx, N.Y.: H. W. Wilson Co., 1961), 393–95; and "Rostow, Walt W(hitman)," in *Current Biography 1961* (Bronx, N.Y.: H. W. Wilson Co., 1961), 395–97. Biographical materials on Walt Rostow include: "Biography of Walt Whitman Rostow," Office Files of John Macy: Rostow, Walt Whitman, Box 502, Lyndon Baines Johnson Presidential Library [hereafter cited as LBJ]; "Resumé: Walt Whitman Rostow," Office Files of John Macy: Rostow, Walt Whitman, Box 502, LBJ;

"Walt Whitman Rostow," in *American Men and Women of Science* [database online] R. R. Bowker, Reed Elsevier, Inc. [cited February 1998], available from LEXIS-NEXIS Academic Universe @ http://web.lexis-nexis.com/univers; "Rostow, Walt Whitman," in *The New Frontiersmen: Profiles of the Men around Kennedy* (Washington, D.C.: Public Affairs Press, 1961), 200.

2. Rostow's comments appear in Lester Tanzer, *The Kennedy Circle* (Washington, D.C.: Robert B. Luce, 1961), 41.
3. W. W. Rostow, "My Life Philosophy," *The American Economist* 30 (1986): 5.
4. W. W. Rostow, *The American Diplomatic Revolution: An Inaugural Lecture Delivered before the University of Oxford on 12 November 1946* (Oxford: Clarendon Press, 1946) and *British Economy of the Nineteenth Century* (London: Oxford University Press, 1948).
5. W. W. Rostow, *Eisenhower, Kennedy, and Foreign Aid* (Austin: University of Texas Press, 1985), 202–3.
6. Rostow commented on the mission of CENIS in an interview with the author, tape recorded in Austin, Texas, on 16 November 1995 (hereafter cited as "Personal interview by author"). His comments reflect one approach to the study of social science and public policy—the "enlightenment paradigm." This paradigm focuses on the diffusion of social scientific information through the communication and teaching activities of social scientists in the university, the mass media, and other channels. For precise explanations of social scientific "enlightenment," see Leslie A. Pal, "Knowledge, Power, and Policy: Reflections on Foucault," in *Social Scientists, Policy, and the State,* ed. Stephen Brooks and Alain-G. Gagnon (Westport, Conn.: Praeger, 1990), 139–58; and Carol H. Weiss, "Policy Research: Data, Ideas, or Arguments?" (paper presented at the Fourteenth World Congress of the International Political Science Association, Washington, D.C., 28 August to 1 September 1988).
7. Rostow, *Eisenhower, Kennedy, and Foreign Aid,* 202.
8. The books Rostow authored as a member of CENIS are: *The Process of Economic Growth* (New York: W. W. Norton, 1952), *The Stages of Economic Growth: A Non-communist Manifesto* (Cambridge: Cambridge University Press, 1960), and *The United States in the World Arena* (New York: Harper & Brothers, 1960). Books he coauthored with other staff members are: Arthur D. Gayer, W. W. Rostow, Anna Jacobson Schwartz, and Isaiah Frank, *The Growth and Fluctuation of the British Economy, 1790–1850* (Hassocks, Eng.: Harvester Press, 1953); W. W. Rostow and Alfred Levin, *The Dynamics of Soviet Society* (New York: W. W. Norton, 1953); W. W. Rostow, Richard W. Hatch, Frank A. Kierman Jr., and Alexander Eckstein, *The Prospects for Communist China* (Cambridge: MIT Press, 1954); W. W. Rostow and Richard W. Hatch, *An American Policy in Asia* (Cambridge: MIT Press and New York: John Wiley & Sons, 1955); and Max F. Millikan and W. W. Rostow, *A Proposal: Key to an Effective Foreign Policy* (New York: Harper & Brothers, 1957).
9. The books, *The Dynamics of Soviet Society* and *The Prospects for Communist China,* emerged from Rostow's commissions from the Eisenhower administration.
10. Rostow provides details of his role in drafting the "open skies" proposal in his book

Open Skies: Eisenhower's Proposal of July 21, 1955 (Austin: University of Texas Press, 1982).

11. Millikan and Rostow's 1957 book, *A Proposal: Key to an Effective Foreign Policy,* emerged from the collaboration with Jackson on the proposal for a world development plan.
12. W. W. Rostow, *The Diffusion of Power: An Essay in Recent History* (New York: Macmillan, 1972), 88.
13. Rostow, *Eisenhower, Kennedy, and Foreign Aid,* 14–15.
14. W. W. Rostow, "On Ending the Cold War," *Foreign Affairs* 65 (1987): 836.
15. Robert A. Packenham, *Liberal America and the Third World: Political Development Ideas in Foreign Aid and Social Science* (Princeton, N.J.: Princeton University Press, 1973), 51.
16. See W. W. Rostow, "The Stages of Economic Growth," *Economic History Review* 12 (1959): 1–16, and *The Stages of Economic Growth: A Non-communist Manifesto* (Cambridge: Cambridge University Press, 1960).
17. Senate Committee on Foreign Relations, *Statement of W. W. Rostow, Center for International Studies, Massachusetts Institute of Technology,* 84th Cong., 2d sess., 3, 17, 18, 19, 26, 27 February and 3, 5, and 10 March 1958, Part 1, 269. Rostow's congressional testimony in 1956 and 1959 occurred in the following hearings: Subcommittee on Foreign Economic Policy of the Joint Economic Committee, *Statement of W. W. Rostow, Center for International Studies, Massachusetts Institute of Technology,* 84th Cong., 2d sess., 10, 12, and 13 December 1956; and Joint Economic Committee, *Statement of W. W. Rostow, Center for International Studies, Massachusetts Institute of Technology,* 86th Congress, 1st sess., 13, 16, 17, 18, 19, and 20 November 1959.
18. Rostow makes this point in his book *Open Skies.*
19. Stephen G. Rabe, *Eisenhower and Latin America: The Foreign Policy of Anticommunism* (Chapel Hill: University of North Carolina Press, 1988), 103.
20. Rostow discussed Kennedy's reasons for supporting foreign aid as a junior senator in W. W. Rostow, interview by Richard Neustadt, tape recording, 11 April 1964, John F. Kennedy Oral History Program, John F. Kennedy Presidential Library (hereafter cited as JFK), 2.
21. Rostow, *Eisenhower, Kennedy, and Foreign Aid,* 71.
22. Rostow discussed Kennedy's collaborations with CENIS in the following interviews: "Interview by Richard Neustadt," 2, and "Personal Interview by Author, 1995." Other accounts of Kennedy's need for materials on foreign policy and his contact with the CENIS group can be found in Rostow, *Eisenhower, Kennedy, and Foreign Aid,* 69–70, and Theodore C. Sorensen, *Kennedy* (New York: Bantam Books, 1966), 73–74.
23. A portion of the Kennedy-Rostow exchange at the 1958 Senate review of foreign policy which reflects the themes the two developed in consultations on aid to India appears in Rostow, *Statement Before the Senate Committee on Foreign Relations,* 84th Cong., 2d sess., 1958, 284–86:

Senator Kennedy: I am very appreciative of your statement Doctor [Rostow]. I have just two or three questions. On the question of India, do you think the proposed economic assistance which the administration has decided to give to India is sufficient to meet the minimum requirements for successful Indian development and American policy in that area?

Mr. Rostow: I believe the present aid program, which amounts to about $290 million this year, is grossly inadequate. . . . This [Five-Year-Plan] is a great adventure for them. Here they are, caught at a moment in that adventure where a lot of pressures have converged on them at once, striking at the one point we can most easily help—foreign exchange. They are subjected to constant Communist propaganda, and to thought of their own: "Well, maybe democracy can't keep a show of this size going through the whole development process."

Senator Kennedy: Could you throw any light on what the Soviet Union is doing for Red China, and Red China's progress in comparison with India's during this same period of time?

Mr. Rostow: . . . Now they [the Chinese] are moving faster ahead, without any doubt, at this moment than India, both overall, and in the industrial sector. But the image of how fast they are moving ahead is stronger than the facts, because the grand tour that is made by journalists and foreign visitors is always this same urban tour. They see the same old plants, and the trains run on time, and it leaves the impression of rapid industrialization and order. In fact, I am pretty well convinced that, if the Indians could get through the next decade maintaining momentum on the pattern they have laid out, they would finish up with a somewhat lesser rate of industrial growth, but with a better overall performance. . . . On the other hand, if the Indians cave in—if one of their motors conks out on take-off—then a really quite mediocre Chinese performance is going to look like the wave of the future throughout the world of underdeveloped countries.

24. The speeches Rostow wrote for Kennedy were: John F. Kennedy, "The Choice in Asia—Democratic Development in India, March 25, 1958," in *A Compilation of Statements and Speeches Made During His Service in the United States Senate and House of Representatives* (Washington, D.C.: Government Printing Office, 1964), 591–608, and "The Economic Gap, February 19, 1959," in *A Compilation of Statements and Speeches Made During His Service in the United States Senate and House of Representatives*, 789–98.
25. Kennedy, "The Choice in Asia," 607.
26. Rabe, *Eisenhower and Latin America,* 102.
27. Rostow's collaborations with Kennedy on the issue of the Development Loan Fund and his lobbying activities while he was in England were discussed in his "Interview by Richard Neustadt," 17, and in his "Personal Interview by Author, 1995."
28. Recent studies of the effect of the Cuban Revolution on American foreign policy include: Martha L. Cottam, *Images and Interventions: U.S. Policies in Latin America*

(Pittsburgh: University of Pittsburgh Press, 1994); Michael J. Kryzanek, *U.S.-Latin American Relations,* 2d ed. (Westport, Conn.: Praeger, 1990); Lester D. Langley, *America and the Americas: The United States in the Western Hemisphere* (Athens: University of Georgia Press, 1989); Abraham F. Lowenthal, *Exporting Democracy: The United States and Latin America* (Baltimore, Md.: Johns Hopkins Press, 1991); John D. Martz, *United States Policy in Latin America: A Quarter Century of Crisis and Challenge, 1961–1986* (Lincoln: University of Nebraska Press, 1988); and Harold Molineu, *U.S. Policy toward Latin America: From Regionalism to Globalism* (Boulder, Colo.: Westview Press, 1986).

29. Castro first delivered the speech at his 1953 trial, after he led a disastrous attack in July on the Moncada army barracks in Santiago. As Lester D. Langley has written in his book *America and the Americas* (190): "At his trial, when he delivered the 'History Will Absolve Me' speech, he spoke largely for the benefit of Cuba's disgruntled professional and business class who lived in a country that boasted the fourth highest per capita income in Latin America and had a vigorous intellectual and political community but suffered under a crass dictator widely regarded as an American puppet." He revised the address while serving time in prison. The speech emphasized to Cubans the ignominy of the American presence on the island, which controlled the nation's utilities and 50 percent of its arable land.
30. After touring Latin America, Milton Eisenhower had warned the president in his report of his travels (Department of State, *Report to the President: United States-Latin American Relations,* publication 5290 [Washington, D.C.: Government Printing Office, 1953], 4): "Highly disciplined groups of communists are busy, day and night, illegally and openly, in the American republics, as they are in every nation of the world." His impressions of the Cold War atmosphere in the Americas remained unaltered well into the 1960s, as he conveyed in his well-known memoir on his experiences in Latin America, *The Wine Is Bitter: The United States and Latin America* (Garden City, N.Y.: Doubleday, 1963), xi: "The Communists and their fellow travelers feed the fury of the underprivileged with half-truths and promises. They nourish a lust for revenge and a cynical conviction that only blood will wash away injustice."
31. Elliot Abrams provides a clear account of the substance and purpose of the exchange of letters between Kubitschek and Eisenhower in "The Alliance for Progress and Today's Development Policy," *Department of State Bulletin* 86 (June 1989): 86–88.
32. L. Ronald Scheman, "The Alliance for Progress: Concept and Creativity," in *The Alliance for Progress: A Retrospective,* ed. L. Ronald Scheman (New York: Praeger, 1988), 5.
33. An early and notable statement by Kennedy on Latin American issues was delivered a few days before Castro entered Havana, on 15 December 1958. He spoke in San Juan, Puerto Rico, where he outlined the need for a "new attitude" on Latin America to arrest the deterioration of United States-Latin American relations and to promote unity in the Western Hemisphere. See: "Remarks of Senator John F. Kennedy (Dem.-Mass.), Democratic Dinner, San Juan, Puerto Rico, Monday Evening, December 15, 1958,"

1960 Campaign Press and Publicity Speeches, Statements and Sections, 1958–1960: Foreign Affairs, Box 1030, Pre-Presidential Papers, JFK.

34. Rostow's contributions to Kennedy's foreign policy are apparent in the election year book the senator published to clarify his positions on national security, foreign aid, and a host of other issues: John F. Kennedy, *The Strategy of Peace* (New York: Harper, 1960).
35. Rostow discusses Kennedy's appeal to Boston-area scholars to assist in his campaign in his "Interview by Richard Neustadt," 19.
36. The phrase appears in Arthur Schlesinger Jr., *A Thousand Days: John F. Kennedy in the White House* (Boston, Mass.: Houghton Mifflin, 1965).
37. Archibald Cox, "Memorandum to John F. Kennedy Regarding the Organization of the Policy-Formulation and Speech-Writing Side of the Election Campaign, 17 June 1960," Richard Goodwin Working Papers, 1958–60: 1960 Campaign Issues, Pre-Presidential Papers, Box 996, JFK, 1–4.
38. Archibald Cox, "Memorandum to Robert F. Kennedy Regarding Speech Writing and Related Activities, 19 July 1960," Richard Goodwin Working Papers, 1958–60: 1960 Campaign Issues, Pre-Presidential Papers, Box 996, JFK, 5–6.
39. Richard Goodwin, "Speech-Writing for the 1960 Post-Convention Campaign—Organization, Procedures, and Personnel," Richard Goodwin Working Papers, 1958–60: 1960 Campaign Issues, Pre-Presidential Papers, Box 996, JFK, 7.
40. W. W. Rostow, *History, Policy, and Economic Theory* (Boulder, Colo.: Westview Press, 1990), 198.
41. Ibid.
42. Rostow reported that, after returning from England in 1959, he "had a sense of rather diffuse uneasiness in the country," so he called Kennedy to suggest the slogan, "Let's Get This Country Moving Again," to capture the need for new direction. He says Kennedy decided to use it first in the Oregon primaries. Rostow's comments appear in: W. W. Rostow, "Interview with Jean W. Ross, 4 Sept. 1981," *Contemporary Authors Database* (Gale Research, Inc.). The phrase "new frontiers" appears three times in his book *The Stages of Economic Growth.* Rostow believes that Theodore Sorensen may have adopted it from the book and speech drafts he provided for the campaign.
43. Schlesinger Jr., *A Thousand Days,* 193.
44. John F. Kennedy, "Excerpts From Address of Senator John F. Kennedy, Stanford University, Palo Alto, California, Feb. 12, 1960," 1960 Campaign and Press Publicity, Speeches, Statements and Sections, 1958–60: Foreign Affairs. Pre-Presidential Papers, Box 1030, JFK, 4.
45. See: "Remarks of Senator John F. Kennedy (Dem.-Mass.), Dartmouth College, Hanover, New Hampshire, Sunday, March 6, 1960," 1960 Campaign and Press Publicity, Speeches, Statements and Sections, 1958–60: Foreign Affairs. Pre-Presidential Papers, Box 1030, JFK, 1, and "Remarks of Senator John F. Kennedy (Dem.-Mass.), St. Mary's College, South Bend, Indiana, Friday, April 8, 1960," 1960 Campaign and Press Publicity, Speeches, Statements and Sections, 1958–60: Foreign Affairs. Pre-Presidential Papers, Box 1030, JFK, 1.

46. Joseph A. Loftus, "Kennedy Is Given a Secret Briefing by C.I.A. Director," *New York Times,* 24 July 1960, 1, 32.
47. John Kenneth Galbraith, "Confidential Memorandum to Theodore Sorensen, Campaign Strategy, 1960," Richard Goodwin Working Papers, 1958–60: 1960 Campaign Issues, Pre-Presidential Papers, Box 996, JFK, 8.
48. C. Douglas Dillon, "The Prelude," in *The Alliance for Progress: A Retrospective,* ed. L. Ronald Scheman (New York: Praeger, 1988), 65–66.
49. Schlesinger Jr., *A Thousand Days,* 193.
50. Richard Goodwin, "Confidential Memorandum, Campaign Strategy, 1960," Richard Goodwin Working Papers, 1958–60: 1960 Campaign Issues, Pre-Presidential Papers, Box 996, JFK, 8.
51. Tony Smith, *America's Mission: The United States and the Worldwide Struggle for Democracy in the Twentieth Century* (Princeton, N.J.: Princeton University Press, 1994), 181.
52. Schlesinger Jr., *A Thousand Days,* 193.
53. Ibid., 194.
54. Max F. Millikan, "Memorandum on a New Organization for the U.S. Foreign Aid Program, November 15, 1960," Transition Files, Task Force Reports, Pre-Presidential Papers, Box 1074, JFK, 6.
55. W. W. Rostow, "Memorandum, The Strategy of Foreign Aid, 1961, December 22, 1960 (forwarded by Fred Holborn)," Transition Files, Task Force Reports, Pre-Presidential Papers, Box 1074, JFK, 4.
56. This view is expressed in Fred Holborn, "Memorandum, An Action Program for a New Approach in Foreign Assistance for the 1960s, November 17, 1960," Transition Files, Task Force Reports, Pre-Presidential Papers, Box 1074, JFK, 1.
57. Holborn, "Memorandum, An Action Program," 3–4.
58. David Halberstam, *The Best and the Brightest* (New York: Random House, 1972), 43.
59. W. W. Rostow, "Personal Interview by Author, 1995."
60. The official documentary historical record of the Alliance for Progress can be found in *American Republics,* vol. 12 of *Foreign Relations of the United States, 1961–1963,* ed. Edward C. Keefer, Harriet Dashiell Schwar, and W. Taylor Fain III (Washington, D.C.: Government Printing Office, 1996). Rostow's recommendations to Richard Goodwin for framing the founding documents of the Alliance can be found in W. W. Rostow, "Memorandum to Mr. Richard Goodwin, June 20, 1961," National Security Files, January through December, 1961, Box 290, JFK.

Chapter 2

1. See: Daniel Lerner and Harold D. Lasswell, *The Policy Sciences: Recent Developments in Scope and Methods* (Stanford, Calif.: Stanford University Press, 1951).
2. The details of the political debate over the purpose and implementation of foreign aid programs in the United States during the 1950s will be covered in chapter three, but it should be noted that Rostow has written of the crusade for foreign aid and his

involvement in it in his book *Eisenhower, Kennedy, and Foreign Aid* (Austin: University of Texas Press, 1985).

3. Richard Bellamy, "Liberalism," in *Ideas That Shape Politics,* ed. Michael Foley (New York: Manchester University Press, 1994), 6.
4. Barry Supple, "Revisiting Rostow," *Economic History Review* 37 (1984): 107.
5. Simon Kuznets is the author of *Secular Movements in Production and Prices: Their Nature and Their Bearing upon Cyclical Fluctuations* (Boston: Houghton Mifflin, 1930). Rostow wrote of Kuznets's criticisms of his model in the preface to *The Stages of Economic Growth: A Non-communist Manifesto,* 2d ed. (Cambridge, Cambridge University Press, 1971), xl: "Professor Kuznets has led the attack on the stages of growth on this question of the appropriate degree of disaggregation; and, quite properly, his extraordinary scholarship as a statistical analyst of growth has influenced others." The passage refers to the schism in macroeconomics between quantitative and qualitative methodologies in developmental theory.
6. Rostow details the differences between his historiographical methods and the statistical methods of the neoclassical economists in "Reflections on Political Economy: Past, Present, and Future," in *Eminent Economists: Their Life Philosophies,* ed. Michael Szenberg (Cambridge: Cambridge University Press, 1992), 222–35.
7. W. W. Rostow, *The Process of Economic Growth* (New York: W. W. Norton, 1952), 3–4.
8. Ibid., 24.
9. Ibid., 10.
10. David S. Kaufer and Cheryl Geisler, "Novelty in Academic Writing," *Written Communication* 6 (1989): 289.
11. Ibid., 290.
12. Ibid., 291.
13. Rostow, *The Process of Economic Growth,* 8.
14. Kaufer and Geisler, "Novelty in Academic Writing," 292.
15. Rostow, *The Process of Economic Growth,* 220.
16. Gene M. Lyons, *The Uneasy Partnership: Social Science and the Federal Government in the Twentieth Century* (New York: Russell Sage Foundation, 1969), 4.
17. Rostow, *The Process of Economic Growth,* 220.
18. Ibid., 256.
19. Ibid., 10.
20. Bert F. Hoselitz, "The Conditions of Economic Growth," review of *The Process of Economic Growth,* by W. W. Rostow, *Journal of Economic History* 13 (1953): 203.
21. J. R. Hicks, review of *The Process of Economic Growth,* by W. W. Rostow, *Journal of Political Economy* 41 (1953): 173.
22. M. M. Postan, "Walt Rostow: A Personal Appreciation," in *Economics in the Long View: Essays in Honour of W. W. Rostow,* vol. 1,, *Models and Methodology,* ed. Charles P. Kindleberger and Guido di Tella (New York: New York University Press, 1982), 10.
23. S. G. Checkland, "Stages and the State: How Do They Relate?" in *Economics in the Long View,* 46.
24. Rostow, *The Process of Economic Growth,* 40.

25. Ibid., 52.
26. Ibid.
27. Ibid.
28. Robert A. Nisbet, *Social Change and History: Aspects of the Western Theory of Development* (New York: Oxford University Press, 1969), 253–54.
29. W. W. Rostow, *Politics and the Stages of Growth* (Cambridge: Cambridge University Press, 1971), 8.
30. Ibid., 7.
31. Ibid., 9.
32. Ibid., 10.
33. Rostow, *The Process of Economic Growth,* 44.
34. Ibid., 23.
35. Ibid., 24.
36. Ibid., 40.
37. Ibid.
38. Timothy W. Luke, *Social Theory and Modernity: Critique, Dissent, and Revolution* (Newbury Park, Calif.: Sage, 1990), 212.
39. Ibid.
40. Rostow, *The Process of Economic Growth,* 254.
41. George Soule, "Important Exploration," review of *The Process of Economic Growth,* by W. W. Rostow, *New Republic,* 8 September 1952, 19.
42. Susan Peck MacDonald, *Professional Academic Writing in the Humanities and Social Sciences* (Carbondale: Southern Illinois University Press, 1994), 29.
43. J. J. Spengler, "Theories of Economic Growth," in *Problems in the Study of Growth* (Washington, D.C.: National Bureau of Economic Research, 1949), 52–53.
44. Shepard Clough, *Essays in Honor of Gino Luzzato* (Milan, Italy: n.p., 1950).
45. James S. Duesenberry. "Some Aspects of the Theory of Economic Development," *Explorations in Entrepreneurial History* 392 (15 December 1950): 68–74.
46. Rostow, *The Process of Economic Growth,* 54.
47. Ibid., 58.
48. Manning Nash, *Unfinished Agenda: The Dynamics of Modernization in the Developing Areas* (Boulder, Colo.: Westview Press, 1984), 2.
49. Franco Ferrarotti, *The Myth of Inevitable Progress* (Westport, Conn.: Greenwood Press, 1985), 22.
50. Rostow, *The Process of Economic Growth,* 28.
51. Seymour Martin Lipset, *Political Man* (New York: Doubleday, 1960), 404.
52. An early article that articulated the "end of ideology" thesis was: Edward Shils, "The End of Ideology?" *Encounter* 5 (November 1955): 52–58. Texts that elaborated on the theme appeared at the end of the 1950s; see, e.g., Daniel Bell, *The End of Ideology* (New York: Free Press, 1960); Lipset, *Political Man.*
53. W. W. Rostow, *History, Policy, and Economic Theory: Essays in Interaction* (Boulder, Colo.: Westview Press, 1990), 274.

Chapter 3

1. John Kenneth Gailbraith, "For Foreign Aid in a New Packaging," review of *A Proposal: Key to an Effective Foreign Policy,* by Max F. Millikan and W. W. Rostow, *New York Times Book Review,* 18 January 1957, 7, 22.
2. The Eisenhower administration's agreement with the terms of the Randall Report is discussed at length in Stephen G. Rabe, *Eisenhower and Latin America: The Foreign Policy of Anticommunism* (Chapel Hill: University of North Carolina Press, 1988). The Princeton Inn group, which was convened unofficially at the request of John Foster Dulles by C. D. Jackson at the Princeton Inn in Princeton, New Jersey, on 15 and 16 May 1954, to study the viability of a world economic plan was presented with an assessment of five key reports to the U.S. government on foreign economic policy—The Gray Report of November 1950, submitted to President Harry S. Truman by Gordon Gray, special assistant to the president, and Edward S. Mason, deputy special assistant; the Rockefeller Report of March 1951, submitted to Truman by the International Development Advisory Board; the Paley Report of June 1952, submitted to Truman by the President's Materials Policy Commission; the Bell Report of February 1953, submitted to President Eisenhower by the Public Advisory for Mutual Security; and the Randall Report of January 1954, submitted to Eisenhower by the Commission on Foreign Economic Policy, composed of seven presidential appointees, five senators, and five representatives, established by an Act of Congress.

   The following comments on the Randall Report, which was of the greatest concern to the Princeton Inn group, are available in "Five Key Reports to the Government: A Summary," C. D. Jackson Papers, Box 83, Princeton Economic Conference, Miscellaneous Correspondence, etc., Dwight D. Eisenhower Library (hereafter cited as DDE), 9:

   > Nearly all felt that the Commission was too narrow in building its report around the dollar-gap problem to the neglect of the wider issue of the proper relationship of foreign economic policy to foreign policy in general. . . . The group felt that the [Randall] Commission lacked any basic philosophy and had not produced "a document from which the nation could derive inspiration or on which it could rest for any length of time."

3. Dwight D. Eisenhower, "Special Message to the Congress on Foreign Economic Policy, March 30, 1954," in *Public Papers of the Presidents of the United States: Dwight D. Eisenhower* (Washington, D.C.: Government Printing Office, 1954), 352–61.
4. During World War Two, Jackson served as deputy chief of the Psychological Warfare Branch of the Allied Force Headquarters at Algiers in North Africa. There, he worked closely with Eisenhower in planning psychological warfare. He also was instrumental in the "Crusade for Freedom," designed to encourage resistance to communism in Europe by establishing Radio Free Europe in Munich—a program that was initiated by a nationwide address by Eisenhower. See Martin J. Medhurst, "Eisenhower and the Crusade for Freedom: The Rhetorical Origins of a Cold War Campaign," *Presidential Studies Quarterly* 27 (1997): 646–61.

5. Rostow recounts the transmission of the report to Eisenhower in: W. W. Rostow, *Eisenhower, Kennedy, and Foreign Aid* (Austin: University of Texas Press, 1985).
6. W. W. Rostow, *The United States in the World Arena: An Essay in Recent History* (New York: Harper, 1960), 330.
7. Max F. Millikan and W. W. Rostow, *A Proposal: Key to an Effective Foreign Policy* (New York: Harper & Brothers, 1957).
8. Ibid., 1.
9. Ibid., 130.
10. Ibid., 131.
11. An examination of how U.S. foreign policy and a great deal of social scientific research in American universities in the twentieth century have adhered to the worldview of realism appears in Robert Hariman and Francis A. Beer, "From Idealism to Post-Realism: The Rhetorical Turn in International Relations," in *Argument and the Postmodern Challenge: Proceedings of the Eighth SCA/AFA Conference on Argumentation,* ed. Raymie E. McKerrow (Annandale, Va.: Speech Communication Association, 1993). The authors discuss how the discursive framework of realpolitik fit the exigencies of a skeptical cold war culture and its economic, social, and political imperatives of power acquisition and self-preservation.
12. G. Thomas Goodnight, "Hans J. Morgenthau *In Defense of the National Interest: On Rhetoric, Realism, and the Public Sphere,*" in *Post-Realism: The Rhetorical Turn in International Relations,* ed. Francis A. Beer and Robert Hariman (East Lansing: Michigan State University Press, 1996), 154.
13. Ibid., 151.
14. Lucian W. Pye, "The Foreign Aid Instrument: Search for Reality," in *Foreign Policy in the Sixties: The Issues and the Instruments,* ed. Roger Hilsman and Robert C. Good (Baltimore, Md.: Johns Hopkins University Press, 1965), 94.
15. C. D. Jackson, "Memorandum to the Secretary of State, April 9, 1954," C. D. Jackson Papers, Box 82, Princeton Economic Conference, Draft Papers, DDE, 4–5.
16. Ibid., 6.
17. Jackson's framing of the four questions, or "Roman numerals," as he labeled them on 15 May 1954 at the Princeton Inn Conference, can be found in: "Proceedings of the Off-the-Record Conference Held under the Auspices of Time, Inc., May 15–16, 1954, Princeton Inn, Princeton, N.J.," C. D. Jackson Papers, Box 83, Princeton Economic Conference, Transcripts, DDE, 8–11.
18. Ibid., 3.
19. Ibid., 26.
20. Ibid., 12–13.
21. See: W. W. Rostow, "Notes on a New Approach to U.S. Foreign Economic Policy," C. D. Jackson Papers, Box 6, Walt W. Rostow, DDE, 15–18.
22. "Proceedings of the Off-the-Record Conference," 18.
23. Ibid., 95.
24. John K. Jessup of Time, Inc., and H. Chapman Rose, assistant secretary of the

treasury, joined the conference on the morning of Sunday, 16 May, to assist in the process of arriving at a final document on the world economic plan.

25. "Proceedings of the Off-the-Record Conference," 223.
26. Ibid., 237.
27. Ibid., 255.
28. Ibid., 280.
29. See "Notes on Foreign Economic Policy," C. D. Jackson Papers, Box 82, Princeton Economic Conference, 5/54—Draft Papers, DDE. The major and minor premises of the argument for a world economic plan were listed in the preparatory document "World Economic Policy: A Simple Outline of a Great Opportunity for the United States," C. D. Jackson Papers, Box 82, Princeton Economic Conference, 5/54—Draft Papers, DDE.
30. "Notes on Foreign Economic Policy," 3.
31. The advantages and disadvantages of shipping U.S. food surpluses to third world countries was discussed in depth during the Princeton Inn conference. In the draft report of the proceedings, Millikan and Rostow advocated the practice. See "Notes on Foreign Economic Policy," 9.
32. "Mr. McDonald's Proposal," C. D. Jackson Papers, Box 82, Princeton Economic Conference, 5/54—Draft Papers, DDE, 1.
33. Ibid.
34. Ibid.
35. President Franklin Delano Roosevelt and British prime minister Winston Churchill drew up the Atlantic Charter in a meeting in Placentia Bay off Newfoundland on 14 August 1941. The document was analogous to President Woodrow Wilson's Fourteen Points, announced during World War One. The Atlantic Charter set out what were to be American and, to some extent, British war aims during the remainder of Word War Two.
36. W. W. Rostow, *The Diffusion of Power, 1957–1972* (New York: Macmillan, 1972), 89.
37. A detailed account of the defeat of the Princeton Inn proposal within the Eisenhower administration based on extensive correspondence between the key figures, is available in Rostow, *Eisenhower, Kennedy, and Foreign Aid*, 95–108.
38. Ibid., 107–8.
39. W. W. Rostow, "Letter to C. D. Jackson, 27 December 1954," C. D. Jackson Papers, Box 91, Rostow, Walt, 1953–54, DDE, 1.
40. Ibid., 2.
41. Rostow provides a short summary of Eisenhower's policy toward the developing world in chapter 8 of *The Diffusion of Power*, 86–93.
42. Millikan and Rostow, *A Proposal*, 5–6.
43. Ibid., 3.
44. Ibid.
45. A foundational statement of the theory of American exceptionalism is Louis Hartz, *The Liberal Tradition in America* (New York: Harcourt, Brace, and World, 1955).

46. The classical model of the rational economic actor is based on the assumption that human behavior is driven by the desire to maximize gain and minimize loss.
47. George F. Kennan treats legalism and moral idealism as interacting components of the American worldview in *American Diplomacy: 1900–1950* (New York: New American Library, 1951).
48. Millikan and Rostow, *A Proposal,* 8.
49. A cogent essay that critiques the developmental models of Rostow, Millikan, and others is Howard J. Wiarda, *Ethnocentrism in Foreign Policy: Can We Understand the Third World?* (Washington, D.C.: American Enterprise Institute, 1985), esp. 4–7. Another perspective, dependency theory, pioneered by Latin American economist Raul Prebisch, argues that an implicit motive behind developmental models, such as Rostow's "stages of economic growth" theory, is to perpetuate center-periphery relationships in which the knowledge and material assistance of a hegemon in effect colonizes the political, economic, and social cultures of reliant nations.
50. Millikan and Rostow, *A Proposal,* 4.
51. Ibid.
52. Ibid., 3.
53. A framework of the propensities for economic growth was initially developed in 1952 by Rostow in his foundational theoretical work, *The Process of Economic Growth,* which is analyzed in chapter 2 of this book. Although, as a model, the propensities schema did not figure as prominently as the early and evolving "stages" model, which served as the theoretical core of Millikan and Rostow's foreign policy proposal, the "propensities" system undergirded the whole of Rostow's work.

    As he wrote in an analysis of his own "dynamic disaggregated theory of production," in his historical survey of the discipline of developmental economics, *Theorists of Economic Growth From David Hume to the Present with a Perspective on the Next Century* (New York: Oxford University Press, 1990), 429: "*The Process of Economic Growth* is the basic statement of the theory I have subsequently elaborated and applied to a wide range of historical and policy problems."
54. Millikan and Rostow, *A Proposal,* 43–44.
55. Ibid., 44.
56. Ibid., 46.
57. Ibid., 47.
58. Ibid., 54.
59. Ibid., 142.
60. Ibid., 59.
61. W. W. Rostow, "The Take-off into Sustained Growth," *Economic Journal* 66 (1956): 25.
62. Ibid.
63. Ibid., 27.
64. Ibid.
65. W. W. Rostow, personal interview by author, 16 November1995, Austin Texas.
66. Millikan and Rostow, *A Proposal,* 58–59.
67. Ibid., 143.

68. Ibid.
69. Bruce Miroff, *Pragmatic Illusions: The Presidential Politics of John F. Kennedy* (New York: David McKay Company, 1976), 135.
70. Millikan and Rostow, *A Proposal,* 150–51.
71. Tony Smith, *America's Mission: The United States and the Worldwide Struggle for Democracy in the Twentieth Century* (Princeton, N.J.: Princeton University Press, 1994), 352–53.
72. Hariman and Beer, "From Idealism to Post-Realism," 261.
73. W. W. Rostow, *Politics and the Stages of Growth* (Cambridge: Cambridge University Press, 1971), 23–24.
74. Millikan and Rostow, *A Proposal,* 136–37.
75. Ibid., 15–16.
76. Ibid., 139.
77. Ibid., 141.
78. W. W. Rostow, "The Challenge Facing the United States: September 1956," C. D. Jackson Papers, Box 91, Rostow, Walt, 1956, DDE, 2–3.

Chapter 4

1. W. W. Rostow, "The Walt Rostow Lectures," C. D. Jackson Papers, Box 91, Rostow, Walt, 1959, Dwight D. Eisenhower Library (hereafter cited as DDE), 1.
2. W. W. Rostow, "The Stages of Growth and the Problems of Peaceful Co-existence, Delivered at the Institute of World Economy and International Relations, Moscow, May 25, 1959," C. D. Jackson Papers, Box 91, Rostow, Walt, 1959, DDE, 2.
3. Rostow, "The Stages of Growth and the Problems of Peaceful Co-existence," 26.
4. Aidan Foster-Carter, "From Rostow to Gunder Frank: Conflicting Paradigms in the Analysis of Underdevelopment," *World Development* 4 (1976): 167–80.
5. Charles P. Kindleberger and Guido di Tella, *Economics in the Long View: Essays in Honour of W. W. Rostow* (New York: New York University Press, 1982).
6. I use the phrase "narrative rationality" in the way that rhetorical theorist Walter Fisher explained it in his book, *Human Communication as Narration: Toward a Philosophy of Reason, Value, and Action* (Columbia: University of South Carolina Press, 1987). Fisher defined narrative rationality as a rhetorical logic of human communication that is tested against probability (coherence) and fidelity (truthfulness and reliability). He wrote in "Narration, Knowledge, and the Possibility of Wisdom," in *Rethinking Knowledge: Reflections Across Disciplines,* ed. Robert F. Goodman and Walter R. Fisher (Albany: State University of New York Press, 1995), 170: "Narration . . . designates a conceptual frame, one that I think is intrinsic to human beings. . . . Thus, all forms of discourse can be considered stories, that is, interpretations of some aspect of the world occurring in time and shaped by history, culture, and character."
7. Martin Gray has provided a serviceable definition of the phrase "frame narrative" in *A Dictionary of Literary Terms,* 2d ed. (Essex, England: Longman York Press, 1992), 124: "In narratives that contain a story within a story, this is the term for the outer,

containing story which is often just a pretext for the larger and more significant narrative, or narratives, embedded within it."

8. For a discussion of Rostow's influence in the modernization movement, see Wil Hout, *Capitalism and the Third World: Development, Dependence, and the World System* (Brookfield, Vt.: Edward Elgar, 1993).
9. For discussions of Rostow's influence in foreign aid policy circles during the 1960s and beyond, see Lincoln Gordon, "The Alliance at Birth: Hopes and Fears," in *The Alliance for Progress: A Retrospective,* ed. L. Ronald Scheman (Westport, Conn.: Praeger, 1988), 73–79; Howard J. Wiarda, "Did the Alliance 'Lose Its Way,' or Were Its Assumptions All Wrong from the Beginning and Are Those Assumptions Still with Us?" in *The Alliance for Progress: A Retrospective,* ed. L. Ronald Scheman (Westport, Conn.: Praeger, 1988), 95–118.
10. Diane B. Kunz, *Butter and Guns: America's Cold War Economic Diplomacy* (New York: Free Press, 1997), 126.
11. W. W. Rostow, *The Stages of Economic Growth: A Non-communist Manifesto,* 3d ed. (Cambridge, Cambridge University Press, 1990), xliv.
12. "Rostow on Growth: A Non-communist Manifesto," *Economist,* 15 August 1959, 409–16.
13. Yuri Zhukov, "Snipe in the Bog," *Pravda,* 19 October 1959; trans. and reprint, *The Economist,* 7 November 1959, 502.
14. Tai Wen, "A Reactionary Theory (of W. W. Rostow) which Serves the U.S. Ruling Clique," *Kuang-ming Jih-pao,* 28 March 1961, 1; trans. and reprint, *Joint Publications Research Service* (SS.1205) Y3.J66: 13/8240.
15. Negative reviews include T. Balogh, "The Changing Fashions of Economics," review of *Economic Development,* by Benjamin Higgins, and *The Stages of Economic Growth,* 1st ed., by W. W. Rostow, *New Statesman,* 30 April 1960, 640, 642; and David McCord Wright, "True Growth Must Come from Freedom," review of *The Stages of Economic Growth,* 1st ed., by W. W. Rostow, *Fortune,* December 1959, 137–212.
16. Saville R. Davis, "Rostow in the World Arena," review of *The United States in the World Arena* and *The Stages of Economic Growth,* 1st ed., by W. W. Rostow, *Christian Science Monitor,* 9 April 1960, 9.
17. Rostow, *The Stages of Economic Growth,* 1st ed. (Cambridge: Cambridge University Press, 1960), 4.
18. W. W. Rostow, *British Economy of the Nineteenth Century* (London: Oxford University Press, 1948), 5.
19. M. M. Postan, "Walt Rostow: A Personal Appreciation," in *Economics in the Long View: Essays in Honour of W. W. Rostow,* vol. 1, *Models and Methodology,* ed. Charles P. Kindleberger and Guido di Tella (New York: New York University Press, 1982), 10.
20. Rostow, *The Stages of Economic Growth,* 145.
21. Ibid., 2.
22. Timothy W. Luke, *Social Theory and Modernity: Critique, Dissent, and Revolution* (Newbury Park, Calif.: Sage, 1990), 212.
23. Rostow recommended to Kennedy that he should make the 1960s a "Development

Decade" in a staff memorandum: "The Idea of an Economic Development Decade, March 2, 1961," President's Office File, Staff Memoranda, Box 64, Rostow, John F. Kennedy Presidential Library.

24. Rostow, *The Stages of Economic Growth,* 2.
25. Ibid., 149.
26. Rostow's vision of the economic actor is based on what he has identified as a tripartite Platonic-Freudian view of human motivation, defined in Platonic terms by the spirited side of man, appetite, and reason. He wrote in his book, *Politics and the Stages of Growth* (Cambridge, Cambridge University Press, 1971), 8: "Freud's id, ego, and super-ego can, for these purposes, be regarded as roughly analogous."
27. Rostow, *The Stages of Economic Growth,* 149.
28. Ibid., 7.
29. Ibid., 163.
30. Ibid., 161.
31. Ibid.
32. In rhetorical scholarship, two representative studies that examine the functions of disease metaphors as symbolic links between holders of political attitudes and values are Edwin Black, "The Second Persona," *Quarterly Journal of Speech* 56 (1970): 109–19; and Steven Perry, "Rhetorical Functions of the Infestation Metaphor in Hitler's Rhetoric," *Central States Speech Journal* 34 (1983): 229–35.
33. W. W. Rostow, "Guerrilla Warfare in the Underdeveloped Areas," *Department of State Bulletin* 45 (7 August 1961): 231.
34. Rostow, *The Stages of Economic Growth,* 11.
35. Ibid., 91.
36. Ibid.
37. Ibid., 92.
38. Ibid., 134.
39. Ibid.
40. Howard J. Wiarda, *Ethnocentrism in Foreign Policy: Can We Understand the Third World?* (Washington, D.C.: American Enterprise Institute, 1985), 5.
41. W. W. Rostow, interview by author, tape recording, Austin, Texas, 16 November 1995.

Chapter 5

1. Arthur Schlesinger Jr., "Myth and Reality," in *The Alliance for Progress: A Retrospective,* ed. L. Ronald Scheman (Westport, Conn.: Praeger, 1988), 68.
2. Jerome Levinson and Juan de Onis, *The Alliance That Lost Its Way: A Critical Report on the Alliance for Progress* (Chicago: Quadrangle Books, 1970), 6.
3. W. W. Rostow, "The Strategy of Foreign Aid, 1961," Pre-Presidential Papers, Transition Files, Task Force Reports, 1960, Box 1074, John F. Kennedy Presidential Library (hereafter cited as JFK), 1.
4. W. W. Rostow, "The Idea of an Economic Development Decade," President's Office File: Staff Memoranda, Rostow, 2 March 1961, Box 64, JFK, 1.

5. "Report to the President-elect of the Task Force on Immediate Latin American Problems," Pre-Presidential Papers, Transition Files, Task Force Reports, 1960, Box 1074, JFK, 1.
6. Stephen G. Rabe, *The Most Dangerous Area in the World: John F. Kennedy Confronts Communist Revolution in Latin America* (Chapel Hill: University of North Carolina Press, 1999), 21.
7. W. W. Rostow, "The 'New Look' in U.S. World Policy," *U.S. News and World Report,* 13 February 1961, 80.
8. "Report to the President-elect of the Task Force on Immediate Latin American Problems," 10–12. The members of the Task Force on Latin America were Adolf A. Berle Jr., chair; Thomas C. Mann, assistant secretary of state for inter-American affairs; John M. Leddy, assistant secretary of the treasury for international affairs; Theodore C. Achilles, counselor of Department of State; Lincoln Gordon, consultant; Haydn Williams, deputy assistant secretary of defense for international security; Wymberly Coerr, deputy assistant secretary of state for inter-American affairs; and Robert M. Sayre, executive secretary.
9. Howard J. Wiarda, "Did the Alliance 'Lose Its Way,' or Were Its Assumptions All Wrong from the Beginning and Are Those Assumptions Still with Us?" in *The Alliance for Progress: A Retrospective,* ed. L. Ronald Scheman (Westport, Conn.: Praeger, 1988), 97.
10. Abraham F. Lowenthal, "Alliance Rhetoric versus Latin American Reality," *Foreign Affairs* (April 1970): 500.
11. "Draft Memorandum From the Consultant to the Task Force on Latin America (Gordon) to the President's Assistant Special Counsel (Goodwin), 6 March 1961," *Foreign Relations of the United States* (hereafter cited as *FRUS*), 1961–63, 12:6.
12. "Report to the President-elect of the Task Force on Immediate Latin American Problems," 1.
13. After travelling to Latin America early in 1961, Arthur Schlesinger Jr. wrote to Kennedy of the need for the rapid promotion of a "middle-class revolution" in Latin America in a "Memorandum from the President's Special Assistant (Schlesinger) to President Kennedy, Washington, March 10, 1961," *FRUS,* 1961–63, 12:12: "The pressing need in Latin America is to promote the middle-class revolution as speedily as possible. The corollary is that, *if the possessing classes of Latin America make the middle-class revolution impossible, they will make a "workers-and-peasants" revolution inevitable;* that is, if they destroy a Betancourt, they will guarantee a Castro or a Peron."
14. John F. Kennedy, "Inaugural Address, January 20, 1961," in *Public Papers of the Presidents of the United States: John F. Kennedy* (Washington, D.C.: Government Printing Office, 1962), 1.
15. John F. Kennedy, "Annual Message to the Congress on the State of the Union, January 30, 1961," in *Public Papers of the Presidents of the United States: John F. Kennedy* (Washington, D.C.: Government Printing Office, 1962), 19.
16. Ibid., 25.
17. Ibid.

18. Ibid.
19. W. W. Rostow, "Memorandum, The Strategy of Foreign Aid 1961, December 22, 1960 (foreword by Fred Holborn)," Pre-Presidential Papers, Transition Files, Task Force Reports, 1960, Box 1074, JFK, 6.
20. Kennedy, "Annual Message to the Congress," 24.
21. W. W. Rostow, interview by author, tape recording, Austin, Texas, 16 November 1995.
22. Gordon makes this point in: Lincoln Gordon, "The Alliance at Birth: Hopes and Fears," in The Alliance for Progress: A Restrospective, ed L. Ronald Scheman (Westport, Conn: Praeger, 1988), 73–79.
23. Gordon, "Draft Memorandum From the Consultant to the Task Force on Latin America," 6–7.
24. John F. Kennedy, "Address at a White House Reception for Members of Congress and for the Diplomatic Corps of the Latin American Republics, March 13, 1961," in *Public Papers of the Presidents of the United States: John F. Kennedy* (Washington, D.C.: Government Printing Office, 1962), 175.
25. Ibid., 171.
26. W. W. Rostow, *The Stages of Economic Growth: A Non-Communist Manifesto* (Cambridge, Eng.: Cambridge University Press, 1960), 26.
27. Rostow, "Memorandum, The Strategy of Foreign Aid 1961," 6.
28. Kennedy, "Address at a White House Reception for Members of Congress and for the Diplomatic Corps of the Latin American Republics," 171.
29. Simon Bolivar (1783–1830) was responsible for leading the liberation of South America from Spanish rule from 1808 onward. He succeeded in driving the Spanish from Venezuela, Colombia, Peru, and Ecuador. Upper Peru was named Bolivia in his honor.
30. Benito Pablo Juarez served as president of Mexico from 1861 to 1864 and from 1867 to 1872. His refusal to repay Mexico's foreign debts led Napoleon III to occupy the country and establish Maximilian as emperor in 1864. When French forces withdrew in 1867, Maximilian was executed and Juarez was rehabilitated within the same year.
31. Kennedy, "Address at a White House Reception for Members of Congress and for the Diplomatic Corps of the Latin American Republics," 171.
32. William D. Rogers, *The Twilight Struggle: The Alliance for Progress and the Politics of Development in Latin America* (New York: Random House, 1967), 34–35.
33. Kennedy, "Address at a White House Reception for Members of Congress and for the Diplomatic Corps of the Latin American Republics," 172.
34. Rogers, *The Twilight Struggle,* 34.
35. Simon G. Hanson, *Dollar Diplomacy Modern Style: Chapters in the Failure of the Alliance for Progress* (Washington, D.C.: Inter-American Press, 1970), 17.
36. Rostow, interview by author, 1995.
37. John F. Kennedy, "Special Message to the Congress on Foreign Aid, March 22, 1961," in *Public Papers of the Presidents of the United States: John F. Kennedy* (Washington, D.C.: Government Printing Office, 1962), 203.
38. Ibid., 204.
39. Ibid., 205.

40. Ibid., 204.
41. Wiarda, "Did the Alliance 'Lose Its Way'?" 99.
42. Arthur Schlesinger Jr., *A Thousand Days: John F. Kennedy in the White House* (Boston: Houghton Mifflin, 1965), 589.
43. Ibid., 588.
44. Robert A. Packenham, *Liberal America and the Third World: Political Development Ideas in Foreign Aid and Social Science* (Princeton, N.J.: Princeton University Press, 1973), 63.
45. Alberto Lleras Camargo, "The Alliance for Progress: Aims, Distortions, Obstacles," *Foreign Affairs,* October 1963, p. 25.
46. William O. Walker III, "Mixing the Sweet with the Sour: Kennedy, Johnson, and Latin America," in *The Diplomacy of the Crucial Decade: American Foreign Relations During the 1960s,* ed. Diane B. Kunz (New York: Columbia University Press, 1994), 59.
47. Rostow, interview by author, 1995.

Chapter 6

1. Bruce Miroff, *Pragmatic Illusions: The Presidential Politics of John F. Kennedy* (New York: David McKay, 1976), 117.
2. Lincoln Gordon, interview by John E. Rielly, tape recording, 30 May 1964, John F. Kennedy Library Oral History Program, 15.
3. An extensive account of Dillon's promises to the Latin Americans at Punta del Este is available in William D. Rogers, *The Twilight Struggle: The Alliance for Progress and the Politics of Development in Latin America* (New York: Random House, 1967).
4. Bill Hadded, "Letter to John F. Kennedy Concerning Problems with the Alliance for Progress, 9 March 1962," President's Office File, Subjects, 25 February 1962 through 26 March 1962, Box 95, John F. Kennedy Presidential Library (hereafter cited as JFK), 1.
5. Rogers, *The Twilight Struggle,* 39.
6. Jack Heller and Miguel S. Wionczek, "The Assumptions of the Alliance," in *The Alliance for Progress: A Retrospective,* ed. L. Ronald Scheman (New York: Praeger, 1988), 132.
7. W. W. Rostow, "Memorandum to Mr. Richard Goodwin, 20 June 1961," National Security Files, January through December 1961, Box 290, JFK, 1.
8. Ibid., 2.
9. This quotation from "The Charter of Punta del Este," and others in this chapter, are from a reprint of the document in Lincoln Gordon, *A New Deal for Latin America* (Cambridge, Mass.: Harvard University Press, 1963), 120.
10. Jerome Levinson and Juan de Onis, *The Alliance that Lost Its Way: A Critical Report on the Alliance for Progress* (Chicago: Quadrangle Books, 1970), 70.
11. Rostow first quoted the figure of an annual growth rate of 2.5 percent for ten years as the basis for the "take-off" in his book *The Process of Economic Growth* (New York: W.W. Norton) in 1952.

12. Gordon, *A New Deal for Latin America,* 120.
13. Rostow, "Memorandum to Mr. Richard Goodwin," 2.
14. L. Ronald Scheman, "The Alliance for Progress: Concept and Creativity," in *The Alliance for Progress: A Retrospective,* ed. L. Ronald Scheman (New York: Praeger, 1988), 20.
15. Tony Smith, *America's Mission: The United States and the Worldwide Struggle for Democracy in the Twentieth Century* (Princeton, N.J.: Princeton University Press, 1994), 225–26.
16. See "Latin America: The Picture When President Johnson Assumed Office," National Security Files of Walt W. Rostow: Latin America File Number One, Box 14, Lyndon Baines Johnson Presidential Library [hereafter cited as LBJ], 1.
17. See W. W. Rostow, "Memorandum to the Secretary of State: Foreign Aid Reorganization, 31 December 1963," National Security File, Subject File, Box 16, LBJ.
18. See Lyndon Baines Johnson, "Remarks of the President to the Ambassadors of the Alliance for Progress in the East Room, 11 May 1964," National Security Files, Agency File, Box 4, LBJ, 5–6.
19. W. W. Rostow, "Memorandum to David Bell, AID: Technical Assistance for National Market Concept, 19 June, 1964," C. D. Jackson Papers, Box 92, Rostow, Walt, 1964, Dwight D. Eisenhower Library [hereafter cited as DDE], 1.
20. W. W. Rostow, "Address by the Honorable W. W. Rostow, Counselor and Chairman of the Policy Planning Council at the Department of State, at the Seventieth Annual Convention of the Farm Equipment Institute, New Orleans, Louisiana, Tuesday, 1 October 1963," C. D. Jackson Papers, Box 92, Rostow, Walt, 1964, DDE, 8. Rostow had expressed his support for applying the national market concept to developing nations and to countries in the Alliance for Progress in two earlier speeches, at Georgetown University on 2 May 1963 and at the Annual Meeting of the American Chamber of Commerce in Mexico City on 13 August 1961. See W. W. Rostow, "Address by the Honorable W. W. Rostow, Counselor and Chairman of the Policy Planning Council at the Department of State, at the Seventeenth Annual Conference of the Middle East Institute, Georgetown University, Washington, D.C., 2 May 1963," C. D. Jackson Papers, Box 92, Rostow, Walt, 1963, DDE; "Address by the Honorable W. W. Rostow, Counselor and Chairman of the Policy Planning Council at the Department of State, at the Annual Meeting of the American Chamber of Commerce, Mexico City, 19 August 1963," C. D. Jackson Papers, Box 92, Rostow, Walt, 1964, DDE.
21. W. W. Rostow, "Letter to President Johnson on CIAP Meeting," National Security Files, Agency File, Box 5, LBJ, 2.
22. W. W. Rostow, "Memorandum: Progress on the World Scene, 27 June 1966," Confidential File FG 11–8–11, Bator, Francis, Box 2, LBJ, 1.
23. W. W. Rostow, "Memorandum to the President: Future of Foreign Aid, 14 October, 1966," National Security File, Subject File, Box 16, LBJ, 1.
24. Ibid.
25. See: W. W. Rostow, "Memorandum for the President: OAS Summit Preparations, 27

February 1967," National Security Files, Memo to the President, Walt Rostow, Box 13, LBJ.

26. W. W. Rostow, "Memorandum for the President: Preliminary Thoughts, 4 April 1966," National Security Files, Files of Walt Rostow, Box 15, LBJ, 1–2.
27. For a list of publicity activities the Johnson administration arranged to promote the OAS Summit of 1967, see Sol M. Linowitz, "Memorandum for Mr. Walt W. Rostow, The White House, Subject: Publicity with Regard to the Summit Conference, 25 March, 1967," National Security Files, International Meetings and Travel File, Inter-American Summit, Vol. 2, Box 16, LBJ.
28. For a complete chronology of the planning of the OAS Summit of 1967, see "OAS Summit Chronology," NSF National Security Council History, OAS Summit Meeting, April, 1967, Box 12, LBJ.
29. W. W. Rostow, "Memorandum for the President, Subject: Visit to the Ranch by Latin American Ambassadors, 30 March 1967," National Security Files, Memo to the President, Walt Rostow, Box 14, LBJ, 30a.
30. See W. W. Rostow, "Memorandum for the President, What USIA Is Doing to Stimulate Public Awareness and Interest in the Summit in Latin America, 15 March 1967," National Security Files, Memo to the President, Walt Rostow, Box 14, LBJ, 14a.
31. Walt Rostow and George Christian, "Background Briefing (Punta del Este Summit Conference), 6 April 1967," National Security Files, International Meetings and Travel File, Punta del Este Summit Conference Press Material, Box 19, LBJ, 3.
32. Ibid.
33. See Sol M. Linowitz, "Memorandum for Mr. Walt W. Rostow, The White House, 25 March 1967," National Security Files, International Meetings and Travel File, Inter-American Summit, Vol. 2, Box 16, LBJ, 1–2.
34. Donald F. Horning wrote to the president concerning communications satellite television coverage of the summit meeting in the following memorandum: "Memorandum for the President: Communications Satellite TV Coverage of the Summit Meeting, 24 March 1967," National Security Files, International Meetings and Travel File, Inter-American Summit, Vol. 2, Box 16, LBJ. The *New York Times* covered the planning for satellite coverage of the conference in Benjamin Welles, "U.S. Weighs Live Telecast of Uruguay Parley via Canary Bird," *New York Times*, 24 March 1967, C15.
35. For an assessment of Latin American reaction to the summit by the USIA, see Leonard H. Marks, "Memorandum for the President, Latin American Reaction to the OAS Summit Conference, 21 April 1967," Papers of Lyndon Baines Johnson, President, 1963–1969, Folder 7, 4/15/67, Box 69, LBJ.
36. For a country-by-country breakdown of media reactions to the OAS Summit of 1967, see Foreign Broadcast Information Service, "Special Memorandum: Latin American Radio and Press Reaction to the Punta del Este Conference, 12 April 1967," National Security Files, International Meetings and Travel File, Inter-American Summit, Vol. 4, Box 17, LBJ.
37. See Lincoln Gordon, "Preliminary Report on the Public Statements by OAS Chiefs of State upon Their Return Home from the Summit, 19 April 1967," National Security

Files, International Meetings and Travel File, Inter-American Summit, Vol. 4, Box 17, LBJ, 1–2.

38. "Charter of the Presidents of the American Republics for the People of the Americas, 7 April 1967," National Security Files, Country File—Latin America, Box 3, LBJ, 6.
39. W. W. Rostow, "Memorandum for the President, Forwarding of Third Progress Report on the Inter-American Summit Decisions by Dean Rusk, 16 October 1967," National Security Files, Country File—Latin America, Vol. 6, 10/67–4/68, Box 3, LBJ, 1.
40. Stephen G. Rabe, *The Most Dangerous Area in the World: John F. Kennedy Confronts Communist Revolution in Latin America* (Chapel Hill: University of North Carolina Press, 1999), 181–82.
41. Heller and Wionczek, "The Assumptions of the Alliance," 133.
42. W. W. Rostow, "Memorandum for the Secretary of State, A Five-Year Economic Development Program for Viet Nam, 23 October 1965," Papers of Walt W. Rostow, Southeast Asia, Box 13, LBJ, 2.
43. W. W. Rostow, "Memorandum for the President, Response to Nixon's Statements on Latin America, 7 February 1968," National Security File, Latin America, Box 4, LBJ. Rostow included in his memorandum to President Johnson a copy of a laudatory *New York Times* article on Nixon's statements about the administration's Latin American policy, published on 7 February 1968.
44. Rostow, "Memorandum for the President, Response to Nixon's Statements on Latin America," 2.
45. Ibid., 1.

Conclusion

1. Herbert W. Simons, "The Rhetoric of Inquiry as an Intellectual Movement," in *The Rhetorical Turn: Invention and Persuasion in the Conduct of Inquiry*, ed. Herbert W. Simons (Chicago: University of Chicago Press, 1990), 5.
2. John Morton Blum, *Years of Discord: American Politics and Society, 1961–1964* (New York: W. W. Norton, 1991), 36.
3. W. W. Rostow, interview by Richard Neustadt, tape recording, 11 April 1964, John F. Kennedy Presidential Library, John F. Kennedy Oral Project Program.
4. Ian Roxborough, "Modernization Theory Revisited." *Comparative Studies in Society and History* 30 (1988): 757.
5. William D. Rogers, *The Twilight Struggle: The Alliance for Progress and the Politics of Development in Latin America* (New York: Random House, 1967), 48.
6. Bruce Miroff, *Pragmatic Illusions: The Presidential Politics of John F. Kennedy* (New York: David McKay, 1976), 136–37.
7. Stephen G. Rabe, *The Most Dangerous Area in the World: John F. Kennedy Confronts Communist Revolution in Latin America* (Chapel Hill: University of North Carolina Press, 1999), 181.
8. Enrique Lerdau, "The Alliance for Progress: The Learning Experience," in *The Alliance*

for Progress: A Retrospective, ed. L. Ronald Scheman (Westport, Conn.: Praeger, 1988), 167.

9. W. W. Rostow, *The Stages of Economic Growth: A Non-communist Manifesto,* 3d ed. (Cambridge: Cambridge University Press, 1990), xxxviii.
10. W. W. Rostow, *The Stages of Economic Growth: A Non-communist Manifesto,* 1st ed. (Cambridge: Cambridge University Press, 1960), 166.

Bibliography

Books

Almond, Gabriel, and James S. Coleman. *The Politics of Developing Areas.* Princeton, N.J.: Princeton University Press, 1960.

Bell, Daniel. *The End of Ideology.* New York: Free Press, 1960.

Black, C. E. *The Dynamics of Modernization: A Study in Comparative History.* New York: Harper & Brothers, 1966.

Blum, John Morton. *Years of Discord: American Politics and Society, 1961–1964.* New York: W. W. Norton & Company, 1990.

Brown, Richard Harvey. *Writing the Social Text: Poetics and Politics in Social Science Discourses.* New York: A. de Gruyter, 1992.

Bulmer, Martin. *Social Science and Social Policy.* London: Allen & Unwin, 1986.

______. *Social Science Research and Government: Comparative Essays on Britain and the United States.* New York: Cambridge University Press, 1987.

Chomsky, Noam. *Intellectuals and the State.* Vertaling: Gerda Telgenhof, 1978.

______. *Language and Politics.* New York: Black Rose Books, 1988.

______. *On Power and Ideology.* New York: Black Rose Books, 1987.

Chomsky, Noam, and Edward S. Herman. *Manufacturing Consent.* New York: Pantheon Books, 1988.

Clough, Shepard. *Essays in Honor of Gino Luzzato.* Milan, Italy, 1950.

Cottam, Martha L. *Images and Interventions: U.S. Policies in Latin America.* Pittsburgh, Penn.: University of Pittsburgh Press, 1994.

Eisenhower, Milton. *The Wine Is Bitter: The United States and Latin America.* Garden City, N.Y.: Doubleday, 1963.

Eisenstadt, S. N. *Modernization: Protest and Change.* Englewood Cliffs, N.J.: Prentice Hall, 1966.

Ferrarotti, Franco. *The Myth of Inevitable Progress.* Westport, Conn.: Greenwood Press, 1985.

Fisher, Walter. *Human Communication as Narration: Toward a Philosophy of Reason, Value, and Action.* Columbia, S.C.: University of South Carolina Press, 1987.

Foucault, Michel. *The Archaeology of Knowledge*, translated by Sheridan Smith. New York: Pantheon Books, 1972.

———. *The Order of Things: An Archaeology of the Human Sciences.* New York: Pantheon Books, 1971.

———. *Power/Knowledge: Selected Interviews and Other Writings, 1972–1977.* New York: Pantheon Books, 1980.

Gayer, Arthur D., W. W. Rostow, Anna Jacobson Schwartz, and Isaiah Frank. *The Growth and Fluctuation of the British Economy, 1790–1850.* Hassocks, Eng.: Harvester Press, 1953.

Giddens, Anthony. *Positivism and Sociology.* London: Heinemann, 1974.

———. *Social Theory and Modern Sociology.* Stanford, Calif.: Stanford University Press, 1987.

Goodman, Robert F., and Walter Fisher. *Rethinking Knowledge: Reflections Across Disciplines.* Albany, N.Y.: State University of New York Press, 1995.

Gordon, Lincoln. *A New Deal for Latin America.* Cambridge, Mass.: Harvard University Press, 1963.

Gramsci, Antonio. *Selections From Prison Notebooks.* New York: International Publishers, 1971.

Gray, Martin. *A Dictionary of Literary Terms.* 2d ed. Essex, England: Longman York Press, 1992.

Habermas, Jürgen. *Communication and the Evolution of Society*, translated by Thomas McCarthy. Boston, Mass.: Beacon Press, 1979.

———. *Legitimation Crisis*, , translated by Thomas McCarthy. Boston, Mass.: Beacon Press, 1975.

———. *Toward A Rational Society: Student Protest, Science and Politics*, , translated by Jeremy J. Shapiro. London: Heinemann, 1971.

Hagen. E. E. *On the Theory of Social Change: How Economic Growth Begins.* Homewood, Ill.: Dorsey, 1962.

Halberstam, David. *The Best and the Brightest.* New York: Random House, 1972.

Hall, Stuart. *The Hard Road to Renewal.* London: Verso, 1988.

Hanson, Simon G. *Dollar Diplomacy: Modern Style: Chapters in the Failure of the Alliance for Progress.* Washington, D.C.: Inter-American Press, 1970.

Hartz, Louis. *The Liberal Tradition in America.* New York: Harcourt, Brace, and World, 1955.

Hout, Wil. *Capitalism and the Third World: Development, Dependence, and the World System.* Brookfield, Vt.: Edward Elgar, 1993.

Inkles, A., and D. H. Smith. *Becoming Modern: Individual Change in Six Developing Countries.* Cambridge, Mass.: Harvard University Press, 1974.

Kennan, George. *American Diplomacy, 1900–1950.* New York: New American Library, 1951.

Kennedy, John F. *The Strategy of Peace.* New York: Harper, 1960.

Kindleberger, Charles P., and Guido di Tella. *Economics in the Long View: Essays in Honour of W. W. Rostow.* New York: New York University Press, 1982.

Kryzanek, Michael J. *U.S.–Latin American Relations.* 2d ed. Westport, Conn.: Praeger, 1990.

Kuntz, Diane B. *Butter and Guns: America's Cold War Economic Diplomacy.* New York: The Free Press, 1997.

Kuznets, Simon. *Secular Movements in Production and Prices: Their Nature and Their Bearing Upon Cyclical Fluctuations.* Boston, Mass.: Houghton Mifflin, 1930.

Langley, Lester D. *America and the Americas: The United States in the Western Hemisphere.* Athens: University of Georgia Press, 1989.

Lerner, Daniel, and Harold D. Lasswell. *The Policy Sciences: Recent Developments in Scope and Methods.* Stanford, Calif.: Stanford University Press, 1951.

Levinson, Jerome, and Juan de Onis. *The Alliance That Lost Its Way: A Critical Report on the Alliance for Progress.* Chicago, Ill.: Quadrangle Books, 1970.

Levy, Jr., Marion J. *Modernization and the Structure of Society: A Setting for International Affairs.* 2 Vols. Princeton, N.J.: Princeton University Press, 1966.

Lewis, W. A. *Development Planning.* London: C. Allen Unwin, 1966.

Lipset, Seymour Martin. *Political Man.* New York: Doubleday, 1960.

Lowenthal, Abraham F. *Exporting Democracy: The United States and Latin America.* Baltimore, Md.: Johns Hopkins University Press, 1991.

Luke, Timothy. *Social Theory and Modernity: Critique, Dissent, and Revolution.* Newbury Park, Calif.: Sage, 1990.

Lyons, Gene M. *The Uneasy Partnership: Social Science and the Federal Government in the Twentieth Century.* New York: Russell Sage Foundation, 1969.

MacDonald, Susan Peck. *Professional Academic Writing in the Humanities and Social Sciences.* Carbondale, Ill.: Southern Illinois University Press, 1994.

Marcuse, Herbert. *One-Dimensional Man: Studies in the Ideology of Advanced Industrial Society.* Boston, Mass.: Beacon Press, 1964.

Martz, John D. *United States Policy in Latin America: A Quarter Century of Crisis and Challenge, 1961–1986.* Lincoln: University of Nebraska Press, 1988.

McClelland, D. *The Achieving Society.* Princeton, N.J.: Princeton University Press, 1961.

McCloskey, Donald N. *The Consequences of Economic Rhetoric.* New York: Cambridge University Press, 1988.

———. *If You're So Smart: The Narrative of Economic Expertise.* Chicago: University of Chicago Press, 1990.

———. *Knowledge and Persuasion in Economics.* New York: Cambridge University Press, 1994.

———. *The Rhetoric of Economics.* Madison: University of Wisconsin Press, 1985.

———. *Second Thoughts: Myths and Morals of U.S. Economic History.* New York: Oxford University Press, 1993.

———. *The Writing of Economics.* New York: Macmillan, 1987.

Millikan, Max F., and W. W. Rostow. *A Proposal: Key to an Effective Foreign Policy.* New York: Harper & Brothers, 1957.

Miroff, Bruce. *Pragmatic Illusions: The Presidential Politics of John F. Kennedy.* New York: David McKay, 1976.

Molineu, Harold. *U.S. Policy Toward Latin America: From Regionalism to Globalism.* Boulder, Colo.: Westview Press, 1986.

Nash, Manning. *Unfinished Agenda: The Dynamics of Modernization in the Developing Nations.* Boulder, Colo.: Westview Press, 1984.

Nisbet, Robert A. *Social Change and History: Aspects of the Western Theory of Development.* New York: Oxford University Press, 1969.

Packenham, Robert A. *Liberal America and the Third World: Political Development Ideas in Foreign Aid and Social Science.* Princeton, N.J.: Princeton University Press, 1973.

Parsons, Talcott. *Societies: Evolutionary and Comparative Perspectives.* New York: Prentice Hall, 1966.

Patton, Michael Q. *Utilization-Focused Evaluation.* Beverly Hills, Calif.: Sage Publications, 1978.

Polkinghorne, Donald E. *Narrative Knowing and the Human Sciences.* Albany: State University of New York Press, 1988.

Rabe, Stephen G. *Eisenhower and Latin America: The Foreign Policy of Anticommunism.* Chapel Hill: University of North Carolina Press, 1988.

———. *The Most Dangerous Area in the World: John F. Kennedy Confronts Communist Revolution in Latin America.* Chapel Hill: University of North Carolina Press, 1999.

Rabinow, Paul. *The Foucault Reader.* New York: Pantheon Books, 1984.

Rogers, William D. *The Twilight Struggle: The Alliance for Progress and the Politics of Development in Latin America.* New York: Random House, 1967.

Ross, Dorothy. *The Origins of American Social Science.* Cambridge, Eng.: Cambridge University Press, 1991.

Rostow, W. W. *The American Diplomatic Revolution: An Inaugural Lecture Delivered Before the University of Oxford on 12 November 1946.* Oxford: Clarendon Press, 1946.

———. *British Economy of the Nineteenth Century.* London: Oxford University Press, 1948.

———. *The Diffusion of Power: An Essay in Recent History.* New York: Macmillan, 1972.

———. *Eisenhower, Kennedy, and Foreign Aid.* Austin: University of Texas Press, 1985.

———. *History, Policy, and Economic Theory.* Boulder, Colo.: Westview Press, 1990.

———. *Open Skies: Eisenhower's Proposal of July 21, 1955.* Austin: University of Texas Press, 1982.

———. *Politics and the Stages of Growth.* Cambridge, Eng.: Cambridge University Press, 1971.

———. *The Process of Economic Growth.* New York: W. W. Norton, 1952.

———. *The Stages of Economic Growth: A Non-communist Manifesto.* Cambridge, Eng.: Cambridge University Press, 1960.

———. *The Stages of Economic Growth: A Non-communist Manifesto.* 2d ed. Cambridge, Eng.: Cambridge University Press, 1971.

———. *The Stages of Economic Growth: A Non-communist Manifesto.* 3d ed. Cambridge, Eng.: Cambridge University Press, 1990.

———. *Theorists of Economic Growth From David Hume to the Present With a Perspective on the New Century.* New York: Oxford University Press, 1990.

———. *The United States in the World Arena.* New York: Harper & Brothers, 1960.

Rostow, W. W., and Richard Hatch. *An American Policy in Asia.* Cambridge, Mass.: MIT Press and New York: John Wiley & Sons, 1955.

Rostow, W. W., Richard Hatch, Frank A. Kierman, Jr., and Alexander Eckstein. *The Prospects for Communist China.* Cambridge, Mass.: MIT Press, 1954.

Rostow, W. W., and Alfred Levin. *The Dynamics of Soviet Society.* New York: W. W. Norton, 1953.

Schlesinger, Jr., Arthur. *A Thousand Days: John F. Kennedy in the White House.* Boston, Mass.: Houghton Mifflin, 1965.

Smith, Tony. *America's Mission: The United States and the Worldwide Struggle for Democracy in the Twentieth Century.* Princeton, N.J.: Princeton University Press, 1994.

Sorensen, Theodore C. *Kennedy.* New York: Bantam Books, 1966.

Tanzer, Lester. *The Kennedy Circle.* Washington, D.C.: Robert B. Luce, 1961.

Wagner, Peter, Carol Hirschon Weiss, Bjorn Wittrock, and Helmutt Wollman. *Social Sciences and Modern States: National Experiences and Theoretical Crossroads.* New York: Cambridge University Press, 1991.

Wiarda, Howard J. *Ethnocentrism in Foreign Policy: Can We Understand the Third World?* Washington, D.C.: American Enterprise Institute, 1985.

Scholarly Articles and Parts of Books

Anderson, Charles W. "The Human Sciences and the Liberal Polity in Rhetorical Relationship." In *The Rhetoric of the Human Sciences: Language and Argument in Scholarship and Public Affairs,* edited by John S. Nelson, Allan Megill, and Donald M. McCloskey, 162–84. Madison: University of Wisconsin Press, 1987.

Bellamy, Richard. "Liberalism." In *Ideas That* Shape *Politics,* edited by Michael Foley, 5–17. New York: Manchester University Press, 1994.

Black, Edwin. "The Second Persona." *Quarterly Journal of Speech* 56 (1970): 109–19.

Bogner, Artur. "The Theory of the Civilizing Process: An Idiographic Theory of Modernization?" *Theory, Culture, and Society* 9 (1992): 22–53.

Bulmer, Martin. "Social Science and Policy-Making: The Use of Research by Government Commissions." *American Behavioral Scientist* 26 (1983): 553–680.

Camargo, Alberto Lleras. "The Alliance for Progress: Aims, Distortions, Obstacles." *Foreign Affairs* (October 1963): 25–37.

Checkland, S. G. "Stages and the State: How Do They Relate?" In *Economics in the Long View: Essays in Honour of W W. Rostow.* Vol. 1. *Models and Methodology,* edited by Charles P. Kindleberger and Guido di Tella, 44–67. New York: New York University Press, 1982.

Dillon, C. Douglas. "The Prelude." In *The Alliance for Progress: A Retrospective,* edited by L. Ronald Scheman, 63–66. New York: Praeger, 1988.

Duesenberry, James S. "Some Aspects of the Theory of Economic Development." *Explorations in Entrepreneurial History* 392 (15 December 1950): 68–74.

Foster-Carter, Aidan. "From Rostow to Gunder Frank: Conflicting Paradigms in the Analysis of Underdevelopment." *World Development* 4 (1976): 167–80.

Goodnight, G. Thomas. "Hans J. Morgentheau *In Defense of the National Interest:* On Rhetoric, Realism, and the Public Sphere." In *Post-Realism: The Rhetorical Turn in International Relations,* edited by Francis A. Beer and Robert Hariman, 143–65. East Lansing: Michigan State University Press, 1996.

Gordon, Lincoln. "The Alliance at Birth: Hopes and Fears." In *The Alliance for Progress: A Retrospective,* edited by L. Ronald Scheman, 73–79. New York: Praeger, 1988.

Hariman, Robert, and Francis A. Beer. "From Idealism to Post-Realism: The Rhetorical Turn in International Relations." In *Argument and the Postmodern Challenge: Proceedings of the Eighth SCA/ACA Conference on Argumentation,* edited by Raymie E. McKerrow, 260–66. Annandale, Va.: Speech Communication Association, 1996.

Heclo, Hugh. "Issue Networks and the Executive Establishment." In *The New*

American Political System, edited by Anthony King, 87–124. Washington D.C.: American Enterprise Institute, 1978.

Heller, Jack, and Miguel S. Wionczek. "The Assumptions of the Alliance." In *The Alliance for Progress: A Retrospective*, edited by L. Ronald Scheman, 131–38. New York: Praeger, 1988.

Hicks, J. R. "Review of *The Process of Economic Growth*, by W. W. Rostow." *The Journal of Political Economy* 41 (1953): 173–74.

Hoselitz, Bert F. "The Conditions of Economic Growth." Review of *The Process of Economic Growth*, by W. W. Rostow. *The Journal of Economic History* 13 (1953): 202–4.

Kaufer, David S., and Cheryl Geisler. "Novelty in Academic Writing." *Written Communication* 6 (1989): 286–311.

Lerdau, Enrique. "The Alliance for Progress: The Learning Experience." In *The Alliance for Progress: A Retrospective*, edited by L. Ronald Scheman, 165–84. New York: Praeger, 1988.

Lowenthal, Abraham F. "Alliance Rhetoric Versus Latin American Reality." *Foreign Affairs* (April 1970): 494–508.

Medhurst, Martin J. "Eisenhower and the Crusade for Freedom: The Rhetorical Origins of a Cold War Campaign." *Presidential Studies Quarterly* 27 (1997): 646–61.

Miller, Carolyn R. "The Rhetoric of Decision Science, or Herbert A. Simon Says." In *The Rhetorical Turn: Invention and Persuasion in the Conduct of Inquiry*, edited by Herbert W. Simons, 162–84. Chicago: University of Chicago Press, 1990.

Nelson, John S. "Political Foundations for the Rhetoric of Inquiry." In *The Rhetorical Turn: Invention and Persuasion in the Conduct of Inquiry*, edited by Herbert W. Simons, 258–89. Chicago: University of Chicago Press, 1990.

———. "Stories of Science and Politics: Some Rhetorics of Political Research." In *The Rhetoric of the Human Sciences: Language and Argument in Scholarship and Public Affairs*, edited by John S. Nelson, Allan Megill, and Donald M. McCloskey, 198–220. Madison: University of Wisconsin Press, 1987.

Nelson, John S., Alan Megill, and D. N. McCloskey. "The Rhetoric of Inquiry." In *The Rhetoric of the Human Sciences: Language and Argument in Scholarship and Public Affairs*, edited by John S. Nelson, Allan Megill, and Donald M. McCloskey, 3–18. Madison: University of Wisconsin Press, 1987.

Pal, Leslie A. "Knowledge, Power, and Policy: Reflections on Foucault." In *Social Scientists, Policy, and the State*, edited by Stephen Brooks and Alain-G. Gagnon, 139–58. Westport, Conn: Praeger, 1990.

Perry, Steven. "Rhetorical Functions of the Infestation Metaphor in Hitler's Rhetoric." *Central States Speech Journal* 34 (1983): 229–35.

Postan, M. M. "Walt Rostow: A Personal Appreciation." In *Economics in the Long View: Essays in Honour of W W. Rostow*. Vol. 1. *Models and Methodology*, edited by Charles P. Kindleberger and Guido di Tella, 1–14. New York: New York University Press, 1982.

Pye, Lucian W. "The Foreign Aid Instrument: Search for Reality." In *Foreign Policy in the Sixties: The Issues and Instruments*, edited by Roger Hilsman and Robert C. Good, 93–112. Baltimore, Md.: Johns Hopkins University Press, 1965.

Rostow, W. W. "My Life Philosophy." *The American Economist* 30 (1986): 3–13.

———. "On Ending the Cold War." *Foreign Affairs* 65 (1987): 831–51.

———. "Reflections on Political Economy: Past, Present, and Future." In *Eminent Economists: Their Life Philosophies*, edited by Michael Szenberg, 222–35. Cambridge: Cambridge University Press, 1992.

———. "The Stages of Economic Growth." *Economic History Review* 12 (1959): 1–16.

———. "The Take-off Into Sustained Growth." *The Economic Journal* 66 (1956): 25–48.

"Rostow on Growth: A Non-communist Manifesto." *The Economist* 15 (August 1959): 409–16.

Roxborough, Ian. "Modernization Theory Revisited." *Comparative Studies in Society and History* 30 (1988): 753–61.

Scheman, L. Ronald. "The Alliance for Progress: Concept and Creativity." In *The Alliance for Progress: A Retrospective*, edited by L. Ronald Scheman, 3–62. New York: Praeger, 1988.

Shapiro, Martin J. "The Rhetoric of Social Science: The Political Responsibilities of the Scholar." In *The Rhetoric of the Human Sciences: Language and Argument in Scholarship and Public Affairs*, edited by John S. Nelson, Allan Megill, and Donald M. McCloskey, 363–80. Madison: University of Wisconsin Press, 1987.

Shils, Edward. "The End of Ideology?" *Encounter* 5 (November 1955): 52–58.

———. "Political Development in the New States–The Will to Be Modern." In *Readings in Social Evolution and Development*, edited by S. N. Eisenstadt, 379–419. Elmsford, N.Y.: Pergamon, 1970.

Schlesinger, Jr., Arthur. "Myth and Reality." In *The Alliance for Progress: A Retrospective*, edited by L. Ronald Scheman, 67–72. New York: Praeger, 1988.

Simons, Herbert W. "The Rhetoric of Inquiry as an Intellectual Movement." In *The Rhetorical Turn: Invention and Persuasion in the Conduct of Inquiry*, edited by Herbert W. Simons, 1–31. Chicago: University of Chicago Press, 1990.

Skocpol, Theda. "Government Structures, Social Science, and the Development of Economic and Social Policies." In *Social Science Research and Government:*

Comparative Essays on Britain and the United States, edited by Martin Bulmer, 27–50. Cambridge, Eng.: Cambridge University Press, 1987.

Supple, Barry. "Revisiting Rostow." *The Economic History Review* 37 (1984): 107–14.

Walker, III, William O. "Mixing the Sweet with the Sour: Kennedy, Johnson, and Latin America." In *The Diplomacy of the Crucial Decade: American Foreign Relations During the 1960s,* edited By Diane Kunz, 42–79. New York: Columbia University Press, 1994.

Weiss, Carol. "The Uneasy Partnership Endures: Social Science and Government." In *Social Scientists, Policy, and the State,* edited by Stephen Brooks and Alain-G. Gagnon, 97–111. Westport, Conn.: Praeger, 1990.

Wiarda, Howard J. "Did the Alliance 'Lose Its Way,' or Were Its Assumptions All Wrong From the Beginning and Are Those Assumptions Still With Us?" In *The Alliance for Progress: A Retrospective,* edited by L. Ronald Scheman, 95–118. New York: Praeger, 1988.

Wittrock, Bjorn, and Peter Wagner. "Social Science and State Development: The Structuration of Discourse in the Social Sciences." In *Social Scientists, Policy, and the State,* edited by Stephen Brooks and Alain-G. Gagnon, 113–37. New York: Praeger, 1990.

Zhukov, Yuri. "Snipe in the Bog." *Pravda,* 19 October, 1959. Translated and reprinted in *The Economist* (7 November 1959): 502.

Magazine and Newspaper Articles

Balogh, T. "'The Changing Fashions of Economics,' review of *Economic Development,* by Benjamin Higgins, and *The Stages of Economic Growth,* 1st. ed., by W. W. Rostow." *New Statesman,* 30 April 1960, pp. 640, 642.

Davis, Saville R. "'Rostow in the World Arena,' review of *The Stages of Economic Growth,* 1st. ed., by W. W. Rostow." *Christian Science Monitor,* 9 April 1960, p. 9.

Galbraith, John Kenneth. "For Foreign Aid in A New Packaging, Review of *A Proposal: Key to an Effective Foreign Policy,* by Max F. Millikan and W. W. Rostow. *New York Times Book Review,* 18 January 1957, pp. 7, 22.

Loftus, Joseph A. "Kennedy is Given a Secret Briefing by C.I.A. Director." *New York Times,* 24 July 1960, pp. 1, 32.

Rostow, W. W. "The 'New Look' in U.S. World Policy." *U.S. News and World Report,* 13 February 1961, pp. 57–81.

Soule, George. "Important Exploration: Review of *The Process of Economic Growth,* by W. W. Rostow." *New Republic,* 8 September 1952, p. 19.

Welles, Benjamin. "U.S. Weighs Live Telecast of Uruguay Parley Via Canary Bird." *New York Times*, 24 March 1967, p. C15.

Wright, David McCord. "'True Growth Must Come From Freedom,' review of *The Stages of Economic Growth*, 1st. ed., by W. W. Rostow." *Fortune* December 1959, pp. 137, 212.

Government Documents

Abrams, Elliot. "The Alliance for Progress and Today's Development Policy." *Department of State Bulletin* 86 (June 1989): 86–88.

"Biography of Walt Whitman Rostow." Office Files of John Macy: Rostow, Walt Whitman, Box 502. Lyndon Baines Johnson Presidential Library.

"Charter of the Presidents of the American Republics for the People of the Americas, 7 April 1967. National Security Country File—Latin America, Vol. 6, 10/67–4/68, Box 3. Lyndon Baines Johnson Presidential Library.

Cox, Archibald. "Memorandum to John F. Kennedy Regarding the Organization and Speech- Writing Side of the Election Campaign, June 17, 1960." Richard Goodwin Working Papers, 1958–1960: 1960 Campaign Issues, Box 996, Pre-Presidential Papers. John F. Kennedy Presidential Library.

______. "Memorandum to Robert Kennedy Regarding Speech Writing and Related Activities, 19 July 1960." Richard Goodwin Working Papers, 1958–1960: 1960 Campaign Issues, Box 996, Pre-Presidential Papers. John F. Kennedy Presidential Library.

Eisenhower, Dwight D. "Special Message to the Congress on Foreign Economic Policy, March 30, 1954." In *Public Papers of the Presidents of the United States: Dwight D. Eisenhower*. Washington, D.C.: Government Printing Office, 1954.

Eisenhower, Milton. Department of State. *Report to the President: United States–Latin American Relations*. Publication 5290. Washington, D.C.: Government Printing Office, 1953.

"Five Key Reports to the Government: A Summary." C. D. Jackson Papers, Box 83, Princeton Economic Conference, Miscellaneous Correspondence, Etc. Dwight D. Eisenhower Library.

Foreign Broadcast Information Service. "Special Memorandum: Latin American Radio and Press Reaction to the Punta del Este Conference, 12 April 1967." National Security Files, International Meetings and Travel File, Inter-American Summit, Vol. 4. Box 17. Lyndon Baines Johnson Presidential Library.

Galbraith, John Kenneth. "Confidential Memorandum, Campaign Strategy, 1960." Richard Goodwin Working Papers 1958–1960: 1960 Campaign Issues, Box 996, Pre-Presidential Papers. John F. Kennedy Presidential Library.

Goodwin, Richard. "Confidential Memorandum, Campaign Strategy, 1960."

Richard Goodwin Working Papers, 1958–1960: 1960 Campaign Issues, Box 996, Pre-Presidential Papers. John F. Kennedy Presidential Library.

———. "Speech-Writing for the 1960 Post-Convention Campaign—Organization, Procedures, and Personnel." Richard Goodwin Working Papers, 1958–1960: 1960 Campaign Issues, Box 996, Pre-Presidential Papers. John F. Kennedy Presidential Library.

Gordon, Lincoln. "Draft Memorandum From the Consultant to the Task Force on Latin America (Gordon) to the President's Assistant Special Counsel (Goodwin), 6 March 1961." *American Republics.* In Vol. 12. *Foreign Relations of the United States, 1961–1963,* 6. Washington, D.C.: Government Printing Office, 1996.

———. "Preliminary Report on the Public Statements by OAS Chiefs of State Upon Their Return Home From the Summit, 19 April 1967." National Security Files, International Meetings and Travel File, Inter-American Summit, Vol. 4. Box 17. Lyndon Baines Johnson Presidential Library.

Hadded, Bill. "Letter to John F. Kennedy Concerning Problems with the Alliance for Progress, 9 March 1962." President's Office File, Subjects, 25 February 1962 through 26 March 1962, Box 95. John F. Kennedy Presidential Library.

Holborn, Fred. "Memorandum, An Action Program for a New Approach in Foreign Assistance for the 1960's, November 17, 1960." Transition Files, Task Force Reports, Pre-Presidential Papers, Box 1074. John F. Kennedy Presidential Library.

Horning, Daniel F. "Memorandum for the President: Communications Satellite TV Coverage of the Summit Meeting, 24 March 1967." National Security Files, International Meetings and Travel File, Inter-American Summit, Vol. 2, Box 16. Lyndon Baines Johnson Presidential Library.

Jackson, C. D. "Memorandum to the Secretary of State, April 9, 1954." C. D. Jackson Papers, Box 82, Princeton Economic Conference, Draft Papers. Dwight D. Eisenhower Library.

Johnson, Lyndon Baines. "Remarks of the President to the Ambassadors of the Alliance for Progress in the East Room, 11 May 1964." National Security Files, Agency File, Box 4. Lyndon Baines Johnson Presidential Library.

Joint Economic Committee. *Statement of W. W. Rostow, Center for International Studies, Massachusetts Institute of Technology.* 86th Cong., 1st sess., 13, 16, 17, 18, 19, and 20 November 1959.

Keefer, Edward C., Harriet Dashiell Schwar, and W. Taylor Fain, III. *American Republics.* In Vol. 12. *Foreign Relations of the United States, 1961-1963.* Washington, D.C.: Government Printing Office, 1996.

Kennedy, John F. "Address at a White House Reception for Members of Congress and for the Diplomatic Corps of the Latin American Republics, March 13,

1961." In *Public Papers of the Presidents of the United States: John F. Kennedy,* 19–28. Washington, D.C.: Government Printing Office, 1962.

———. "Annual Message to the Congress on the State of the Union, January 30, 1961." In *Public Papers of the Presidents of the United States: John F. Kennedy,* 19–28. Washington, D.C.: Government Printing Office, 1962.

———. "The Choice in Asia—Democratic Development in India, March 25, 1958." In *A Compilation of Statements and Speeches Made During His Service in the United States Senate and House of Representatives,* 591–608. Washington, D.C.: Government Printing Office, 1964.

———. "The Economic Gap, February 19, 1959." In *A Compilation of Statements and Speeches Made During His Service in the United* States *Senate and House of Representatives,* 789–98. Washington, D.C.: Government Printing Office, 1964.

———. "Excerpts From Address of Senator John F. Kennedy, Stanford University. Palo Alto, California, Feb. 12, 1960," 1960 Campaign and Publicity, Speeches, Statements and Sections, 1958–1960: Foreign Affairs, Box 1030, Pre-Presidential Papers. John F. Kennedy Presidential Library.

———. "Inaugural Address, January 20, 1961." In *Public Papers of the Presidents of the United States: John F. Kennedy,* 1–3. Washington, D.C.: Government Printing Office, 1962.

———. "Remarks of Senator John F. Kennedy (Dem.-Mass.), Dartmouth College, Hanover, New Hampshire, Sunday, March 6, 1960." 1960 Campaign Press and Publicity, Speeches, Statements and Sections, 1958–1960: Foreign Affairs, Box 1030, Pre-Presidential Papers. John F. Kennedy Presidential Library.

———. "Remarks of Senator John F. Kennedy (Dem.-Mass.), Democratic Dinner, San Juan, Puerto Rico, Monday Evening, December 15, 1958." 1960 Campaign Press and Publicity, Speeches, Statements and Sections, 1958–1960: Foreign Affairs, Box 1030, Pre-Presidential Papers. John F. Kennedy Presidential Library.

———. "Remarks of Senator John F. Kennedy (Dem.-Mass), St. Mary's College, South Bend, Indiana, Friday, April 8, 1960." 1960 Campaign Press and Publicity, Speeches, Statements and Sections, 1958–1960: Foreign Affairs, Box 1030, Pre-Presidential Papers. John F. Kennedy Presidential Library.

———. "Special Message to the Congress on Foreign Aid, March 22, 1961." In *Public Papers of the Presidents of the United States: John F. Kennedy,* 203–12. Washington, D.C.: Government Printing Office, 1961.

"Latin America: The Picture When President Johnson Assumed Office." National Security Files of Walt W. Rostow: Latin America File Number One, Box 14. Lyndon Baines Johnson Presidential Library.

Linowitz, Sol M. "Memorandum for Mr. Rostow, The White House, Subject:

Publicity with Regard to the Summit Conference, 25 March 1967." National Security Files, International Meetings and Travel File, Inter-American Summit, Vol. 2, Box 16. Lyndon Baines Johnson Presidential Library.

Marks, Leonard H. "Memorandum for the President, Latin American Reaction to the OAS Summit Conference, 21 April 1967." Papers of Lyndon Baines Johnson, President, 1963–1969, Folder 7, 4/15/67, Box 69. Lyndon Baines Johnson Presidential Library.

Millikan, Max F. "Memorandum on a New Organization for the U.S. Foreign Aid Program, November 15, 1960." Transition Files, Task Force Reports, Pre-Presidential Papers, Box 1074, John F. Kennedy Presidential Library.

"Mr. McDonald's Proposal." C. D. Jackson Papers, Box 82, Princeton Economic Conference, 5/54—Draft Papers. Dwight D. Eisenhower Library.

"Notes on Foreign Economic Policy." C. D. Jackson Papers, Box 82, Princeton Economic Conference, 5/54—Draft Papers. Dwight D. Eisenhower Library.

"OAS Summit Chronology." NSF National Security Council History, OAS Summit Meeting, April, 1967, Box 12. Lyndon Baines Johnson Presidential Library.

"Proceedings of the Off-the-Record Conference Held Under the Auspices of Time, Inc., May 15–16, 1954, Princeton Inn, Princeton, N.J." C. D. Jackson Papers, Box 83, Princeton Economic Conference Transcripts. Dwight D. Eisenhower Library.

"Report to the President-elect of the Task Force on Immediate Latin American Problems." Transition Files, Task Force Reports, Pre-Presidential Papers, Box 1074, John F. Kennedy Presidential Library.

"Resume: Walt Whitman Rostow." Office Files of John Macy: Rostow, Walt Whitman, Box 502. Lyndon Baines Johnson Presidential Library.

Rostow, W. W. "Address by the Honorable W. W. Rostow, Counselor and Chairman of the Policy Planning Council at the Department of State, at the Annual Meeting of the American Chamber of Commerce in Mexico City, 19 August 1963." C. D. Jackson Papers, Box 92, Rostow, Walt, 1963. Dwight D. Eisenhower Library.

______. "Address by the Honorable W. W. Rostow, Counselor and Chairman of the Policy Planning Council at the Department of State, at the Seventeenth Annual Conference of the Middle East Institute, Georgetown University, Washington, D.C. 2 May 1963." C. D. Jackson Papers, Box 92, Rostow, Walt, 1963. Dwight D. Eisenhower Library.

______. "Address by the Honorable W. W. Rostow, Counselor and Chairman of the Policy Planning Council at the Department of State, at the Seventieth Annual Convention of the Farm Equipment Institute, New Orleans, Louisiana,

Tuesday, 1 October 1963." C. D. Jackson Papers, Box 92, Rostow, Walt, 1964. Dwight D. Eisenhower Library.

———. "The Challenge Facing the United States: September 1956." C. D. Jackson Papers, Box 91, Rostow, Walt, 1956. Dwight D. Eisenhower Library.

———. "Guerrilla Warfare in the Underdeveloped Areas." *Department of State Bulletin* 45 (7 August 1961): 231.

———. "Ideas and Action, Address Made at the Carnegie Institute of Technology, June 11, 1962."*Department of State Bulletin* 47 (9 July 1962): 60.

———. "The Idea of an Economic Development Decade, March 2, 1961." President's Office File, Staff Memoranda, Box 64, Rostow. John F. Kennedy Presidential Library.

———. "Letter to C. D. Jackson, 27 December 1954." C. D. Jackson Papers, Box 91, Rostow, Walt. Dwight D. Eisenhower Library.

———. "Letter to President Johnson on CIAP Meeting." National Security Files, Agency File, Box 5. Lyndon Baines Johnson Presidential Library.

———. "Memorandum for the President: Forwarding of Third Progress Report on the Inter-American Summit Decisions by Dean Rusk, 16 October 1967." National Security Country File—Latin America, Vol. 6, 10/67–4/68, Box 3. Lyndon Baines Johnson Presidential Library.

———. "Memorandum for the President: OAS Summit Preparations, 27 February 1967." National Security Files, Memo to the President, Walt Rostow, Box 13. Lyndon Baines Johnson Presidential Library.

———. "Memorandum for the President: Preliminary Thoughts, 4 April 1966." National Security Files, Files of Walt Rostow, Box 15. Lyndon Baines Johnson Presidential Library.

———. "Memorandum for the President, Response to Nixon's Statements on Latin America, 7 February 1968." National Security File, Latin America, Box 4. Lyndon Baines Johnson Presidential Library.

———. "Memorandum for the President, Subject: Visit to the Ranch by Latin American Ambassadors, 30 March 1967." National Security Files, Memo to the President, Walt Rostow, Box 14. Lyndon Baines Johnson Presidential Library.

———. "Memorandum for the President,What USIA Is Doing to Stimulate Public Awareness and Interest in the Summit in Latin America, 15 March 1967." National Security Files, Memo to the President, Walt Rostow, Box 14. Lyndon Baines Johnson Presidential Library.

———. "Memorandum for the Secretary of State, A Five-Year Economic Development Program for Viet Nam, 23 October 1965." Papers of Walt W. Rostow, Southeast Asia, Box 13. Lyndon Baines Johnson Presidential Library.

———. "Memorandum on the Strategy of Foreign Aid, 1961, December 22,

1960 (forwarded by Fred Holborn)." Transition Files, Task Force Reports, Pre-Presidential Papers, Box 1074, John F. Kennedy Presidential Library.

———. "Memorandum: Progress on the World Scene, 27 June 1966." Confidential File FG 11-8-11, Bator, Francis, Box 2. Lyndon Baines Johnson Presidential Library.

———. "Memorandum to David Bell, AID: Technical Assistance for the National Market Concept, 19 June 1964." C. D. Jackson Papers, Box 92, Rostow, Walt, 1964. Dwight D. Eisenhower Library.

———. "Memorandum to the Secretary of State: Foreign Aid Reorganization, 31 December 1963." National Security File, Subject File, Box 16. Lyndon Baines Johnson Presidential Library.

———. "Memorandum to the President: Future of Foreign Aid, 14 October 1966," National Security File, Subject File, Box 16. Lyndon Baines Johnson Presidential Library.

———. "Memorandum to Mr. Richard Goodwin, June 20, 1961." National Security Files, January through December, 1961, Box 290. John F. Kennedy Presidential Library.

———. "Notes on a New Approach to U.S. Foreign Economic Policy." C. D. Jackson Papers, Box 6, Walt W. Rostow. Dwight D. Eisenhower Library.

———. "The Stages of Growth and the Problems of Peaceful Co-existence, Delivered at the Institute of World Economy and International Relations, Moscow, May 25, 1959." C. D. Jackson Papers, Box 91, Rostow, Walt, 1959. Dwight D. Eisenhower Library.

———. "The Strategy of Foreign Aid, 1961, Dec. 22, 1960." Transition Files, Task Force Reports 1960, Box 1074, Pre-Presidential Papers. John F. Kennedy Presidential Library.

———. "The Walt Rostow Lectures." C. D. Jackson Papers, Box 91, Rostow, Walt, 1956. Dwight D. Eisenhower Library.

Rostow, Walt, and George Christian. "Background Briefing (Punta del Este Summit Conference), 6 April 1967," National Security Files, International Meetings and Travel File, Punta del Este Summit Conference Press Material, Box 19. Lyndon Baines Johnson Presidential Library.

Schlesinger, Jr., Arthur. "Memorandum from the President's Special Assistant (Schlesinger) to President Kennedy, Washington, March 10, 1961." In Vol. 12. *Foreign Relations of the United States, 1961–1963,* 12. Washington, D.C.: Government Printing Office, 1996.

Senate Committee on Foreign Relations. *Statement of W. W. Rostow, Center for International Studies, Massachusetts Institute of Technology.* 84th Cong., 2d sess., 3, 17, 18, 18, 26, 27 February and 3, 5, and 10 March 1958, Part 1.

Spengler, J. J. "Theories of Economic Growth." In *Problems in the Study of*

Growth, 52–53. Washington, D.C.: National Bureau of Economic Research, 1949.

Subcommittee on Foreign Economic Policy of the Joint Economic Committee. *Statement of W. W. Rostow, Center for International Studies, Massachusetts Institute of Technology.* 84th Cong., 2d sess., 10, 12, and 13 December 1956.

Wen, Tai. "A Reactionary Theory (of W. W. Rostow) Which Serves the U.S. Ruling Clique." *Kung-ming Jih Pao*, 28 March 1961, 1: trans. and reprint. *Joint Publications Research Service* (SS. 1205) Y3.J66: 13/8240.

"World Economic Policy." C. D. Jackson Papers, Box 82, Princeton Economic Conference, 5/54—Draft Papers. Dwight D. Eisenhower Library.

Unpublished Material

Weiss, Carol H. "Policy Research: Data, Ideas, or Arguments?" Paper Presented at the Fourteenth World Congress of the International Political Science Association. Washington, D.C., 28 August to 1 September 1988.

Interviews and Correspondence

Gordon, Lincoln. Interview by John Reilly, tape recording, 30 May 1964. John F. Kennedy Oral History Program. John F. Kennedy Presidential Library.

Rostow, W. W. Interview by the author, tape recorded in Austin, Texas, on 16 November 1995.

———. Interview by Jean Ross, 4 September 1981." *Contemporary Authors Database.* Gale Research, Inc.

———. Interview by Richard Neustadt, tape recording, 11 April 1964. John F. Kennedy Oral History Program. John F. Kennedy Presidential Library.

Index